BLOOD AND CIRCUSES

A FOOTBALL JOURNEY THROUGH
EUROPE'S REBEL REPUBLICS

BLOOD AND CIRCUSES

ROBERT O'CONNOR

\Bb\
Biteback Publishing

First published in Great Britain in 2020 by
Biteback Publishing Ltd
Westminster Tower
3 Albert Embankment
London SE1 7SP
Copyright © Robert O'Connor 2020

Robert O'Connor has asserted his right under the Copyright, Designs and Patents Act 1988 to be identified as the author of this work.

All rights reserved. No part of this publication may be reproduced, stored in a retrieval system or transmitted, in any form or by any means, without the publisher's prior permission in writing.

This book is sold subject to the condition that it shall not, by way of trade or otherwise, be lent, resold, hired out or otherwise circulated without the publisher's prior consent in any form of binding or cover other than that in which it is published and without a similar condition, including this condition, being imposed on the subsequent purchaser.

Every reasonable effort has been made to trace copyright holders of material reproduced in this book, but if any have been inadvertently overlooked the publisher would be glad to hear from them.

ISBN 978-1-78590-511-7

10 9 8 7 6 5 4 3 2 1

A CIP catalogue record for this book is available from the British Library.

Set in Times New Roman

Printed and bound in Great Britain by
CPI Group (UK) Ltd, Croydon CR0 4YY

For ASJ

CONTENTS

Introduction	The Dead Zone	ix
Part One	Raised by Wolves: Kosovo	1
Part Two	Buried at the Mountains: Armenia, Azerbaijan and Nagorno-Karabakh	63
Part Three	Breathing Corpses: Georgia, Abkhazia and South Ossetia	131
Part Four	Baptised in the River: Moldova and Transnistria	193
Part Five	After Hades: Ukraine and the Donbass	259
Conclusion		315
Timeline of Key Events		319
Acknowledgements		331
Index		333

INTRODUCTION

THE DEAD ZONE

'Do you know what's going on over that border?' asks the checkpoint guard, narrowing his eyes into an inquisitive glare. 'Aren't you scared?'

I smile a broad, forced smile, showing my teeth and leaning back slightly in my seat to create the impression of being at ease.

'Nope,' I reply with a nonchalant shrug that I doubt would gull the most naïve inquisitor. The guard fixes me with a look that is almost sympathetic, and as he slips a cigarette neatly between his narrow lips, his dark, silent eyes seem to sneer, 'Yeah, right.'

The truth is I am scared. But not for the reason the guard thinks. It's true that the city for which I am headed, Donetsk in far-eastern industrial Ukraine, was until recently under siege, bombarded by daily airstrikes and artillery fire from enemies staked out a couple of kilometres away in the sprawling countryside.

Today, those hardy, damned souls still fighting in the Donbass War suffer weekly casualties amongst their number, the victims of pot-shots fired by soldiers under the command of the Ukrainian capital, Kyiv.

The war in Donbass is still hot, active, alive. But it's not bullets or bombs that frighten me.

It's him and his colleagues that I'm scared of. The guard – I have no clue as to his role here at the camp, since the place is crawling with officials all in different uniforms – looks to have been brought to life from the pages of a picture book on Soviet-era enforcers.

His black, close-cropped haircut exaggerates the angular contours and high, handsome cheekbones of his face, and his deep, sunken eyes greedily swallow the space around them like black holes. Whatever mess I've walked myself into here on the fringes of Ukraine's Donbass, neither he nor his colleagues are going to offer me any sympathy.

One hour ago, I was hauled off the bus I had boarded early this morning in the nearby Russian city of Rostov-on-Don and told I was being denied further passage by the camp authorities, who are the ordained guardians of the self-proclaimed *Donetskaya Narodnaya Respublika* – the Donetsk People's Republic (DPR).

Instead, I was sent back to the customs house on the Russian side of the crossing, but as I wandered lost and bewildered around the camp, I was herded into line to cross back over the border by two dead-eyed officials who flatly ignored my protestations that I was attempting to cross the other way. 'Welcome to Russia,' they kept repeating as I tried to get my words in order in pidgin Russian. 'Welcome to Russia. Welcome to Russia. Welcome to Russia.' This is serious, because passing back over the border will be a one-way ticket. There will be no hope of reaching Donetsk from there. It will also leave me stranded in the Russian outback, a hundred miles from nowhere with the sky darkening and a biblical storm collecting in dirty black clouds overhead.

I still don't know how I negotiated my way out of the line back towards Rostov-on-Don. It's possible that my mind responded to the stress and the chest pains that were soaring through my lungs by simply scrubbing the memory out.

All I know is that, sat here in the dilapidated customs house in the nowhere land between Russia and the DPR, my options are limited.

I am trapped in the dead zone between a super-state and an unrecognised military-ruled pariah republic, unable to move in either direction,

INTRODUCTION

a diplomatic pawn that nobody seems to know quite what to do with. Here, my documents are not recognised, which renders me technically stateless. Legally, I am a non-entity. It's checkmate. I no longer exist.

I have plenty of time to reflect, whilst sitting in this crumbling room. My overwhelming feeling is that this has been coming to me for a long time.

I've spent the past three and a half years negotiating some of the world's most hostile international borders, entering territories that are not recognised under international law and that live in a constant state of conflict with the outside world.

I've met paranoid border guards who regarded me with the deepest suspicion, merely for attempting to cross into their land, and who have treated my presence as an excuse to exercise a petty macho nationalism that ordinarily remains frustratingly dormant. In truth, I asked for my current predicament.

This isn't the usual fare of a jobbing football journalist. The ebb and flow of life as a sports writer never managed to quieten my curiosity to discover a different kind of football. Eastern Europe was always an interest, I think because of the chaos of the region's attempts to integrate with the free world during my lifetime. The building blocks of the world's favourite game in the land of Communism are so utterly different from those that created the Hollywood football culture of Western Europe as to require a completely new vocabulary in order to understand them.

During these years I have watched football in some of Europe's most obscure outposts – cities, towns and villages with sad, troubled histories where the game has served as both a tonic and a lightning rod in the bloody process of post-Communist state-building. Sport and politics are familiar bedfellows here.

I suppose I feel mournful for the heyday of Soviet and Yugoslav football that I missed out on experiencing. During the days of the Communist one-party state, the game was in most technical respects just one more state asset, controlled and manipulated by party apparatchiks who bent the rules or simply invented new ones in nakedly self-serving attempts to get ahead. A tiny closed-off elite controlled the football giants of Yugoslavia and the USSR, which meant that the best players were simply plucked from lesser sides by order of the Communist Party and inserted into the starting XI for Spartak Moscow, Dynamo Kyiv, Red Star Belgrade and a tiny handful of choice clubs that were run by the most powerful government ministries in the capital cities of Russia, Ukraine and Serbia. Match-fixing was a fact of life, as was the influence of the 'shadow economy', the illegal funnelling into clubs of private wealth creamed off by enterprising crooks from the rigid but grossly ineffective command economy.

But the system also created wonderful, eternal rivalries: Red Star Belgrade v. Dinamo Zagreb; Dynamo Kyiv v. Spartak Moscow; Ararat Yerevan v. Neftçi Baku. These teams rarely meet in competition football now, and when they are thrown together by the serendipity of a European draw the diminished status and financial power of the former Eastern Bloc leagues means that the games have little more footballing significance than simple nostalgia for those who are lucky enough to remember. But these matches had a national as well as a football significance.

When Dinamo played Red Star in Zagreb in May 1990, it caused a riot between Croat and Serb supporters that many believe was one of the key events in escalating what became the Croatian War of Independence. And as Thomas de Waal writes in his work *The Caucasus: An Introduction*, 'people knew to stay off the streets of Yerevan and Baku whenever Ararat played Neftçi'.

Football also had implications for the Yugoslav and Soviet treatment of nationality. Both states operated on a system of 'ethno-federalism', the dividing up of their vast territories into semi-autonomous political units that reflected the ethnic realities of those regions, where the 'titular' nations were given special privileges. Yugoslavia divided

INTRODUCTION

itself into six federal republics, the USSR into fifteen. Even though, in reality, the local governments in the republics did not have autonomy – particularly so in the case of the Soviet Union – the arrangement created two key sets of circumstances that would prove to be crucial in the way both sets of countries eventually broke up and have continued to develop into the twenty-first century.

First, it built the governmental and administrative framework that would provide the infrastructure for state building when the moment came to grab independence. And second, it incubated and preserved a sense of cultural separateness amongst these titular nations; a feeling of destiny that eventually gave these republics the confidence to fight the failing central powers in Moscow and, more alarmingly, the minority nations in their own backyards.

Why is football a useful lens through which to try and understand the bloodshed of the Soviet and Yugoslav collapse? The crushing power of central government in both countries destroyed civil society. The free press, political opposition, even art and literature that challenged central authority became non-existent. Football supporters in the Soviet and Yugoslav republics embraced their local clubs and local players as a form of collective self-expression.

As the centre weakened and the regions became more openly nationalist, football clubs also became imbued with exaggerated meaning. In the words of one Georgian dissident, football became 'the most valuable weapon in the fight against Soviet power'. When the fight turned away from Moscow and was directed inwardly towards local minorities – sparking the separatist wars that are the subject of this book – the game retained its peculiar, volatile meaning, and football clubs became great symbols of resistance and political expression.

What are the technical facts of those inter-ethnic wars of independence? The Communist economy of the USSR was notoriously inefficient. The black market – where locally produced goods were shifted through private hands and taxes generally went unpaid – became the lifeblood of the republics. Political power, though nominally concentrated in Moscow, became de-centralised as local ethnic leaders built up feudal fiefdoms that, bit by bit, transferred real control from the Kremlin to Tbilisi, Minsk, Chişinău and Yerevan. These nationalistic overlords were the reason why the republics were successful when they grabbed independence after the USSR collapsed in 1991.

But such figures are also to blame for the civil wars and ethnic fighting that followed independence. What began as an experiment in the 1920s – the Bolshevik policy of encouraging national expression amongst the USSR's border peoples and the acknowledgement that such people had not been conquered by an empire, but rather welcomed as equals into a new kind of fraternal state in which national differences would eventually disappear beneath the powerful waves of class-consciousness – turned out to be, not just a defining feature of the union's seventy-year existence, but the wrecking ball that would eventually bring it crashing down.

The border guard snaps my attention back into the room by clicking his fingers and ordering me to my feet. Someone on-site at the camp has arranged to link my phone to a civilian's 4G connection – it would, apparently, be illegal for one of the military officials to have done so. I can message my fixer in Donetsk city, and ask for someone to drive two hours to the border to negotiate with the camp's commander on my behalf.

I don't know how this ends. The heavens have opened now, and I'm poked outside onto the muddy footpath and told to wait 'a while' before attempting the 100-metre path back to the Donetsk officials who turned me away the first time.

Even if I make it into the DPR, I've no way of knowing if my message has been successfully received in the city.

But then I suppose I've only got myself to blame.

PART ONE

RAISED BY WOLVES: KOSOVO

Today there's no sun peaking
Only icy rain falling, and expecting screams from pain, she starts crying
Who will assault her when that creaking door opens?
But against her will, she must obey the stranger's voice
ANDREW CRISCI, KOSOVAN POET

© Burmesedays, amendments by Globe-trotter / CC BY-SA

1

Just after midnight on the night of 27 April 1999, Genc Hoxha was woken by the sound of Serb soldiers breaking down the door of his family home.

Along with his wife, parents, grandparents and two children, he was ushered outside into the street alongside other families in the neighbourhood who had been herded from their homes and into the night. It was freezing.

Hoxha was thrown against the outside wall of his house, whilst his family were led away by the soldiers.

One of the attackers began to interrogate Hoxha in Russian, correctly assuming that he couldn't be understood. Hoxha knew enough to pick out a few words and realised that he was being asked to name his profession. He searched frantically in his mind but was unable to find the right words.

What he eventually blurted out was 'Oleg Blokhin'.

The soldier paused at the mention of Blokhin, the Ukrainian who had been one of the USSR's most gifted footballers. 'You are a footballer?' he asked.

A boy from Gjakova in the west of the country, Hoxha had made his name with the city's leading club KF Vëllaznimi in the 1980s, before moving on to play for KF Liria in nearby Prizren. In the Kosovan football league's maiden season in 1991, he had been named footballer of the year.

'Yes, I am a footballer,' Hoxha stuttered in reply. The soldier looked at him.

'I don't want to kill a footballer,' he said. 'So, here's what is going to happen. I am going to fire my gun twice into the air, and you are going to fall to the ground. You will stay there for ten minutes. Then you will leave this place.'

For a moment, Hoxha didn't answer. 'Can I go back to look for my family?' he asked finally.

'If you want to live, you will do as I have said,' replied the Russian-speaking soldier. Then he fired his gun twice into the sky. As he did so, Hoxha fell to the ground. 'Is it over?' he heard one of the Serbs ask as the Russian-speaking soldier returned to the street. 'Yes,' he replied. 'It's over.' Then they left.

Once he was sure the soldiers would not return, Hoxha went to a neighbour's house to start the desperate search for his family. Time passed in a blur.

'I had assumed that the Serbs had taken them down onto the main street, away from the house,' he tells me. Throughout our meeting, what strikes me most is the calmness of Hoxha's bearing, as he matter-of-factly retells the tale of the day that Oleg Blokhin saved his life.

'At first, I thought maybe it would have been better if they'd killed me. I went over the road to my neighbour's house, he was a footballer also, and we just moved then from house to house, waiting for the Serbs to return.'

By this time, the streets of Gjakova were ablaze. Hoxha's own house was burned to the ground that night as the attackers scorched the earth that had borne witness to their crimes.

'Everything around us was burning, but we kept moving. The only thing we could do was move. We weren't going anywhere. Just trying to stay alive, waiting for the Serbs to return.'

By 3 a.m., three hours after the massacre had begun, the remaining Serbs had left Gjakova. In those first few hours of 27 April, 379 people were killed.

With the village smouldering, the remaining residents began the march into the centre of Gjakova, the war's latest refugees, but they would be far from the last.

'We began the trek out of Gjakova towards Albania,' says Hoxha. 'Then two of my neighbours came and grabbed me and said, "Follow us." They didn't say why, they just pulled me away.

'They brought me to a clearing within the crowd, and there were my wife and children. Everyone just started to cry. Everyone was hugging and crying. It was very emotional. After that we got on trucks and left Kosovo for Albania.'

The Gjakova massacre, committed in the village of Meja just outside the town, is thought to have been the worst atrocity during Kosovo's civil war, in terms of the number of people killed. A little over six weeks later, the first NATO ground troops entered the country, which signalled the end of a three-month aerial campaign and pushed Kosovo tentatively in the direction of peace.

II

A cold wind blows in from the Klina highway, and as the sun starts to fade in the sky, the little Kosovan town of Skënderaj feels like a dot on a wild landscape. Spring has started. The cold, though, is perishing.

Dust clouds rise up off the road where the route in and out of town joins a tarmacked forecourt from where the last bus service of the day has just departed for the capital Pristina. Two children kick a well-worn football against the wall of the bus station, its leather panels flapping as it bounces off the corrugated steel. The stitching has long since disintegrated from months, perhaps even years of being kicked around on the dirty concrete.

The dull throb of history beats endlessly beneath the soil of Skënderaj. The town is in the district of Mitrovica in northern Kosovo. It is a crumbling wreck.

The drive north out of the capital Pristina and up into the battered countryside offered the first sobering indications as to what went on here at the end of the last century.

Much of the roadside is lined with rubble, great hulking shards of grey mortar and discarded brick. Huge fields, thick with cloying marsh and mud, roll away into some undeterminable distance, maybe to the horizon and back. It isn't clear what purpose they serve, save for dividing up the forsaken villages and townships that have been left out here in the wild in the middle of nothing and nowhere.

The road winds through the village of Likovac, which was used as a Serb military base during Kosovo's brutal civil war and is just kilometres from Gornje Obrinje where another of the conflict's most despicable massacres took place. Today, crumbling villages form a backdrop to martyrs' cemeteries that mark the roadside with memories of the dead.

There is something deliberate about how these memorials have been placed along the route between Pristina and Skënderaj, they serve as a reminder to all that pass by that the last war of the murderous twentieth century was as blood-soaked as any that came before it.

At the edge of this sprawling mass of rural nothingness, Skënderaj awaits.

I've driven out here from the capital with a friend of a friend, a cameraman from the local TV station RTV21, named Sahit. He is manning the media gantry today in Skënderaj for the Superleague match between FC Prishtina – former champions but with fading fortunes – and local side KF Drenica; a relegation battle that promises blood and sweat, but little quality.

Sahit speaks a small amount of English, just enough to share his opinion of Kosovan football as it stands on the brink of a new era: 'Football in Kosovo is no good,' he mutters, pulling his beaten old Volvo out onto the highway. 'No money.'

Sahit makes his living watching this impoverished league through his camera lens, and although I'm wary of his cynicism, I've no reason to doubt his authority. Hereafter, the hum of the road soundtracks our drive beneath the drawl of Sahit's dreadful Turkish rock cassette.

At 8 a.m. on the morning of 26 September 1998, Serb forces stationed in Likovac began shelling the Delijaj family compound in the village of Gornje Obrinje. Their targets were the guerrilla fighters of the Kosovo Liberation Army (KLA), who had a stronghold in Drenica.

The bombardment continued through the day and into the following morning, during which time the compound was almost entirely evacuated into the surrounding forest, and only those who were too old, frail or sick to follow were left behind. In the days that followed, the Serbs obliterated the buildings that had formerly housed the Delijaj clan, before taking to the woods to hunt down those that had fled.

Over the next three days, they satisfied their bloodlust by massacring the people hiding amongst the trees. In all, the bodies of twenty-one Kosovar-Albanian civilians were recovered from the compound and the surrounding forest at Gornje Obrinje. Some were mutilated beyond recognition. One elderly victim had had his brain removed and strewn across a mattress beside him.

A thick mist descends as we pass along this road near Likovac. Sahit looks unaffected by the history surrounding the route of our pilgrimage, and the car rumbles onwards towards the Bajram Aliu Stadium at Skënderaj.

Kosovo has changed. It is still changing. The seeds of the liberal-democratic, West-leaning identity that has helped the country to forget its troubled relationship with Serbia and its violent civil war were sown long before the NATO intervention that ended the conflict, which drove out the Serbs and brought an end to decades of oppression.

A rebooted Kosovan identity has been germinating since the 1950s. During this time Albanian social resistance to Serb rule was embraced by local collectives, using centuries-old traditions of art, literature and culture to shield themselves from Yugoslavia's grey, immovable Communism which, somehow, never felt like a fit here.

This 'otherness' is a filter through which Kosovo's history must be viewed. In the lottery that was twentieth-century state-building – the archaic practice of clumping together ethno-linguistic groups into polities designed to find harmony through homogeneity – the Muslim Albanians of Kosovo drew the short straw, and were forced to toil under the Orthodox Slavic regime that tormented them for their differences but refused to acknowledge these differences in the form of adequate self-governance. In this way, Kosovo spent half a century walking towards the civil war of 1998 to 1999.

The country today is cash poor, but it has found friends in Europe. Investment, grants and loans from the EU have been channelled into rebuilding Kosovo's infrastructure. And although at the time of writing there are still eighty-two UN member states that do not recognise the 2008 Kosovo declaration of independence – including Russia, China and most of Asia and South America – the country is slowly being made to feel at home amongst the family of world nations. The International Court of Justice proffered recognition in 2010 and various roadmaps have been agreed with Brussels as Kosovo carves out a prospective path towards EU membership (the country has used the euro as its currency since 2002).

But there are still pieces of the puzzle missing. Though 58 per cent of UN members recognise Kosovo's independence, the Pristina government still has no seat at the UN table. Serbia still claims the territory of Kosovo as its own, a quirk of history traceable to a Serb defeat to the Ottoman Empire in 1389 at the Battle of Kosovo which is, inexplicably, celebrated as a kind of sacred rebirth of the Serb nation.

And, crucially for a country looking to leave any kind of cultural or political stamp on the world map, there is, as of March 2016, no recognition in the world's most cherished sport. But all that is about to change. I've come to Kosovo to watch the countdown to their acceptance into UEFA.

* * *

The Bajram Aliu Stadium in Skënderaj is a cold, grey place to spend a Saturday. Two long concrete blocks lie either side of a filthy brown pitch, one with a thin steel roof, the other bare and exposed to a biting wind. Today, there is an early spring breeze in the air, but there's something about the poverty of the stadium that seems to take an extra couple of degrees off. The cold nips near to the bone.

This is a stadium where men think nothing of relieving themselves against the wall outside, and where stray dogs – all skin and bone – parade up and down the terraces, shivering and coughing. Greasy teenagers scoop peanuts from vats into the open palms of supporters, and the shells have created a skin on the concrete that splinters and crunches underfoot. It's unclear whether the housing estate beyond the west stand is still being built or is in the process of falling down. The dank smell of mud drifts all around the ground and gets into my clothes; it will be days before I'm able to shift it.

The bleakness of the stadium is a joy compared to the drive to Skënderaj from Pristina. Although here, like on the road that bore us, the past demands it be heard. The man they call the father of modern Kosovo, the KLA leader Adem Jashari, was killed in combat just over a mile from the Bajram Aliu Stadium. His picture hangs in the president's office inside the freezing bunker – one could hardly call it a boardroom – that Drenica refers to as a clubhouse.

The media gantry at the stadium is an improvised platform of damp wooden pallets, all rotten and unsteady. It houses three TV cameras, all mounted on rickety tripods and manned by chain-smoking technicians done up in denim and leather. The small crowd is easily divisible into two groups, those sat freezing on the rock-hard terrace and those who had the foresight to bring makeshift cardboard seats to spare their backsides from the ice-cold stone. Nobody looks pleased to be here.

Typically crowds in Kosovo's Superleague fill out as the game progresses, since by the second half nobody is bothering to check for tickets on the permanently open gates. So, when Granit Arifaj puts KF Drenica in front against FC Prishtina with a flying volley twenty minutes from time, it's greeted with a healthy roar from the home fans. Struggling Drenica beat their relegation rivals 1–0; a huge win that takes them one step closer to avoiding dropping out of the top tier.

But then, every game in the Superleague this season is significant. A little over six weeks from now in May, an assembly of the UEFA Congress will meet in Budapest to vote on Kosovo's full membership in the European football family. It will mark the end point of a journey that began in 1991 when a plucky band of rebels broke with Yugoslavia and risked their lives to start an illegal football league in the mud and marshes.

If the assembly confirms Kosovo's full membership in the European football family, it will open up access to the qualifying stages of the World Cup. There will also be passage into European competition for Kosovo's clubs, including the UEFA Champions League. The country's financial fortunes will transform overnight. Cash injections will come from UEFA and FIFA coffers, throwing a lifeline to a football industry that is currently un-sellable and flirting with bankruptcy.

Under UEFA there will be new support from private industry, and the country will be freed from its unwanted rebel status. Kosovo's football clubs will be given protection by the international transfer system, contracts will be recognised by the European and world governing bodies and investors will see potential in the domestic game, buoyed by the country's increased visibility on the world stage.

The road that carried Kosovo from the embers of a burned-out Yugoslavia into this century was marked with horrors.

For anyone born before 1990, the very name of the country casts a spell. To a child growing up in middle-England suburbia, Kosovo was the place where war was born. Or at least war in the age of colour broadcasting, as our televisions beamed footage of skin-headed men in camouflage gear sat atop tanks into our homes.

Some names and phrases stick out in my memory from those news broadcasts. Prekaz was one, where much of the trouble seemed to be happening. The antagonist of the drama was Slobodan Milošević, a Serb, whose crimes were the 'ethnic cleansing of the Albanians'; a term that still feels grossly sanitised.

As the perception of a world outside of my own came into focus, it was Kosovo, and the struggle between the Albanians and Milošević – between good and evil, in that binary framework that children use to make sense of things morally – that became the centre of the earth.

Since the beginning of the 1980s, a kind of social apartheid had split Kosovo in half. Albanian culture came under attack from the Serb government, access to education was curbed – as was use of the Albanian language – and civil administration became a Serb-only domain. Year on year, the crisis got worse, until civil war became inevitable.

Football changes in the same way that life changes. Whereas in the troubled 1980s the game was used as a tool to unite the Albanian resistance, by the 1990s it was outlawed amongst Albanians, with serious, often violent repercussions for those who disobeyed. Football became heavily politicised, and playing the game was transformed into being an unyielding act of rebellion, a demonstration of subversive defiance of the status quo.

This origin story was recounted to me on a cold day in March 2016 by the effortlessly charming Eroll Salihu in his office at the Football Federation of Kosovo (FFK) headquarters on Rruga Agim Ramadani in central Pristina.

It was the first time I'd met Salihu, general secretary of the FFK. He is 6ft tall, firm of jaw and is so animated that his energy sometimes lifts his toned, lean frame clean out of his seat when he is talking.

Salihu is a football man. He is also a serious man who is highly educated, having graduated in law from the University of Pristina in 1991, with an excellent grasp of English to boot. As a young player he was a trailblazer; he was one of a tiny minority of youngsters from Kosovo who were picked to play for Yugoslavia at youth level.

In September 1991, he made a call that would change Kosovan football for ever.

'After playing one match [of the 1991/92 season] we were asked if we wanted to keep playing,' he says, leaning forward in his chair inside the tiny office that the FFK shares with the governing bodies of a handful of other sports.

'We had already missed two matches by then because it had become difficult to play in Serbia and in Bosnia. We were the only non-Slavs in the federation and everyone thought that war was about to break out in Kosovo. It didn't happen, but we felt by then that it had become impossible to play football in Yugoslavia. So, when we were asked if we wanted to keep playing, I said no. I was the first to say no.'

What followed was the creation of the first independent football league of Kosovo, which effectively siloed the nation from the rest of the footballing world.

The new Kosovan league, its players and its clubs, were rebels against the authority of their Serb masters. Teams in the new competition were forced out of their stadiums, as they were facilities owned by the Serb-led municipal authorities. They were forced to play matches on scrap land, whilst dodging Serb police and a volunteer militia whose mandate was to suppress all expressions of Kosovar-Albanian consciousness.

As Yugoslavia was torn apart along its ethnic seams, Kosovo's Albanians were battered into submission. 'They were the most difficult circumstances you can imagine,' says Salihu, leafing through a volume compiled by the FFK detailing the league's troubled first twenty years. The book is a statistician's dream, a comprehensive account of records and results brought brilliantly to life by a gallery of pictures cataloguing Kosovan football's darkest years. It documents the country's unyielding act of defiance through football. 'We had no freedoms,' he says. 'We played football under pressure and under terror. Players were beaten by police. Ninety-five per cent of the footballers in Kosovo were Albanian, but the 5 per cent who were Serbs were the ones who were allowed to play in our stadiums.'

'*Urra per fitore*' ran the opening line in a Kosovar newspaper article the day after the new league's maiden fixture. 'Hurray for victory.' Victory, though, for whom?

KF Flamurtari, for one. The opening game of the new league took place on 13 September 1991 between FC Prishtina and Flamurtari, a team also from the capital. Prishtina led early through a goal from Salihu, but found themselves two behind, before a late consolation halved the arrears. At the final whistle it was 3–2 to Flamurtari, with an 'official' attendance of 300 hardy supporters. Prishtina wouldn't lose again all season; they took the maiden championship by a point from KF Trepča '89 at the beginning of what was to be a decade of dominance.

In this way, football life continued. Players risked serious injury by playing on hard, uneven ground, alongside the threat of arrest that stalked every kick. But the league survived. In the mud and in the marshlands, it even started to thrive.

At a rally outside Pristina to mark the 600th anniversary of the Battle of Kosovo in June 1989, Serbian President Milošević took to the stage and stoked up nationalist resentment towards Albanians in the province. He sought to poison the conversation about nationality with his rhetoric and concocted a dangerous fiction about race war, whilst depicting the local Albanians as a threat to the safety of those Serbs living in the region. Succeed, and he could install himself as the ordained saviour of the Serb nation.

In the months and years that followed, discrimination against

Kosovo's Albanians became enshrined in law. Public officials were thrown out of their jobs, medical staff were sacked, and Albanian-language schools were closed down.

By 1991, a resistance had formalised in the shape of an underground, alternative government, headed up by the Albanian writer and pacifist Ibrahim Rugova. The resistance provided schooling in the Albanian language, a rudimentary health service and, above all else, hope. The new football league became a big part of that.

'The reaction to the Prishtina team when we visited Serb stadiums was terrible,' says Kushtrim Munishi, who played alongside Salihu as a striker for Prishtina in 1991. Like his teammate, he was one of the few Albanian players to represent Yugoslavia at youth level – usually the phone numbers of players from Kosovo would be conveniently 'lost'.

'They would offend us with racial taunts,' he says. 'The home fans and the political situation we were in made it very difficult.'

My fixer for this part of my trip who has arranged the meeting with Munishi is a young eccentric called Valon Hoxha. When we meet, the day after my interview with Salihu, he is decked out in a migraine-inducing button-down shirt and his head is peeking out from above a lumberjack's jacket with sheepskin trim. With his pristinely tailored beard and round, wide-rimmed spectacles, he looks more east London than east Kosovo. He hasn't let the freezing cold stop him from bowling down central Pristina's Mother Teresa Boulevard in knee-length shorts.

Here, the city presents itself in the way in which it would most like to be seen. The boulevard is a wide, expansive concourse peppered with bars and trendy restaurants that take their aesthetic cue from London and Berlin rather than Yugoslavia's socialist past.

Valon grows mushrooms – purely culinary, he insists – and

climbs mountains. He works for a local NGO writing EU funding bids for regeneration projects around the country, and there is plenty of money up for grabs, which is being pumped from Europe into Kosovo as it rebuilds after the war.

When the country became unstable, Valon's family became part of a large Albanian diaspora that migrated to Macedonia, though his worldview was formed when he left the Balkans to study in Missouri. Today, he is part of a Kosovan community that has links to the UK, which is what led him to me.

'The guy said he's going to be maybe thirty minutes late,' he says, shaking my hand. 'We can take a walk or we can just sit and have a beer?' He's already most of the way through the door of the nearest bar, and I feel it polite to follow to where I'm being led.

Valon is my fixer and translator, but he is also particularly keen on nudging me towards Pristina's after-hours culture. He had promised earlier in the day that he'd take me to a jazz bar after our afternoon meeting with Munishi – a plan I'm trying to wriggle out of since I'm due on a 5.30 a.m. bus to Tirana – but he hasn't stopped twisting my arm, and I wonder whether it might not be simpler just to power through and sleep on the *marshrutka*. As it happens, the interview takes the wind from both our sails.

'The pressure on Albanians playing in a Yugoslav league was intense,' says Munishi. 'It was hard in a way that I cannot explain. It would be difficult for anybody who didn't experience it to imagine what it was like being in an Albanian football player's shoes in those days.

'So the Serb government basically gave us a choice. "You need to make a decision. Are you Serbian or are you Albanian?" We answered that in our actions.

'Usually, the police were after the head people, those that had organised the games, not necessarily the players. The league officials were usually beaten up and arrested. Both sides kept pushing. They'd play the game again and the police would come again.'

Prishtina lost their title after the maiden season of the new league. In 1993 it went to KF Trepča from the mining community in the Serb stronghold of Mitrovica. It was fitting that these two teams were the first champions as they had been the only Kosovan teams to have played in the Yugoslavian top-flight.

The day before travelling to Skënderaj, I had shared a ride with a friend from the FFK, Bajram Shala, from the federation headquarters to the Pristina bus station. 'For the first two years after 1991 people just played football so that it would survive,' he told me. Bajram, a charming young man in his mid-twenties, is the FFK's team manager, handling all non-football matters for the national team. He grew up at the same time the new league was finding its feet.

He remembers being startled at the way spectators came to support teams, who just a few years before had been hailed as being at the pinnacle of Balkan football, and were now reduced to playing football in mud baths, washing themselves in filthy rivers at the end of games.

'But after one or two years, like in every league and in every sport, the real rivalries began between clubs and investors,' Bajram said. 'Even though the clubs were in completely unacceptable conditions, they started to have rivalries. Pressure came on sponsors to invest more money, to get better players.

'There was no such thing as international transfers, the situation was too fucked up for that. The conditions were impossible and yet, people put in their money to make the best teams. That's what football does to people.'

The Independent League of Kosovo lasted until 1997, when it was suspended at the outbreak of the civil war. FC Prishtina were its final champions, after retaining the title they'd won the previous year. KF Drenica, playing in the heartland of Albanian resistance – and the location where the war would begin a few months later – came bottom and were relegated.

'The whole trick was not getting caught,' says Munishi. 'As soon as they had you, you were done.'

Eventually, both Prishtina strikers felt compelled to leave Kosovo. Munishi, who had already turned down FK Partizan in Belgrade and Dinamo Zagreb – two of Yugoslavia's biggest clubs – accepted an offer to play for Zagłębie Lubin in Poland in 1993. He didn't return until after the war.

Salihu was given the chance to return to the professional ranks with a Serb incarnation of FC Prishtina that had remained part of Yugoslavian football. Unsurprisingly, he declined, and instead settled in Switzerland with the help of another former Prishtina star of the 1980s, the hard-case midfielder Agim Cana (Cana's son Lorik would go on to captain Albania in their first-ever international tournament at Euro 2016).

The Serbs continued their pursuit of Salihu throughout the 1990s. During a visit home from Turkey in 1996 he was approached by the notorious warlord Arkan, who had made himself president of Serbian Pristina. Salihu's family were pestered and harassed by officials, and his father was interrogated almost daily by Serb police. 'I would die before I played for Arkan,' exclaims Salihu. 'They were like the Gestapo, the way they pursued us.'

'I can't believe how casually that guy talked about those things,' states Valon after Munishi had supped the last of his beer and departed into the night. 'All that war and death and violence. And yet he was so calm.'

I suppose he's right. No one could have blamed Munishi or Salihu if they'd decided to never speak about their experiences again. But then maybe telling their story provided some form of catharsis.

Stepping back onto Mother Teresa Boulevard, the air's got colder, and I instinctively shove my hands deep into my pockets. Valon squeezes my arm – 'Till next time, my friend' – before he wanders off into the night. And I'm left alone, with just the gentle hum of revelry buzzing behind me.

* * *

Inside the KF Drenica clubhouse back in faraway Skënderaj, I meet Daut Geci, who is a man who looks like he has lived through a war. He has small eyes and a rugged face, the bottom half of which is covered by a thin layer of coarse stubble, and when he shakes me by the hand his expression doesn't change.

Today, he serves as club president at Drenica alongside his day jobs as an officer in the Prekaz police and as partner in a local building firm, but his ties to this club and to this province run deeper. If there is a man to tell the tale of how football survived Kosovo's war, it is Daut Geci.

Geci played for Drenica as a midfielder during the 1990s when football clubs all over the country were being chased out of their grounds and into the woods. 'There is a field just over there where we moved to play a lot of our games,' he says, standing and gesturing out of the window of the freezing bunker that Drenica calls a clubhouse. The draught in here is bitter, and every word between us visibly carries on the cold air.

'But when the war started, we were the first club in Kosovo to have to stop our activities, because it was here in Drenica that the war began.

'The truth is that our club didn't really survive the war. We had to restart completely. There was nothing left. No structures survived, only the pitch survived. Most clubs didn't suffer in this way, because a lot of areas weren't so exposed to the violence.

'But we were destroyed. We went down to the Second League [the third tier] after the war and had to begin over. But within two seasons, we were back in the Superleague.'

Looking out from the Drenica bunker into the muddy wastelands where the war first began, a sense of a kind of Kosovan exceptionalism reveals itself. Geci's memories of what went on here as the Serbs lashed the whip still haunt him.

'We were playing a game in Mitrovica, which isn't far from Skënderaj, in I think 1997. It was Drenica against KF Trepča. We were interrupted by soldiers from the special unit of Arkan, who entered the pitch with guns and stopped the game. When people realised who they were they ran. They ran for their lives.

'Now, the players were young and they could run. They got away. But they caught the referee and some of the older fans who were less mobile and couldn't get away from the pitch.

'They made those old people dismantle the goals and carry them around the field on their backs, just for fun. It was ritual humiliation. Because at that time, the club at Drenica refused to accept the Serbian government as our government, and so the club was outlawed. Officially you had to deny the Kosovo state, but we refused to do that. Wherever we went to play football we were chased away. The club basically became illegal.

'That was the formal reason for what happened. The real reason as we all know is that the Serbs didn't want Albanians to live in this country.

'Once we had been driven away, we could never return to the

same place again. But every time it happened, we had a huge boost in motivation. We were young and we just wanted to play football. And we absolutely didn't want to bow down to the regime. Our incentive was incredible, and we would play football everywhere we went. We were determined that that's how it would be. Everywhere we could find a suitable place, we would play.'

KF Drenica have led a workmanlike existence. Founded in 1958, the side was a provincial speck on the Yugoslavian football map, tucked away here in the never-ending countryside, slogging it out in the dirt in their dreary black and red jerseys. They were relegated a few months before the attack on the Jashari family compound at the start of the war in March 1998, but they'd never finished much higher than halfway up the league. KF Drenica existed because there was no reason not to. They played football because it gave the illusion of making the time pass.

The KLA leader Adem Jashari used to play football in the fields of Skënderaj. He also watched Drenica at the Bajram Aliu Stadium. It is the wall behind Geci's desk on which Jashari's picture hangs, stony-faced and clad in khaki green. He has a thick black beard and eyes like smooth stones.

In 1995, when the US-brokered peace deal was struck to bring an end to the wars in Croatia and in Bosnia-Herzegovina, there was hope that foreign intervention would also bring resolution to the problem of Kosovan independence. There were even hopes that borders for a new ethnic Albanian state could be drawn up under the protection of the international peacekeeping community.

When this failed to materialise, the disappointment was palpable. Out of that disappointment, after years of peaceful resistance under Ibrahim Rugova's Democratic League of Kosovo, the KLA emerged under Jashari's helmsmanship and armed to the teeth.

On 7 March 1998, Serb forces attacked the Jashari family compound, just 1km away from the Bajram Aliu Stadium, killing Adem himself and more than sixty other members of the Jashari family. The date is seared into the Kosovan national consciousness. Nowhere is this starker than here in Skënderaj. Adem Jashari is a martyr for the Albanian resistance. For many in Kosovo, they owe him their independence. Some owe him their lives.

'Adem Jashari loved Drenica,' says Geci. 'When the club went illegal and we moved onto a new field, it was close enough to the Jashari house that they would watch from their home. The club was special to him.

'It shows how deep football is connected to everything here in Drenica. He was the founder of our nation, but he still came here to watch Drenica play football.'

Jashari's death marked an escalation in the conflict that was to become the civil war. For some, 7 March was the day the war began. Certainly, it was for those living in Skënderaj. This connection between the Jashari clan and KF Drenica has survived into Kosovo's new era – his nephew Bekim served for many years here before Geci as the club president.

The community at Skënderaj is tight. Kosovo's tragedy turned it into a beacon of resistance. Even in death, Jashari sits as its almost mythical figurehead.

'There are no words to describe him,' says Geci. 'He gave his life for this country. He was one of the greatest men who ever lived.'

Today, his name is given to the country's only commercial airport in Pristina, and to the old national stadium in the Serb stronghold of Mitrovica.

III

Set against a backdrop of classically rolling Balkan hills, the Kosovo B Power Station on the outskirts of Pristina looks like something out of steampunk fiction. Its mammoth concrete chimney stretches some 200 metres above the city, obfuscating the landscape with a fatuous entitlement, spewing its foul clouds. A 2008 report by the World Bank called part of the Kosovo Power Station the 'worst single-point source of pollution in Europe'.

Beneath the thick plumes of smoke sits the tidy municipality of Obilić. As well as being home to the country's three major operating coal mines, the town has an Albanian majority population, and so to most people here it is known by another name, Kastriot, after the medieval Albanian national hero George Kastrioti Skënderbau. The name Obilić hails from a chapter in Serbian history, that of the warlord Milos Obilić who, as legend has it, killed the Ottoman Sultan at the Battle of Kosovo in 1389, a date held sacred in Serb mythology. As the energy centre of Kosovo, Obilić generates 97 per cent of the country's electrical power in 2016. The city is also a battleground between competing Albanian and Serb interpretations of the past.

It isn't easy to understand why Serbs and Albanians are so protective of Kosovo. What is certain is that the region has always been a melting pot of peoples and cultures – Orthodox and Muslim, Albanian and Slav, imperially ruled and free tribes – all of which have come under the dominion of different invading military powers and swapped sovereignty with the rise and fall of the Eurasian continent's great powers. Since the nineteenth century, and particularly since the break-up of Yugoslavia, Serb and Albanian historians have fought each other to put their own people in Kosovo first, thus casting the region ad infinitum in the colours of either nation.

The official history from Belgrade states that the Serbs were chased out of Kosovo and into Hungary by the Ottomans in 1689, which thus allowed Albanian settlers to fill the demographic gap, an event seared into the popular consciousness as '*Velika Seoba*' – the Great Migration. The Great Migration serves as the second part of the Holy Trinity for the Serb nation. The first is the defeat of the Serbian army by the Ottomans at the Battle of Kosovo in 1389, whilst the third is the re-conquest of Kosovo by the Kingdom of Serbia in 1912.

The Great Migration lends Kosovo considerable significance in the Serb sense of place in history. Unsurprisingly, this narrative is rejected out of hand by Albanians who argue, with some merit, that the Great Migration had a negligible impact on the demography of Kosovo.

A slightly less heroic take on the Serb obsession with this region is that between the late thirteenth century and 1766, the town of Peć in western Kosovo was the seat of the patriarchal head of the Serbian Orthodox Church. In an age when sovereignty was won and squandered cheaply and the nation-state identity had not yet taken root, this gave Peć the status of a kind of spiritual national capital.

The fact that the Patriarchate had originally been located at Žiča about 160km north of Kosovo before the monastery was burned by nomadic Turks, together with the awkward reality that other central stories relating to Serb nationhood were only co-opted into prominence much later – such as the 1389 Battle of Kosovo defeat, which was largely forgotten about by the Serbs for centuries until re-emerging as a focus of national reawakening in the nineteenth century – suggest that the modern obsession with Kosovo is at least partially a political project propped up by a system of carefully curated national myths.

Sitting beneath the doom-inducing cooling towers of the Kosovo power plant, little Obilić is home to one of the country's oldest football clubs, KF KEK, founded in 1928 by the town's coal miners and for most of its ninety-year existence known as FK Obilić (rather prosaically, the team's nickname is 'the Electricians').

In March 1992, FK Obilić welcomed their great rivals FC Prishtina onto their patch for a much-anticipated derby in the newly formed Independent League of Kosovo in the shadow of the country's filthy wreck of a power station.

The game was still young, 0–0, when it happened. Play was interrupted suddenly by commotion from the sidelines, followed by a swift pitch invasion by the local Serb police. The game was broken up. Some, including players and spectators, dispersed quickly, knowing that if they were caught they would be arrested. Others were taken into custody by heavy-handed officers and carted off to the nearby police station in Obilić.

One of those taken was FC Prishtina's Jusuf Tortoshi. Tortoshi was Kosovan football royalty. He had been a member of the Prishtina side of the 1980s that achieved legendary status in Kosovo with a series of spectacular results in the Yugoslav First League, most memorably a 3–1 win at the Marakana in Belgrade in 1983 against Serb giants Red Star.

In Yugoslavia, where the suppression of ethnic identity had been central to Josip Broz Tito's means of keeping the federation intact, the republics looked to their best football clubs as a way of expressing their nationhood. Victory at the Marakana was ecstasy for Prishtina but a humbling experience for Belgrade, and it hardened the Serb determination to crush Kosovo. As a member of that Prishtina side, Tortoshi's name carried considerable weight, ten years on.

The police held him for three hours on that day in Obilić. When it was over, he emerged distressed, his face swollen and bearing rich-blue bruises from a sound beating.

Tortoshi's relationship with FC Prishtina was dyed in the wool. Having joined the club's youth ranks at the age of seven, he had been there throughout the wonder years of the 1980s when Prishtina held their own with zest and style in the Yugoslav First League.

When the crackdown began, he was used by the authorities to send a message. A blow to the face of Tortoshi was a blow to Kosovan civic pride, and in Obilić in 1992 that blow was firmly dealt.

'That day, we just sat in a friend of ours' restaurant and waited,' says Tortoshi's former Prishtina teammate, Edmond Rugova. He had been at the game and had watched his friend being dragged away still wearing his FC Prishtina kit. 'We just sat and sipped our coffee, looking over our shoulders not really knowing what was going to happen next.

'This was a time when people were being dragged out of their homes, people would disappear overnight sometimes. You would hear the most horrendous stories – so-and-so was beaten up or he is nowhere to be found. Then Tortoshi came out of the police station, bruised and beaten. His face was swollen.

'When everything deteriorated in the 1990s you couldn't speak to Serbs in the street. Even if I saw them and they saw me. We couldn't do it and they couldn't do it either because the tension was so high that they would be reprimanded if they were seen speaking to us. It would be "What do you have to talk to those guys about? You've seen what they're doing to us." I would see my best friend on the street and would pretend I didn't see him.'

Rugova left Kosovo in 1985 for a new life in the United States, building a career with the New York Cosmos before retiring to Kansas at the start of the 1990s.

He returned periodically to Pristina over the next decade and was saddened to see the deterioration in the quality of life there. Ever since Milošević's speech at the Battle of Kosovo memorial in 1989, the republic had been sleep-walking itself towards civil war, despite the efforts of the underground resistance.

Rugova longed for a return to the old ways. On a return visit home in 1995, he was moved to take action.

'If I don't go back and see that place, my eyes are gonna fall out,' he pleaded.

'It's not a good idea,' Tortoshi snapped back. 'Not with the way things are.'

It was a warm day in the tiny village of Llukar just outside of the capital. A match between FC Prishtina and some now-forgotten opponent had just been broken up by a single armed Serb police officer, and the crowd had dispersed quickly and quietly.

This was unfortunate. The game's organisers had found a perfect spot for football, a clearing with soft ground in what was an otherwise heavily wooded area. It was still and beautiful, somehow seeming to remain so even as tackles flew in and studs raked down shins. Llukar was calm that day, at peace.

Rugova never missed Tortoshi play with Prishtina during visits home. Sometimes, he would watch his friend being taken straight from the pitch into police custody, as had happened on that day at Obilić three years before. Today, there was to be no interrogation, no rough treatment, and the two friends travelled together back to Pristina, collecting their thoughts.

'I just want to go inside, feel the grass, look around,' Rugova persisted, refusing to let it lie. 'Then I'll be satisfied.'

It wasn't the first time that Rugova had pressed this issue, and it wasn't the first time that Tortoshi had fought to dissuade him. Tortoshi was a realist. It was 1995, and two Albanians couldn't simply walk into a football stadium in Kosovo.

This time, no scolding from his friend would keep Rugova from taking one last trip to the City Stadium, the scene of the two friends' greatest triumphs in the 1980s. He was going, and he was taking a reluctant Tortoshi with him.

In their day, Albanians made up the majority of the FC Prishtina team with a handful of exceptions. One of those exceptions had been Kosta Lalic, a larger-than-life eccentric goalkeeper with an immaculate chest-length beard and a wicked smile.

Years later, Rugova would swear that the long-haired Serb was the greatest goalkeeper ever produced by Yugoslavia. Lalic was another player whose spiritual connection to the club kept him close by, and by 1995 he was head coach of the Serb incarnation of FC Prishtina, which had been left to compete in Yugoslavia after the Albanian contingent had upped sticks and made for the woods.

The three friends had been tight. They had travelled the length and breadth of the federation together, turning their unfashionable little football club into one of the most talked-about teams in the country.

When Tortoshi and Rugova arrived they found structural renovation work being carried out at the stadium. This at least meant that access wouldn't be a problem. The dressing rooms had been replaced by a temporary portacabin. The pair snuck up to the door and listened to what was going on inside.

Players wandered in and out, but when they saw the two men standing outside the atmosphere changed. Everybody recognised these elder figures of Kosovan football, but nobody dared say a word. As Rugova and Tortoshi stood awkwardly at the door as the tension built, amidst the sounds of their former home they heard a familiar voice.

Despite his imposing masculine frame and unmistakable hair and beard, Kosta Lalic had an endearing tendency to blush like a schoolgirl whenever he felt overawed. Stepping out of this rickety cabin, coming face to face not only with his two former teammates and comrades but with a huge part of his own past, was one such moment. His face, framed by his thick blond hair like a lion's mane, flushed crimson.

After a few minutes of awkward niceties, whilst all three tried hard to pretend that this wasn't all happening in such circumstances, Rugova found the courage to ask the question.

'We wondered if we might just come in, have a look around?'

Lalic's face cracked into a grin. 'You son of a bitch,' he bellowed. 'What kind of a question is that? This is your stadium.'

Rugova doesn't remember how long he spent out on the pitch. But he does recall looking up to the part of the terrace where, as a fourteen-year-old in 1973, he had watched his beloved Prishtina lose to a last-minute goal from NK Osijek of Croatia, missing out on promotion to the Yugoslav First League.

He remembers walking down to the goal where his teammate and club legend Fadil Vokrri had headed two goals in May 1983 on the day that Prishtina had celebrated an historic promotion to the Yugoslav First League with a processional 3–0 victory over FK Sutjeska. A crowd of 45,000 had packed into the City Stadium that day, before flowing out into Pristina for the greatest street party the city had ever known.

Rugova's memories hung on every corner of the pitch. As he reached down to touch the turf with his fingers, ten years of pain and loss slipped from his shoulders. When he got back to his feet, he stood twice as tall.

And then it was over. He reeled Tortoshi back in from his own cathartic daydream, and the two headed back towards the makeshift dressing rooms.

Lalic by now had resumed work with his team. On the way out, Rugova paused and shouted over to him.

'Hey!'

Lalic turned. As he did so, his old friend raised his arms silently in a shrug. For a moment, the three men stood in silence, separated by a few yards of the battered old pitch of the Pristina City Stadium, but with history now driven immovably between them.

'What the hell is this all about?'

Lalic shrugged his giant shoulders, and the two visitors left. Three days later, Rugova returned to Kansas. He never saw Kosta Lalic again.

'It was heartbreaking to see the country in that condition,' he tells me. 'But for those people to do what they did, under those circumstances, the only thing that can possibly drive you is the love for the game.'

* * *

Days after leaving Skënderaj, I arrange to meet with Fisnik Isufi, president of Superleague side KF Drita from the city of Gjilan in the east. We meet on Rruga Agim Ramadani in the capital on a freezing afternoon in March 2016.

Drita won the league championship way back in 2003, but since the death of the side's wealthy benefactor there has been little to get excited about. The highlights of their calendar are games against city rivals SC Gjilani, a seething rivalry that packs the streets with throngs of ultras when the teams meet.

I had heard about Gjilan before meeting Isufi. No one had a positive word to say. Even in the late bars of Agim Ramadani and Mother Teresa Boulevard, where buoyant locals befriend foreign explorers and try to sell them the cultural delights in the re-booted version of their country, the word on Gjilan is lukewarm.

The bar Isufi has suggested is packed, so I'm made to sit outside and endure the twin gut-punch of the fumes from Pristina's busiest thoroughfare and the piercing spring air.

Isufi is one hour and fifteen minutes late. When he arrives, I am barely visible beneath a winter coat, hat and scarf, with just my eyes and nose braving the wild elements.

It was only a week earlier that I'd sat drenched in sunshine in this same spot, and watched Liverpool lose 3–2 to Southampton in the Premier League through the open windows of the bar on a TV above the counter. The sudden deterioration in the weather is something I am becoming used to in Kosovo.

'I began at Drita as just a fan,' says Isufi, ordering coffee and apologising for his tardiness. The shallow afternoon sun glistens off his balding pate, and the rolled-up sleeves of his shirt suggest he isn't particularly troubled by the cold. 'Then I became the leader of one of the fan groups that we call *Intelektualët* – the Intellectuals.'

Isufi is an archetype of post-war Kosovo. Born before the conflict, he was too young to fight, but is old enough to remember the fear. By trade, he is a project manager, that most Westernised of job titles. His passions are football and jazz. And he believes deeply in his fledgling country.

Young professionals with energy and business skills are a sought-after commodity here. Money, or the lack of it, is a thorn in the side of Kosovan football. Since 1991, a desperate scramble to meet deficits and plug holes has made survival, rather than growth, the name of the game.

'We don't have any sponsorship system in Kosovo,' says Isufi. 'So, it's very difficult. In fact, Drita has never had proper sponsorship.

'You just have to find the occasional backer that has passion about football. You get a bit of money from the people who come to watch the games, but it's small.

'A big part of my job is to negotiate with our fans.'

Negotiate?

'There are a lot of people who love this club. Sometimes they don't ask about what is the financial reality. They just expect victory. I have to play bridge between the fans' expectations and the club's resources.'

Drita have been cut adrift financially. Extravagances such as transfer fees and stadium repairs are a no-go. The country's recognition from UEFA is the only prize that matters.

Without exposure to international football, Kosovo's horizons would be restricted. Players cannot be sold abroad, transfers don't take place and investors fail to engage. 'At the moment, clubs are straightforward, just training and training and training. But football isn't just training. It's much more. It's life,' states Isufi.

The road east from Pristina towards Gjilan runs through rough and raw countryside. The driving rain that pounds the windshield creates a dramatically eerie atmosphere, which complements the tangled wildness of the Balkan outback. The road passes alongside the glorious Byzantine fourteenth-century Orthodox monastery at Gračanica, where Milos Obilić watches over the town atop his horse in full battle dress and a poignant sculpture, which is clad in photographs of local people whose bodies were never found after the war, mournfully spells out the word MISSING.

After the 1999 conflict, the Orthodox Bishop of Prizren moved his official seat here to Gračanica in muted solidarity with the Serb nation, making the town the spiritual home of the Serbs in Kosovo.

In these rural townships, history counts for nothing. The Serb villagers in the poorer provinces languish in poverty from one month to the next in much the same way as their Albanian neighbours. The grindstone knows no creed. It is a reminder that, even in fiercely tribal Kosovo, economic dislocation is a common enemy that dictates the lives of ordinary people.

The rain lets up as we roll into Gjilan, but it leaves in its wake a biting wind. The town bears testimony to the fact that, across most of Kosovo, Serb populations are disappearing. Between 1953 and 2011, the proportion of Serbs living in Gjilan has plummeted from just under 40 per cent to a little over 0.5 per cent. Aside from a small number of Roma and other groups, the place is now almost entirely Albanian.

Each January, heirs to Albania's freedom fighters congregate in Gjilan to celebrate their culture. Since 1992, people from across the Albanian territories in the Balkans have flocked here for a city-wide celebration of Albanian arts, music and culture. *Flaka e Janarit* is richly symbolic, and drenches the city in noise, colour and life.

But not today. The streets of Gjilan are wet and grey.

There is a famous footballing son that hails from this town. Xherdan Shaqiri, once of Bayern Munich and Inter Milan and now of Liverpool, left Gjilan with his family aged two, finding refuge in Switzerland. He never played at the Gjilan City Stadium, the sparse concrete amphitheatre tucked in the centre of town just off the main thoroughfare.

Gjilan is small and cramped, and seems to have been assembled in a hurry without any kind of design in mind. The traffic en route to the ground crawls along bumper to bumper, with car horns ringing out amongst the patchwork of doddering corner shops and shabby hair salons that line the cracked pavements.

On this miserable Monday afternoon, Drita's great rivals that they share their city with, SC Gjilani, are hosting Trepča '89 from Mitrovica in the country's northern Serb stronghold.

Trepča have the title in their sights. Just a few points separate them from KF Feronikeli at the league's summit, although this doesn't translate into urgency or quality on the pitch.

The Gjilan City Stadium possesses a beguiling Ottoman-era

charm. Its bobbly, unkempt pitch sits between two banks of cold concrete with a draughty, dilapidated clubhouse tucked up in one corner. The Trepča match is played to a soundtrack of the Islamic call to prayer, bellowed out from the half-dozen mosques which are visible amongst the red-tiled roofs from the stadium's open terraces. When it rains – and it rains frequently in Gjilan – supporters get soaked, but it doesn't matter. They're a hardy sort here, made this way by decades of grey, bloodless Communism.

The turn-out, even for a Monday afternoon, is uninspiring. The single cameraman working on behalf of the FFK sets up his tripod so close to me I have to drag myself away down the terrace as he curses and grimaces his way through his afternoon's work. The atmosphere is a far cry from the derby day between Drita and Gjilani.

Known as the 'Kosovo Derby', Drita v. Gjilani is concentrated energy. It represents not just the city's historic struggles, but those of the country at large. The old order's footprint is stamped across this bitter rivalry.

'You probably won't want to write the things I have to say about them,' begins Isufi, sipping his coffee back on Agim Ramadani. 'When we have to make a toilet, we say we have to make a Gjilan.'

Isufi's Drita are no heavyweights in Kosovo. Founded in 1947, the club has a traditionally right-wing nationalist following.

'After the Second World War, Albanians in Yugoslavia were not treated right,' he says. 'Students in Gjilan founded what you would call a freedom movement. They couldn't find jobs, so they found themselves gathering at football.' Drita, meaning 'light', was a space where Albanian intellectuals and dissidents could gather to share ideas without attracting the attention of the Serb authorities, who were less quick to crack down on sports clubs than on political groups.

'It was cleverly done,' says Isufi, lighting a cigarette and casually swinging one leg over the other. 'They said they were meeting to play and watch football, but when they met they would discuss freedom.'

Folk bands, poetry societies and dance groups all emerged; a swathe of collectives that promoted and celebrated Albanian heritage. Though keenly nationalist, the movement didn't subscribe to resistance through violence, and the group's weapons were the pen and the softly plucked strings of the *çifteli* rather than the butt of a rifle.

'They just wanted to not be persecuted by Serbs,' says Isufi. 'That was the strategy of the intellectuals. They would gather to recite Albanian poetry and sing Albanian hymns and tell old Albanian stories. And of course, to play football. That's where we took the name *Intelektualët* from.'

This was a crystallisation of the way in which Albanians viewed themselves within the federation, the heirs to an ancient, vibrant culture, smothered by a bureaucratic and repressive Communism. Such an act of resistance could not go unchallenged.

After the Tito–Stalin split in 1948, which led to Yugoslavia being expelled from the Communist Information Bureau and being thrust on a separate path from Moscow, the Yugoslav authorities began to be suspicious that Albanians in Kosovo were pro-Soviet saboteurs. In Gjilan, the local Serb-dominated Communist Party responded to Drita's dissidents by creating a football club of their own: Red Star, in the image of their namesakes from Belgrade.

'The Serb directors of the club at Red Star destroyed many promising careers,' says Isufi. 'The owners of the industrial companies that controlled the club, it was their brothers that played, or it was their sons. They destroyed legends who could have become great players.'

Red Star forcibly absorbed the best players from the city's small local talent pool. They had the money and more importantly they had the support of Yugoslavia's anti-Albanian, pro-Serb governors.

'Say you are English, and I am Albanian,' says Isufi. 'You are a good player, but you won't play, my Albanian players will play instead. Then you will know my message. You are not welcome here.'

As Red Star took an iron grip over the city, Drita could scarcely find eleven players to wear their blue and white stripes. In 1952, under intense pressure, the club temporarily folded, the first in a succession of club closures.

When the Serbs were forced out of Kosovo, Red Star became SC Gjilani, but despite now being run by Albanians, the Drita supporters haven't forgotten the team's Serb connections.

'They weren't actually connected to the Serbs by the 1990s,' explains Isufi of SC Gjilani's bloodline.

'The Serbs actually didn't care too much about them. "Not in my stadium, not in my city, you can do what you want in the fields and such." But the Albanians found money from somewhere. Football fans with money came together to make SC Gjilani happen. But it took time.

'This was around the time that Dinamo Zagreb and Red Star Belgrade played that game that basically started the Yugoslav war [the teams met in Zagreb in May 1990 weeks after Croatia had elected its first pro-independence Parliament, and a huge riot erupted between Serbian and Croatian supporters which left more than sixty people wounded]. The aggression had become so bad that the Albanian players were forced to quit and it stayed bad, so there was no possibility of football between Serbs and Albanians. No way.

'Somehow those clubs were provoking that ego for Albanians. We were supposed to recognise only Serbia, we were supposed to write only in Cyrillic letters. People didn't want their team name to be written in Cyrillic and didn't want to play in those kind of conditions.

'There was always resistance to that, but the government were increasing the standard of Serb orthodoxy that the Albanians were expected to conform to. The enforced use of Cyrillic instead of Latin was a big provocation.'

Drita's recent fortunes have been defined by the patronage of a local businessman, Selami Osmani, who by the time of his death in 2008 had ploughed €1 million into the club.

Driven half-mad by fantasies of what the club could grow into in an independent Kosovo, Osmani was famously difficult to work with, and never consulted or allowed others into his decisions. Whatever mistakes he made, and there were plenty, he made up for them with money.

He was also a huge public donor during the period of Serb rule, investing in the institutions of the rebel leader Ibrahim Rugova and his allies in the underground government. That sports, education and humanitarian infrastructure were able to survive amongst Albanian communities during the Serb occupation was in large part down to Osmani.

In the 2002/03 season, Drita defied the odds to win a first ever Superleague title. To this end, Osmani is an idol in Gjilan, with one obituary waxing lyrical that 'for Drita, he has spared nothing of himself'. To mark his passing, a plaque was installed at the City Stadium. It reads: 'Selami Osmani – Your Work Makes Light'.

The problem for the club now, says Isufi, is that the mentality of being able to spend money and the expectation of success has remained for the club's current owners, but the means to pursue those expectations have long since dried up.

Curious to see what Gjilan makes of Osmani and his legacy in

2016, I put the question to a handful of passers-by as I traipse away from the ground after watching SC Gjilani's 1–0 defeat against Trepča. Not many in town speak English, but Granit, who serves me a black tea not far from the bus station, is happy to talk.

'If Osmani accidentally brought in two right-sided strikers, he would say, "OK, we'll just buy two left-sided strikers to go with them,"' says Granit. 'But he was a great man. Many years ago, he threw a celebration for fifty years of Drita. They all came; Ibrahim Rugova, the politicians, everyone.'

And what about the blackout years, those troubled times between 1991 and 1999 when football was forced underground?

'Prishtina were the best team, they were supported by the Albanian students. At matches, they would sing the name of Enver Hoxha.'

Surely not the Albanian dictator Enver Hoxha, the man who ran the country's economy into the ground and who interned and executed thousands of political prisoners inside forced labour camps? Granit gives a wry smile.

'They didn't truly know who was Enver Hoxha, but they were desperate to identify as Albanians because of what the Serbs were doing here. Where you are from?'

England, I tell him, spilling tea on myself.

'Ah, Shaqiri,' he replies, in reference to the town's most famous son, Xherdan, who had recently signed for Stoke City. 'No charge for the tea, my friend. For Shaqiri.' I bid Granit goodbye and walk out, confused but grateful.

Isufi is the face of the new Kosovo, forward-looking and ambitious as it emerges from its troubled birth. He is a far cry from the cigarette-smoking men in khaki gear riding atop tanks I remember from the news.

Kosovo used to be the poorest province in all of Yugoslavia, with massive federal subsidies needed in the 1960s and 1970s to restart an economy that had tanked. Owing to the unchecked pretentions of the province's Communist governors, these funds were often badly invested, and led to the 'marble sidewalks but troubled industries' that were observed by foreign visitors from the early 1980s onwards.

When Slobodan Milošević revoked the province's autonomy, Kosovo's problems worsened. A cocktail of dire economic policies reacted with international sanctions and internal ethnic tensions, damaging an already crumbling economy. Then came the war, and financial as well as physical ruin.

Though it is still one of Europe's poorest regions, the country is finally showing signs of recovery. Innovators like Isufi have built upon Osmani's legacy to make this recovery possible. For the first time, Kosovan culture can freely afford broader horizons than simple resistance to Serb hegemony.

* * *

Rruga Agim Ramadani is a great sprawling boulevard that cuts through the centre of the Kosovan capital like a jugular artery. Pristina owes its greying, frail appearance to the decaying Serb colonial style that dominated town planning from the 1970s onwards.

Money was spent by Tito's government to stave off unrest amongst impoverished Albanians and to snuff out nationalist grumblings. In a triumph of Communist bureaucracy, most of it lined the pockets of the crooked League of Communists of Kosovo Party leaders, who wasted little time in erecting brutalist aberrations, whilst public infrastructure crumbled.

Chief offender is the Grand Hotel on Mother Teresa Boulevard. It's a pompous hulk of rectangular concrete that looms thirteen storeys above the city and bears down on everything below like an untreated weed. Those responsible for erecting the Grand Hotel and its fatuous stone cousins owe the people who now live amongst them a sincere and unconditional apology.

Back on Agim Ramadani, another of the city's carbuncles, the House of Sports – which is home to the Football Federation of Kosovo – sits awkwardly.

It's hard to imagine a less ceremonious building which could house the headquarters of the country's most popular sport. At first glance one would believe the place has been left to rack and ruin, abandoned as an afterthought whilst the city struggles towards its future. There are windows, but all along the ground floor they are blacked out, and though the place sits just metres from Pristina's bustling heart, no one would ever believe there was anything going on inside the House of Sports. It's a mark of the neglect with which football has been treated here.

Standing outside the building, I'm struck by the sulphur-like smell that hangs in the air all across Pristina. It's a smell that anyone who has ever smelled burning gunpowder might imagine bullets and bombs leave behind.

The glass front door opens to a dark entryway, with a few empty pigeonholes clumsily nailed to the wall opposite. It's from here on the first floor, one up from a cheap sporting goods store, that the FFK operates, crammed into a few square yards of office space alongside a handful of other sporting governing bodies. Lancaster Gate, it is not.

Inside, the stairs that lead up to the FFK's offices are poorly lit. Not that the peeling walls offer up much of interest. It's not until one reaches the top of the stairs that it becomes clear that the building has any function at all, and the first indications of the struggles that have brought the country to this point begin to reveal themselves.

A handful of neatly framed pictures are dotted along the walls, a handpicked selection of football highlights from the short history of this tiny nation. The first to catch the eye, nailed to the wall outside the office of the general secretary, shows the national team all in white before a friendly against Saudi Arabia in Ankara, Turkey, in June 2007.

Back-row, first on the left, stands a broad-shouldered, tracksuited man with olive skin, thick dark hair and a domineering nose. He is beaming with pride.

As a player Edmond Rugova had been part of Kosovo's golden generation of the 1980s. This was a time when FC Prishtina had held their own with skill and zest against far better-resourced outfits in the Yugoslav First League, the federal pyramid system that spanned the great old footballing republic.

'We had the greatest success in the club's history, in the history of any club from Kosovo,' describes Rugova.

Briefly, brilliantly, these sons of little Kosovo stood on the shoulders of giants, the likes of Partizan Belgrade and Dinamo Zagreb who were celebrated as the 'Brazil of Europe'.

Rugova was part of the same Prishtina team as Fadil Vokrri who inspired the club to its most famous victory, a 3–1 win at the fortress home of Serbia's Red Star Belgrade in 1983, and who went on to be the FFK president. The victory was as magnificent as it was impertinent – how dare the primitive Albanian upstarts believe they could win in the backyard of the grand masters of Yugoslavia and then dance rings around the champions.

I've been lucky enough to meet Vokrri – widely regarded as Kosovo's best-ever player – twice. The first time was here at the offices of the FFK on my first day in the city in early 2016. He strode manfully into the room and swallowed my hand in his huge sweaty palm. He doesn't speak English, but that gave him a mystic kind of aura that left me feeling embarrassed and star-struck.

I've watched his performance against Red Star Belgrade more

times than I'm comfortable admitting. Vokrri played that day like a man possessed. He didn't score, but Prishtina could not have won without him.

'Vokrri was the best player in Yugoslavia,' says Fadil Muriqi, the powerhouse Prishtina midfielder who earned the nickname Maradona for his magical feet and brilliant billowing hair. I first made Muriqi's acquaintance after my first visit to Kosovo, via telephone from his home in Australia.

'I was good, but Vokrri was better. A great player and a great man. Talent, organisation, communication. A very intelligent soccer player. We were lucky to have him.

'We played a little more on the counter-attack that day [against Red Star] than we would usually be happy with. Red Star missed a lot of chances though. They missed a penalty. But after that our confidence was huge. That was when we believed we could beat them.

'It was different playing in Serbia than anywhere else. There was an arrogance about the Serbs. It was very hard to go there. But our motivation to show them what we as Kosovans could do, to show Serbia how good we were – that was a huge motivation.'

Tito, who had suppressed all nationalism in Yugoslavia, died in the summer of 1980. Immediately afterwards, a new generation of explicitly nationalist politicians began to squabble over his legacy. In Kosovo, the problem was particularly acute because of historic tensions between Albanians and Serbs. Both sides saw an opportunity in Tito's succession – the Serbs saw a chance to finally neutralise the threat posed by their barbarous ethnic neighbours, whilst young Albanians saw a chance to emerge from decades of impoverishment and cultural isolation.

'At that time, we Albanians were being sidelined,' says Rugova. 'There was a clear political decision by the Serbian government to slowly but surely close down Albanian schools. Albanian people were kicked out of work and institutions were being closed down.'

Rugova was born in 1957 in the western town of Peja. When he was six months old, his family moved to Pristina, and later he enrolled in the youth outfit for local side Obilić in the shadow of the hideous Kosovo Power Station. Years later, he watched on helplessly as his friend and Prishtina teammate Jusuf Tortoshi was dragged away into police custody by Serb militia.

But in the early 1980s, the future of football in Kosovo had never looked brighter. Edmond Rugova, with his electric pace and lightning feet, was at its beating heart.

He signed for Prishtina in 1979. Playing at the 20,000-capacity City Stadium, they were the best-supported club in the province.

Founded as FC Kosova by Yugoslav soldiers at the Pristina Garrison in 1922, the team went through a succession of names up to the Second World War, during which Kosovo was briefly annexed to fascist Albania, eventually returning to Yugoslav football under their current name when peacetime resumed.

The relocation of Kosovo's regional administration from Prizren to Pristina after the war strengthened the team with new recruits, and the side was buoyed by ex-soldiers returning from the front line. This was the beginning of Pristina as Kosovo's governmental and cultural capital. The same people that directed the evolution of public life were also responsible for creating the first professional structures for the football club.

'The party committee members worked very hard to bring in a lot of talent from all over Kosovo,' explains Muriqi. 'By 1982, we really started to see the benefit of that work in the quality of the team. To have made it to the First League of Yugoslavia with such a young squad, it was incredible really. That was one of the toughest leagues in Europe. They started bringing in different kinds of coach, experienced men from all over Yugoslavia.'

Muriqi and Rugova's Prishtina careers dovetailed with the ascent of Milošević to political prominence. President Milošević couldn't legally revoke Kosovo's autonomous status – only the republic's provincial assembly could do that. So, he used the powers available to him and attacked Albanian culture in its existential form.

The first public unrest erupted during a demonstration of students from the University of Pristina in March 1981, where roughly three quarters of the intake were ethnic Albanian. The strike began as a stand against the poor living conditions, but quickly broke out into a general protest in opposition to Albanian subjugation on their own territory.

Within days, the student protests had come to embody the anger at Kosovo's cultural isolation within Yugoslavia, and a lack of economic opportunity for the local people. Protests became so frequent and violent that FC Prishtina were briefly forced to leave the city and play matches in nearby Kragujevac.

'Yugoslavia wanted their strongest teams to come from Serbia at that time,' says Muriqi. 'Partizan Belgrade and Red Star – they were the favoured teams. It was very hard for Albanian footballers to play then.

'I was the best player in the First League of Yugoslavia. I was the fittest player. Yet I was never picked to play for Yugoslavia. They looked at us in a different way. Something happened there. It was very wrong, the politics of Yugoslavia. Very wrong.'

The protests were about justice. Albanians in Kosovo had the lowest living standards of any region in Yugoslavia. It was also one of the most heavily subsidised provinces in the federation, with much of that subsidy being directed by local party officials into the advancement of Albanian studies at the university. It created an explosive sense of injustice, where Albanian national consciousness grew concurrently with a distrust for the regime.

'We were being deprived of our basic rights around that time,' says Rugova. 'But as athletes, I believe we were always privy to some kind of a privilege, if you will.

'In the 1980s, we never felt the animosity of the Serb authorities, not really. Some of our best friends were Serbs, we grew up speaking the language fluently. We played with many of them, side by side.'

Most weren't so fortunate. Between 26 March and 2 April, eleven people died in street violence started by Albanian nationalists around Pristina. A state of emergency was declared in the capital.

Belgrade pumped out declarations that the hunt for 'the enemy' was ongoing, and scores of suspects were rounded up and arrested. Uniformed and undercover police arrived en masse from Belgrade, eyes and muscle, to stop the decline in law and order.

The propaganda war raged on. Albanians were accused of setting fire to the Patriarchate of Peć, one of the oldest symbols of Serb culture in Kosovo, and Albanian provincial leaders of fermenting nationalism through clandestine organisations dedicated to unifying ethnic Albanians into a single state. To the Serbs, Albanian nationalism became shorthand for terrorism.

Meanwhile, at the Pristina City Stadium, a legend was about to be born.

FC Prishtina were eking out an existence in the wilderness of Yugoslavia's second division. In charge of the team was a newly appointed Hungarian Serb, born in 1923 in Zrenjanin in the northern province of Vojvodina. His name was Béla Pálfi.

An experienced coach who knew Yugoslavian football like the back of his hand, Pálfi was fifty-eight by the time he arrived in Pristina from the Greek club Egaleo, following spells managing FK Sloboda Tuzla in Bosnia, whom he coached in the Yugoslav

First League, and the Serb outfits Proleter Zrenjanin and Radnički Kragujevac. As a player, he had represented Yugoslavia at the 1948 Olympics in London, as well as at the 1950 World Cup in Brazil.

Pálfi held the rare accolade of having played for both Belgrade clubs, pathological enemies Red Star and Partizan, whose complicated hate for each other is a product of the Nazi occupation of Yugoslavia.

An anti-fascist guerrilla resistance was carried out by two groups – the Communist Partizans, who believed strongly in federalism and were led by a young Tito; and the Chetniks, crazed Serb evangelists loyal only to Belgrade and drunk on fantastical notions of the Serb nation's destiny as a chosen race. During the occupation, rivalry between the two groups became so fierce that, by the end of the war, the Chetniks had begun to collaborate with the Nazis against the Partizans.

When Partizan Belgrade was founded at the end of the Second World War, Pálfi – recognised as one of the country's best players – was brought in as a member of the club's first-ever team, the 1947 first league title winners, before going on to spend the best years of his career at Red Star, where he won the league twice more in 1951 and 1953.

Playing amongst both Partizans and Chetniks gave Pálfi a unique and timeless understanding of the emotional politics that afflicted Yugoslavia, and taught him how to harness and control the prejudices that shaped the national consciousness.

Tall, broad and with thick black hair framing his strong, angular forehead, he was an old-fashioned gentleman. He was educated, empathetic and emanated calm, which was unusual amongst the demonstrative masculinity of Balkan football. He never shied away from seeking to tame this wildness with a rational hand.

'He was very, very intelligent,' says Muriqi. 'He was an

experienced coach who brought something new to Prishtina. More discipline, more teamwork. He was an older man and that made the players respect him. Tactically he was very aware. There's no doubt that it was his tactical ability that got Prishtina into the First League of Yugoslavia.'

Pálfi was also a specialist. As a football coach he had few equals in terms of how well he understood what was going on politically and socially in the country. He knew that success could only be achieved by working through the very peculiar set of challenges that football in different parts of Yugoslavia faced.

In Pristina in the early 1980s, this meant tapping into the disenfranchisement felt by the Albanian community as Belgrade cracked the whip. The football team traditionally had a Serb majority, but in a city where relations between Albanians and Serbs were deteriorating daily, something needed to change if the club wanted to keep its supporters on side during the troubles.

It wasn't the case that people would refuse to get behind a team with Serb elements. Certainly, it was true that relations between the government and the city's educated dissidents were declining – such that on the customary evening promenade down Rruga Agim Ramadani, Albanians kept to the north side of the street and Serbs to the south – but it was quite different to the seething hatred that would pound Yugoslavia during the 1990s. That said, the battle lines had been drawn; Albanians sided with Albanians, Serbs with Serbs.

'Pálfi realised very quickly that this wasn't going to work unless FC Prishtina had a make-up where local kids, Kosovar-Albanian kids, made up the bulk of the starting line-up,' says Rugova.

The Albanians in Kosovo had always felt a special kind of otherness about their place within Yugoslavia. They were the only non-Slavs in the federation, and formed a tiny minority that subscribed to the doctrines of neither Orthodoxy nor Catholicism.

Geographically, Kosovo is penned in. To the north is Serbia with its Cyrillic script and Orthodox culture, and north-west is the culturally and ethnically Serb republic of Montenegro. To the south-east, North Macedonia speaks a variant of Bulgarian and also follows the traditions of the Orthodox Church. Where else in the federation were the people of Kosovo to look to reinforce their cultural identity if not inwardly, to their own customs, heritage and kin?

This was something that the great Serbian Real Madrid manager Miljan Miljanić had observed years before when he predicted that 'they will never have any success at Prishtina until the ethnic background of the club is changed'.

As a result, Pálfi set about making some changes, and through the door came a cadre of Albanians. The flying full-back Ramiz Krasniqi arrived from Radnički Pirot in Serbia. Agim Cana was brought back to play in midfield from FK Vëllaznimi in Gjakova, the club he had left Prishtina to join just a year earlier. Faruk Domi came in at left-back, and to the heart of midfield was added a stalwart with First League experience, the rock-solid Ramadan Cimili who had represented Mitrovica side FK Trepča in their single season in the top flight in 1979.

'The reason for our success is that we all played for each other,' states Muriqi. 'Vokrri was the best of us, but the other Albanian players that Pálfi brought in worked so hard for each other.'

Pálfi had inherited a side that already had a strong pool of Kosovar Albanians. Alongside Rugova in attack were the powerhouse winger Fadil Muriqi and the mazy centre-forward Fadil Vokrri, with utility man Jusuf Tortoshi filling in where needed. All four had been born and raised within a short taxi ride of the centre of Pristina. Suddenly, this was a team no longer just Kosovan in name.

'We were incredibly fortunate to have someone come in who

understood the region so well,' says Rugova. 'Pálfi knew what was needed and what was necessary to change things, because he knew Yugoslavia so well. He knew what that ethnic situation was that needed to be created and he went and he created it.

'I don't think we will see another coach like that.'

The team idolised their manager. When, one weekend in 1982, Pálfi found himself needing to take an urgent trip to his hometown of Zrenjanin to tend to a family emergency, his players clubbed together their state-issued fuel vouchers to see that their coach could make it home.

'People just loved the guy, and so did we,' explains Rugova. 'There was a tremendous respect for the man, a quiet-natured guy. He would come in and stick everything up on the board, everybody's names, so that everybody would know exactly what they were doing for the day.

'Then he designed this dream for us, that at the time seemed like an unreachable dream.'

* * *

'We were being pushed around as a people and everything had begun to deteriorate,' recalls Rugova in 2017. 'Because of that there was a big political connotation to what we as a football club were doing.

'Béla Pálfi could sense the crowd. He knew the political structure, he knew what was going on in the country at the time.'

In the summer of 1981, Prishtina weren't pulling up trees. Marooned in the bottom half of the Second League's eastern division, there had been little to recommend the City Stadium to the football world outside of Kosovo for years.

The team had never played in the top flight. But they had come frustratingly close to doing so in 1974, losing in the promotion play-offs to NK Osijek of Croatia.

It was a muggy day in Pristina on the day Osijek came to town, one that began with the city preparing for a party that never arrived.

'I was fourteen or fifteen when the team played Osijek,' continues Rugova. 'What made that defeat hard to take was that we had such a great generation of players. To my mind they were probably a stronger, more talented generation than we were.

'The stadium was full, there was the noise and the flags. It was an incredible thing to see.'

The year 1974 was an optimistic one. The Yugoslav Constitution was redrawn to strengthen Kosovo's position within the federation, and Albanian people believed they were being heard. Prishtina's promotion to the First League seemed like fate. The city became paralysed with anticipation for the Osijek game. It was even arranged that the match ball would be delivered to the centre circle for the kick-off by a man parachuting into the ground from a plane above the city.

'It's hard to explain exactly what we went through as a nation when we lost that game,' expresses Rugova. As the team of 1974 drifted one by one on to new challenges in the top tier, Prishtina were relegated from the Yugoslav Second League into the obscurity of the third tier.

The 1982/83 season began with little sign of what was to come. After a routine opening-day win at home to FK Sloboda Tuzla, the team were dismantled on their first away trip of the season; 3–0 at FK Bor in eastern Serbia. It was the start of a difficult autumn. More defeats followed in Macedonia to FK Teteks and in Montenegro to OFK Titograd.

By the time the leaves were falling from the trees, Prishtina straightened up. They went seven unbeaten to climb up to third, a point behind league leaders FK Teteks. Pálfi took his team to Serbia to face FK Rad on 21 November knowing a win would put them top of the league for the first time.

They got thrashed. A 4–1 defeat exposed 'little Prishtina' as parochial nearly men without the spirit to dethrone their Slav cousins. They were the heirs of the class of 1974, still haunted by the spectre of NK Osijek. As the team floundered, the crisis in the streets intensified.

Days after Prishtina returned from Rad, three bombs exploded in the city. One went off just yards from the Communist Party headquarters. The same week, a gang of Albanian children were accused of setting fire to a young Serb boy in the street.

The month also brought foreign interest in the crisis. At New York City University, an international conference on Kosovo was convened, and the Kosova Relief Fund USA was established to collect funds to aid the families of political prisoners of the regime in Pristina.

Yugoslavia sent police, soldiers and military intelligence to Pristina on what was formally dubbed 'service work'. Reports say that Belgrade spent $30 million on increased security during the months when the protests were at their worst.

Prishtina needed to restart their season. Béla Pálfi ordered four deep trenches to be dug behind each goal and along the touchlines at the City Stadium, into which were installed platforms that were each capable of housing an extra 5,000 fans. The old ground's 20,000 capacity was doubled in a stroke, though it still wasn't enough to accommodate the dozens of other supporters who would watch from nearby buildings and from the branches of trees. It helped Pristina create a blitzkrieg environment, smothering opposition teams against a wall of noise.

'It was go, go, go, go, go, right from the kick-off,' exclaims Rugova. 'A team that comes in with some sense of anxiety already just could not cope with that kind of relentless attacking style and would give in most of the time. And then away from home we just sat back and waited to rip teams up with this perfectly designed counter-attacking game. It was a perfect system.

'The supporters wanted to see that we were giving something back, in light of what was happening to them. Because of the relationship between the Albanians and the Serbs, those fans, they always favoured a hardman on the pitch. Someone who was ready for a fight.' When the league resumed after the long winter break, Prishtina climbed to the top of the table.

'You have to appreciate it in the context of what was already happening in the country,' states Muriqi. 'The country was living almost through the football club of Pristina.'

The extent to which football had afflicted ordinary people became clear on an away day in May 1983. The team were in first place with seven games to go when they travelled to the city of Bitola in western Macedonia for a fixture against FK Pelister. Three minutes in, the flying full-back Ramiz Krasniqi burst into the box and was brought down, and the referee blew for a penalty. Rugova stepped forward.

Facing him was the Serb goalkeeper Živan Ljukovčan, a Yugoslavia international who famously played with three fingers missing from his left hand. Ljukovčan had a reputation for playing mind games with his opponents when facing penalties. Rugova caved under the pressure. Ljukovčan dived low to his left and clawed the ball away with the two fingers of his left hand. In the second half, Rugova struck the inside of the post but there was to be no reprieve, and the game finished goalless.

The story goes that back in Pristina an unlucky supporter, who was listening in by radio to the match commentary from Bitola, dropped dead of a heart attack when Ljukovčan stopped Rugova's kick.

Returning home, even Rugova's own parents shunned him. 'Why did you change your mind?' raged his mother. 'What were you thinking?' It was a tense and suspicious time. Some suspected that Rugova had been 'got to' by influencers for whom a promotion to the First League for Prishtina would not have been a good thing. The city was on a knife-edge.

'I used to joke with Kosta Lalic during practice when we would take penalties,' remembers Rugova. 'I would say, "Hey, that's the corner I'm going to put it in." So, when that kick was saved everyone wanted to know why; why I changed my mind. That bus ride back from Bitola was the longest of my life.'

'For me to have grown up and lived through the generation of players that came before, to have watched the team that fell short against Osijek in 1974 ... I was just lucky to have been part of this generation, the "golden generation", they called us. I'm embarrassed sometimes to have people compare us to the 1974 side.'

The title run-in was less a procession than a stumble. Prishtina crossed the line only because FK Sutjeska from Montenegro failed to. But cross it they did. The following season, they finally laid the ghosts of 1974 to bed, and took up their place in the First League of Yugoslavia.

It was to be the last great episode in Kosovo's football history for years. Their six seasons in the top flight were blighted by more unrest and worsening persecution. Prishtina were relegated in 1989. A decade later Kosovo was at war.

IV

In October 2014, a European Championship qualifier between Serbia and Albania in Belgrade was abandoned when fighting broke out on the pitch and in the stands. The catalyst for the violence came when a drone was flown over the pitch carrying the flag of the hypothetical 'Greater Albania', an irredentist idea that promotes the incorporation of Kosovo into an enlarged Albanian state.

The Albania captain that night, who was in the thick of the chaos, was Lorik Cana. Born in Pristina, he moved to Switzerland as a child to escape the Yugoslav war. He is the son of the FC Prishtina legend Agim Cana and consequently, he attended virtually every game the team played from the age of five.

I spoke with Cana in Rome shortly before Albania and Serbia were due to meet in the return fixture in Elbasan, twelve months on from the abandoned game.

'I feared for the safety of my teammates,' argued Cana, who fought back against the Serb supporters. 'I tried to neutralise the first fan, but they were coming at us from all around the pitch and it became impossible.'

From the moment Serbia defender Stefan Mitrovic pulled the drone out of the Belgrade sky, which prompted the start of the melee, the whole thing lasted a little more than three minutes. However, the fall-out was far-reaching. But Cana has no regrets about his actions that night.

'I'd do exactly the same thing again,' he said. 'When you're a team, and especially when you are one of the older members of that team and are leading by example, you consider them to be your brothers. If someone from outside of the pitch is going to come and attack one of my teammates, my first instinct is to protect him. It was just something completely natural. If it had happened to me my teammates would have done the same thing.'

Assigning blame for the fight has proved to be difficult, although the drone pilot was revealed as being an Albanian called Ismail Morina.

Precautions were taken before the game. No visiting supporters had been issued tickets without first presenting an Albanian passport; a move intended to keep Kosovan fans from gaining entry to the stadium and inflaming the situation.

This was supposed to have been a cooler period in Balkan relations. Earlier in 2014, diplomatic channels had been opened between Serbia and Albania following the Kosovo crisis, and political extremism had been criticised in both countries. There had been sufficient confidence amongst UEFA officials for the game to be allowed to go ahead. What happened inside the Partizan Stadium looked strangely out of place in the 21st-century Balkans.

Serbia were docked three points for failing to control their fans but were also given a 3–0 walkover after the Albania players refused to return to the pitch. The ruling drew sharp criticism in Albania, not least from the defender Bekim Balaj, who had been attacked by a supporter wielding a chair. He tweeted sarcastically, 'Sorry [Michel] Platini [UEFA president], for the stool I almost broke with my head. Bravo UEFA.'

Some accused the ruling of disregarding UEFA's stated aim to tackle racism in its stadiums, especially since the sanctions failed to address the anti-Albanian chanting heard from the Serbian fans during the short period that the game lasted. Albanian Football Federation (FSHF) board member Cimi Shakohoxha derided the decision and argued that it '[flew] in the face of UEFA's aim to eradicate racism from the game. It's not about the points,' he protested. 'It's about fighting racism.'

The Albanian reaction worked. In July 2015, an appeal was lodged with the Court of Arbitration for Sport. The court sided with the FSHF, and ruled that the match had been forfeited by Serbia, reversing the 3–0 walkover and awarding the victory to Albania.

'I was in the stadium that night and what I saw there will remain forever in my mind,' FSHF president Armand Duka told me. 'Nothing that happened in that nightmare in Belgrade should be reflected on the pitch in Elbasan. Our players, but even the opponents who were like friends to us in their home, will simply play a football match.' Albania did play a football match and Serbia beat them 2–0.

None of this helped Kosovo's UEFA bid. In January 2014, an agreement was reached between the FFK, FIFA and the Football Association of Serbia that allowed Kosovo to compete in friendly international fixtures against other FIFA members, provided that no national symbols, such as flags or the national anthem, were displayed. It was also stipulated that the team would not be permitted to arrange fixtures against countries of the former Yugoslavia.

'Until now, football in Kosovo has only survived,' says Eroll Salihu. 'How can we talk about development? How? We have been totally isolated for twenty-five years. And especially so since 2000 when we became de facto independent. We have only survived.

'We have so many talented young players here, but once they reach sixteen or seventeen, it's not enough to be talented. They have to be developed. Our infrastructure is non-existent, players and coaches are not paid well. We have lost a generation of players. That is down to isolation.'

UEFA and FIFA's opposition to Kosovo's membership precipitated this political gridlock.

'UEFA statutes say that countries must be recognised by the United Nations,' says Salihu. 'Not members, but recognised. What does "recognised" mean? It is undefined.'

According to the United Nations, 'recognition' means a readiness by other states to assume diplomatic relations, which an increasing number of countries have shown. But Salihu is irritated by a process that has been ongoing since 2008, with little cooperation offered by UEFA.

The international picture is changing. At last count, Kosovo has been recognised by 108 of 193 UN members (far from the necessary two thirds, but moving in the right direction) as well as by the UN's International Court of Justice and the International Olympic Committee.

Salihu's point was that the arguments had become overwhelming. 'We are recognised now in sports and in politics, so there cannot be much argument any more.'

And yet there was always leverage. Salihu reaches into his desk and brings out a photocopy of a document, signed by the Serbian and Kosovan governments in 2013, stating that 'neither side shall block or encourage others to block the other side's progress in their respective EU path'.

'I said to the Serbian delegation in Zurich, "What are you saying? You cannot be against any proposal that helps us on our European path. Because your state signed this!" The FFK was never a member of the Football Association of Serbia, never! They have never had our registration!'

Despite the enmity, there was still a respect that existed between the two federations on a personal level. The FFK's previous president Fadil Vokrri was a legend of Partizan Belgrade, where Serbian football chief Tomislav Karadžić also served as president. When Vokrri, the only Kosovan to represent the Yugoslavia national team, made his international debut in a friendly game against Brazil, the FIFA delegate was the previous president, Sepp Blatter, who chaired the 2013 meeting between the three parties. This has helped lubricate the workings of the machine, if only a little.

And in the end the weight of this argument forced the issue in Kosovo's favour.

* * *

The rain is coming down harder now. Not that anyone's bothered. It's gone midnight and there is little by way of attraction to keep anybody out at this hour in this shabby little town.

The rain pours through the awnings of cafes and shops having long since eaten its way through the gutters, amplifying the thrumming of the downpour. This is Shkodër in northern Albania, an Ottoman-style town that somehow has still acquired a dull 21st-century homogeneity to it.

The Catherine wheels that had fizzed and smoked a few hours before have now burned out. Not long ago in this ramshackle town, clouds of blue and yellow smoke had bellowed along the main street, and air horns had rung out like sirens right across Shkodër. But the party is over now.

A few hours from now, heavy storms will rack the city, multiplying the grey puddles that have been collecting steadily since afternoon. Just off the strip, the Loro Boriçi Stadium stands empty, its floodlights still burning brightly despite the party having long since fizzled out. After the party comes the hangover.

In the stadium car park, a tall, broad-shouldered man politely chats with two reporters in the dark, before waving them off into the night with a smile. It's a gracious smile, almost apologetic, but it would have fooled no one had there been anyone left in town to see it. The man is Eroll Salihu. He has had a chastening night.

'Our two central defenders were so slow tonight,' he says, shaking me by the hand, finally allowing the pretence to fall and his face to drop. When I met Salihu in March at the offices of the FFK, the mood was quite different to how it is now. He was excited that day, agitated even, as the UEFA ruling on Kosovo's membership approached.

On 3 May, that passage was granted. Tonight, Kosovo have played their first competitive match on Albanian soil, a World Cup qualifier against Croatia. It has not gone well.

In the end it was 6–0 to Croatia, and this was not even Croatia at their strongest. Kosovo had expected a difficult night, but few people, neither those inside the sold-out Loro Boriçi Stadium in Shkodër, nor those watching in their thousands on the big screen in Mother Teresa Square back in Pristina, had expected anything quite as bad as this.

It has been an embarrassment, a thrashing. No one feels this more than Salihu. He expects so much of his countrymen.

'It wasn't a 6–0 game I don't think,' he bemoans, tired. 'But it wasn't good. Not at all.'

The game was prefaced by the first-ever playing of the country's national anthem on Albanian soil. Even as an outsider it was hugely emotional, and at the same moment the home fans unfurled a giant flag that covered the terrace with the words:

THE DARDANIANS
RAISED BY WAR, STRONGER THAN FEAR

But tonight has not been about pageantry. It has been about football. And Kosovo have been found wanting.

What now? The question hangs in the air with the rain.

Things have come so far since the dark days when Salihu and his peers sought refuge in the woods. But for the general secretary, it was never enough simply to gain recognition and sit back.

The team showed moments of promise in tonight's match, but it never looked like being enough. Their opponents Croatia gained their own independence at the same moment that Kosovo's struggles were just beginning, and they have now enjoyed two decades competing at the top of international football.

Conversely, Kosovo have lost a generation of players during their time in the football wilderness. So, whilst Croatia's striker Mario Mandžukić was helping himself to a first-half hat-trick in Shkodër, the Dardanians (named after the ancient Balkan Kingdom of Dardania) could not call on stars such as Xherdan Shaqiri and Granit Xhaka, who could have played for Kosovo had they not chosen to play for the national team in Switzerland.

Internationalism is at the heart of this team, which is ironic given the side has spent so many years outside of UEFA in the football wilderness. Most of the players were born and raised abroad, drawn from the sprawling Kosovan diaspora across Europe.

The right full-back Fanol Perdedaj, then of German team FSV Frankfurt, made a good show, as did midfielder Milot Rashica of Vitesse in the Dutch league. Up front, Bersant Celina showed flashes of the skill that saw him make his first-team debut for Manchester City in early 2016 – he later joined Swansea City – although Croatia's dominance meant he did not see much of the goal.

The feeling in the camp is that, after the long fight for recognition, Kosovo's problems are just beginning. The national team set-up here has been run on an almost amateur basis for so long that it could take years for the infrastructure to catch up. In the meantime, there will likely be more sobering nights like the one in Shkodër for Salihu and his countrymen to endure.

External forces continue to be unkind to Kosovo. Prior to their very first World Cup qualifier against Finland in September 2016, half a dozen of the squad didn't receive clearance from FIFA until a matter of hours before kick-off, as they had already represented other countries, mostly Albania.

Three days from now, the team are due to play a World Cup qualifier against Ukraine on neutral ground in Poland, after the government in Kyiv said they wouldn't recognise the players' travel documents.

Domestically, things are a little more promising. Salihu's old club FC Prishtina sit at the top of the country's Superleague, but two weeks ago their manager Kushtrim Munishi walked out on them, after the club refused to formalise his relationship in the form of a contract.

'We are supposed to be professional now,' he told me as we were re-acquainted two days previously in the same Pristina bar where I'd first met him with the mountain-climbing mushroom fanatic Valon. 'I said, "I want to be on a contract or I will go." They didn't do it, so I went.'

Our meeting should have been full of optimism, at the start of a historic week for the young republic. Instead, the self-inflicted implosion of the country's biggest club dominated our agenda.

Crossing the car park at the Loro Boriçi Stadium, I wonder what Salihu makes of the situation at his old stomping ground, and with the domestic game at large. 'There are still problems, yes,' he hesitantly admits. It doesn't seem as if he's going to proffer up much more tonight. By now, his cheerful demeanour has evaporated entirely, and his exhausted tone is telling me what he is not saying. We say our goodbyes and he disappears into the night.

As the rain falls harder and Shkodër welcomes in the early hours of a new day, the lights of the Loro Boriçi Stadium stay brightly lit, and it's tempting to wonder what the coming days, months and years hold for Kosovo.

Suddenly, the lights flicker out.

PART TWO

BURIED AT THE MOUNTAINS: ARMENIA, AZERBAIJAN AND NAGORNO-KARABAKH

So in Nagorno-Karabakh
These were my fears
Forty thousand dead windows
Are visible there from all directions
The cocoon of soulless work
Buried at the mountains
OSIP MANDELSTAM, RUSSIAN POET

© Peter Fitzgerald / CC BY

I

It was one of those sleeps that is deep enough for you to forget where you were when you drifted off.

'Passport registration!' A man's voice barks in heavily accented English down to the back of the *marshrutka* microbus where I had been sleeping, now utterly and suddenly awake. None of the other fifteen passengers move, but they turn their faces towards the bleary-eyed foreigner sitting alone on the back row.

Armenians are a striking people, with an olive skin tone, pronounced brows and piercing eyes, which means that although I haven't spoken a word since the bus left Yerevan in Armenia, my otherness is clear to everyone.

It takes a frantic search through all of my pockets before I finally place a clammy hand on the documents that will allow me to continue along the road. I clamber through a gauntlet of legs and rucksacks and then drop from the *marshrutka* to the dirt track below.

The early afternoon sun hits me hard in the face. It's only a fifty-metre walk from where the bus has stopped to the border checkpoint, but it feels longer. The mountains of the Lesser Caucasus rise up on both sides of the road and pen you in, leaving the short walk down to the border guard the only way to go.

This is the point, tucked away deep in the hills, where Armenia meets the border of the de facto Nagorno-Karabakh Republic. All consular protection terminates here as I enter the Mountainous Black Garden – a name that derives from the Russian and Turkic cultures that built the region (*'nagorno'* means mountainous, *'kara'* means black and *'bagh'* means garden). This is, in diplomatic language, rogue territory, the edge of a frozen conflict that has sat on ice for almost twenty-five years, the people in the region in limbo and none of the protagonists quite knowing how to proceed.

We are in the Lachin corridor, not legally a part of Armenia, rather an occupied buffer zone within neighbouring Azerbaijan, held on to by the Armenian military in order to provide a safe route from the border town of Goris into Karabakh. In international law though, this whole territory is part of Azerbaijan and is central to a dispute that has kept the two states at loggerheads since 1988 and the final days of the USSR.

The animosity between the two countries though dates back much further. In *The Caucasus: An Introduction*, Thomas de Waal cites the football rivalry between Azeri and Armenian football fans as one of the earliest forms of popular expression in a Soviet world that supressed all aspects of civil society. 'Ordinary people knew to stay at home whenever Neftçi Baku were playing Ararat Yerevan,' he writes of the simmering tension that existed between the two communities as far back as the 1960s. Today, the war over Karabakh has reduced relationships between the two neighbours to hatred.

The journey to this place is hypnotising. From the moment Yerevan begins to sink into the distance and the first views of the peak of biblical Mount Ararat piercing the overcast sky appear, the vistas are breath-taking. The snow that carpets the mountainsides is undisturbed and crisp, and the rural towns and villages that pepper the route are seemingly untouched by the world beyond these hills.

Late in the afternoon, the cloud breaks, and the sun washes over Goris and the road that links Armenia to Nagorno-Karabakh. The rocky surroundings seem to glow gold.

The drive from Yerevan should take six hours, but today it has taken nine. For all the natural beauty of this place, there is no escaping the isolation that Karabakh, the rogue state that emerged out of the mess of the Armenia–Azerbaijan war, is subject to, even from its Armenian sister. Though the fighting has largely stopped, there is no apparent end in sight to the impasse that keeps the capital city

Stepanakert and its surrounding provinces in diplomatic lockdown. The paranoia it breeds is infectious.

At the kiosk window, my passport is handed along a long line of khaki-clad men, each taking longer than feels comfortable to study my visa, which was issued the previous day at the permanent representation to Nagorno-Karabakh in Yerevan. The last of them leers forward at me through the hatch.

'Why have you come here?'

For a moment, I don't answer. In this corner of Europe, tetchiness amongst officials seems to intensify near the borders, but even so this feels extreme. I play it safe.

'Football.'

My stamped passport is handed back almost reluctantly through the window, but my interrogator isn't finished. He fixes me with a deliberate stare, the kind that only someone blessed with these God-given Armenian eyes could inflict. He holds it as we sink into a pregnant pause.

Maybe it's the heightened state of paranoia, brought on by the imposing surroundings coupled with the fatigue from a long journey, but his parting words linger like a threat.

'Good luck…'

II

This is not quite Asia, but by no obvious metric is it still Europe either. The Transcaucasian republics of Azerbaijan, Armenia and Georgia are locked together in a shared history and by geopolitics, but this part of the Eurasian borderland seethes with unresolved conflict.

This used to be one country, not once but three separate times during the twentieth century. In April 1918, the territories surrounding the Lesser Caucasus mountains, sandwiched between Russia to the north and Turkey and Iran to the south, and with the Caspian and Black Seas to the east and to the west, came together to form the short-lived Transcaucasian Democratic Federative Republic. Latterly, under Soviet rule, they were collected together by Stalin into a single state, before seeing out the remainder of Soviet history as lone republics within the USSR.

Before that, the lands that surround the ancient capital cities of Yerevan, Tbilisi and Baku were the playthings of empires. For centuries the imperial powers of Russia, Persia and the Ottomans divided this place up according to their own interests and created volatile, complicated national psyches in the process. The Communist state acted as a buffer to whatever violent potential was incubated in the region. When the Soviet system began to collapse, it was like a pin had been pulled from a grenade.

On the night of 18 February 2004, Ramil Safarov walked into a branch of Tesco near the Ferenc Puskás Stadium in central Budapest and purchased an axe.

Safarov, an Azerbaijani soldier, was in Budapest as part of a NATO English-language camp. He was billeted at the city's National Defence University, sharing a room with a Ukrainian officer whom on the night in question was back in Kyiv attending the funeral of a relative. Safarov was alone in his room, and as he sharpened his axe with a honing stone he was not disturbed.

At 5 a.m., he walked to the dorm of Gurgen Margaryan, an Armenian officer from Yerevan. Taking his axe, he murdered Margaryan as he slept, almost decapitating him. Safarov was arrested at the scene.

'I regret that I hadn't killed any Armenians before this,' he said in his statement to Hungarian police. 'My job is to kill because [whilst] they live, we will suffer. If there were more Armenians here, I would kill all of them.' He was sentenced to thirty years.

Then, something very peculiar happened. Back in Azerbaijan, the state's human rights commissioner sensationally denounced the Hungarian courts for sentencing Safarov too harshly, declaring, '[He] must become an example of patriotism for the Azerbaijani youth.'

Baku began to lobby for Safarov's extradition. After eight years of applying pressure, the Hungarian government relented. Safarov was returned to Azerbaijan, whereupon he was pardoned by President Ilham Aliyev and rewarded with eight years' worth of back pay and a military promotion.

A spokesman for Aliyev offered the following statement on Safarov's release: 'Yes, he is in Azerbaijan. This is great news for all of us. It is very touching to see this son of the homeland, who was thrown in jail after he defended his country's honour and dignity of the people.'

It is strongly alleged that Safarov's release was used as leverage in a deal between Baku and Budapest over $1.6 billion in Hungarian bonds. Yerevan promptly severed all diplomatic ties with Budapest and protesters besieged the Hungarian embassies in Armenia and in the United States.

In Azerbaijan, money talks.

A lucrative oil trade has shaped the port city of Baku. Back in the 1920s, when the USSR was embryonic and fighting to survive, Moscow attacked the city in order to gain control of its natural gas supplies, which marked the beginning of seventy years of Soviet rule.

In the post-independence era, oil money from the Caspian has financed a ruthless crusade of urban renewal. The city's poorer citizens in turn are being marginalised, as was the case most brutally in the building of the 70,000-seater Olympic Stadium for the city's successful Euro 2020 bid, a project which saw the tearing down of low-income housing and the forcible relocation of residents.

Baku is two cities, rich and poor, living not so much side by side, as one inside the other. A tiny, secretive elite controls the town's vast resources. There are almost no political or press freedoms.

The leafy settlement of Surakhani sits at the base of Azerbaijan's Absheron Peninsula. Like the majority of neighbourhoods in the capital, this is not a wealthy area; the decaying vestiges of the country's Soviet-era petrochemical industry that pepper the streets bear witness to a town that has been forgotten. The Caspian Sea, from which the country has extracted its vast oil wealth, is not much more than 10km away. The petro-dollars, though, have not made it this far downtown.

Amongst Surakhani's dusty streets and ramshackle apartment blocks, one building takes pride of place. The Azersun Arena only reveals itself when you are up close as it has been neatly tucked away amongst the town's creaking bones. Inside, the grubby streets of Surakhani give way to the lush white-tiled corridors of Azerbaijan's footballing epicentre. This is the home of the country's champions, Qarabağ FK.

Qarabağ – nicknamed 'the Horsemen' after a poem written by Alexander Pushkin in honour of loyal Karabakh Azeris who defended the Russian-held city of Kars against Turkish attack in the early nineteenth century – are the nomads of Azerbaijan. Since their re-founding in 1987 they've moved from city to city, stadium to stadium, driven by circumstances outside of their control, manipulated by heavy and complex politics.

'This club means everything to the people of Azerbaijan,' I'm told by the club's press officer, Nurlan Ibrahimov, on my first visit to the stadium in February 2017. 'Our lands are being occupied. It's through success with Qarabağ that we bring that to the attention of the world.'

This is not the empty hyperbole of a football media department. In July 1993, Qarabağ fled their hometown of Ağdam, forced out by a war of which the club still sits at the political, if no longer the geographic centre.

Today, Ağdam is a ghost town, the buildings that once housed communities are crumbling into dereliction and are being slowly reclaimed by nature. Of Qarabağ's former home, Imarat Stadium, there is nothing left.

'We will always use football to stand up for ourselves,' exclaims Ibrahimov. 'We will always play to keep the memory of Ağdam alive.'

The 1988 to 1994 war between Azerbaijan and Armenia claimed between 25,000 and 35,000 lives, and displaced more than a million people, most of whom have never been able to return to their homes.

The two sides fought for control of Nagorno-Karabakh, the mountainous region within Azerbaijan's borders where in 1988 an Armenian majority lobbied Moscow for unification with the Armenian Soviet Republic. The Kremlin rejected the petition, and in the years that followed, low-level fighting between Armenian and Azeri villages slowly took on greater and greater political significance, until upon the dissolution of the USSR the fighters acquired military-grade weapons from the Soviet army and what had been an internal civil conflict erupted into a full-scale interstate war.

In 1994, a Russian-brokered ceasefire created a fragile peace in the region. However, dozens of casualties are still recorded each year along the line of contact between Azerbaijan and the self-proclaimed Nagorno-Karabakh Republic, which is governed by the Armenians. Diplomatic relations between the belligerents remain frozen. The international border is closed – the propaganda war, white-hot.

At first, the war was fought between intellectuals, historians that pored over source material in search of evidence that their own people were the first to settle in the hills of ancient Karabakh. The Karabakh Armenians were traditionally the eastern-most people of an Armenian nation centred largely on Ottoman eastern Anatolia (modern Turkey), and the Christian highland dwellers around Stepanakert (then called Khankendi) were surrounded in the lowlands by Muslim Turkic communities that spread out to the shores of the Caspian.

Stalin decided to award Soviet Karabakh to the Azeri rather than the Armenian Soviet Socialist Republic in 1923, as part of an attempt to appease Turkey which sat just over the border. Subsequent petitions were lodged throughout the 1950s, 1960s and 1970s for the region to be re-allocated to Yerevan, until the rise of the Karabakh movement of 1988 collided forcefully with the weakening of central power in Moscow and growing nationalist independence movements locally – the Karabakh Committee in Stepanakert was the first organised political opposition to form in the entire Soviet Union, and set a precedent that was repeated across the USSR in its final years – which led to mass bloodshed.

Mushfig Huseynov sits forward in his chair and widens his already broad chest and shoulders. The 46-year-old is employed today as number two to Qarabağ's first-team coach, Azerbaijan legend Gurban Gurbanov. We are meeting in February 2017 in the plush offices of the Azersun Arena's management complex, from where the club's operations are orchestrated. He was eighteen years old when war came to Ağdam.

In those days, he was an up-and-coming striker for Qarabağ in the fourth tier of the former Soviet football league system. Despite their position, the team drew regular attendances that dwarfed those in the rest of Azerbaijan. Composed of local players, Qarabağ played with a slick, technical swagger that was in stark contrast to the classical Soviet hustle and bustle.

Football in Azerbaijan went through a fallow patch in the 1980s. It followed a golden period during which Baku's Neftçi PFK finished third in the Soviet Top League and Azeri striker Anatoliy Banishevskiy played in a World Cup semi-final, as the Soviet Union narrowly lost 2–1 to West Germany at Goodison Park in July 1966.

When Huseynov made his Qarabağ debut at the age of just fourteen, Ağdam was still a bustling town with a passion for the game, and a thirst for free-flowing, attacking football. He was at a football camp in Baku the day the first shells fell on his hometown.

'We never believed that it would last,' he recalls. 'Suddenly every part of life became a risk in Ağdam. Travelling to and from training. Even training itself, and matches. The projectiles were falling all the time.'

The early months of the conflict were characterised by flashes of interethnic violence between Azeris and Armenians, largely localised within those neighbourhoods where the two communities lived. On 27 February 1988, 35km from Baku in the city of Sumgait, in a pogrom targeting local Armenians carried out by Azeris, thirty-two people were killed, although some sources have since asserted that hundreds of people in fact lost their lives. Those that survived fled and became the first refugees in an exodus that would purge Azerbaijan of its Armenian minority.

Ağdam sits just on the Azeri side of the border of what was then the Nagorno-Karabakh Autonomous Oblast (*'oblast'* is a Russian word meaning province). It was traditionally one of the most affluent towns in the South Caucasus, owing to its thriving black market. 'These were Soviet times, remember,' I'm reminded by my journalist colleague Aydin Bagirov, who grew up in Ağdam and is now the most famous face of football TV punditry in Baku. 'But despite that we had foreign cars in our city – Fords, Mercedes. After Baku, you could only find those cars in Ağdam. We were the trading capital of Azerbaijan. Anything and everything could be bought or sold in Ağdam.'

But the town was dominated by the criminal gangs that were the protagonists of the early stages of the war. Ağdam was controlled by six mafia-type gangs, that by all accounts fought with each other just as much as they did with local Armenian villages, and it was this low-level criminality and pillaging that provided the motivation to fight in the early days of the conflict as much as any belief in a national cause. The combination of this violent material opportunism with the political projects formulated by nationalist leaders in Baku and Yerevan ultimately created the war.

Ağdam owed its strategic significance to its usefulness as a base for Azerbaijan forces to launch missile attacks against the Karabakh capital Stepanakert, which sits just 10km away. As the 1980s rolled into the 1990s, and local militia acquired more and more sophisticated weaponry from the collapsing Soviet military, the two towns rained fire down on each other.

At first, Ağdam carried on much as before. As the months became years and the crisis worsened, people clung to what remained of their old life.

'During that period, the people demanded more than ever that we play good, attractive football,' recalls Huseynov, running a giant hand through his close-cropped and greying hair. 'We had 15,000 people in a stadium that was built for only 10,000. Even for our training sessions we had more people trying to watch than we could really fit. Qarabağ became an event. It was something extraordinary. They loved great football in Ağdam, and that's what we gave them.'

In 1988, Qarabağ won the Azeri national league championship and secured promotion to the all-Soviet Second League (the third tier). This was a mark of the cauldron that the team's supporters had created at Imarat Stadium. The ground was built on the site of the seventeenth-century winter palace of the ruling Karabakh khans, which was constructed in the lowlands to provide refuge from the freezing cold of mountainous Shushi (also known as Shusha), the capital of ancient Karabakh. The body of the daughter of one of the khans, Khurshidbanu Natavan, is said to be buried at the site of the former palace, and when the stadium was built in 1952 it was named in honour of the *'Imarat'* – beautiful house – that had stood there years before.

In the 1989 season, Qarabağ won seventeen out of their twenty-one home games in the Second League, losing none, yet won only once all season on the road, at bottom side MCOP Lokomotiv Tbilisi. All seventeen of the team's defeats came away from Imarat Stadium, where the royal spirit of Khurshidbanu Natavan's daughter was said to watch over them on matchdays. But even her protection ultimately withered before the pen-pushers of Soviet bureaucracy. At the end of 1989, the resignation of the Baltic states from the Soviet football league system led to a reorganisation, and Qarabağ were booted back down to the fourth tier.

'We were like a lot of Azerbaijan teams in that we were very technical,' explains Shahid Kasanov, who captained the side during their final season in Ağdam. Kasanov is a surly, authoritarian character when he joins Huseynov, Ibrahimov (Qarabağ's press officer) and me in the manager's office at the Azersun Arena. 'But we were physically tough too. We needed to be, to stand up against the physical power of the Soviet teams.'

Kasanov grew up watching Azerbaijan's golden generation of the 1960s. It helped inform his own game when he inherited the captain's armband for his hometown team. Ibrahimov tries to get the former skipper to open up about his skill as a player: 'He is very modest, but on the pitch he was the best,' but Kasanov is deep in thought now.

'Before one match in 1992, we had to bring earth to fill in a hole in the pitch made by a bomb before we could play,' says Kasanov. 'By then, we knew we were in a war. The planes were overhead most days. But we weren't afraid of dying. Ağdam was our home and it was our duty to play football there, for these people.'

'The calm in Ağdam was gone,' states Huseynov. 'We continued to play football, but it had become an obligation. Every minute you knew that a bomb could fall and change your life.

'How could I compare with life before the conflict? I couldn't. There is no comparison. When peace turns to war, it is every difference you can imagine. It is impossible for you to imagine the kind of traumas Ağdam experienced in such a short time. Every day we would wake up to news of more martyrs.'

The expectation amongst young men of fighting age was that they would answer the call to arms and join the military effort. Ideas about duty and about the homeland are taken seriously here. The footballers of Qarabağ, however, had their requests to join up and fight alongside their neighbours turned down. The decision was made at the very top of Ağdam's military command – no footballers from Qarabağ were to be admitted to the army.

The call to bar footballers from serving was taken by Asif Maharammov, a factory worker from Ağdam who rose to the rank of lieutenant colonel after forming his own battalion at the outbreak of the war. Throughout his career, Maharammov was known to his colleagues as Fred Asif, a nickname acquired as a child due to his appreciation for the pop band Right Said Fred. The moniker followed him through his military career, although when he received the National Hero of Azerbaijan medal after his death in 1994 for his services to the country, his given name of Maharammov was used.

As the conflict worsened, Fred Asif's message was carefully tailored to go out to the people of the besieged town. It was to be business as usual, with civilian life preserved in as close to its fullest form as was possible amongst the shelling and the bombing.

'Before the war, we were the only club I think in Azerbaijan that existed using only local players,' says Kasanov. 'The team was native for the people. Everybody was from Ağdam; the players and the fans. They were their relatives and their neighbours. It was special, it was native. The team was their own. The club and the stadium became a temple.'

The Imarat Stadium was hit by Armenian projectiles in those first two years of the war, twice, although fortunately on both occasions the stands were empty. Huseynov says this occurred only by the grace of God – no one could have survived the devastation caused when the bombs hit. The club's training base was targeted too, one night in 1992. Had the missile hit a few hours earlier, the casualties would likely have numbered more than a dozen. Instead, the players cleared away the debris from the ruined buildings that had fallen on their pitch and continued with training as normal.

The end of 1991 brought an escalation in the Armenian aerial campaign against Ağdam. But still the Imarat Stadium remained full on matchdays. During the 1992 season – the first of the newly independent Azerbaijani Top League – Armenian forces shelled the area around the stadium during Qarabağ's home game against İnşaatçı Sabirabad FK from the city of Sabirabad, over 160km from Ağdam. When the bombs exploded, the İnşaatçı players hit the ground, terrified by the sounds of the nearby bombardment. Huseynov and his teammates, hardened against the carnage all around them, simply carried on playing.

'It's a strange thing,' he reflects, 'how quickly you become used to war.'

When the team were promoted back to the third tier at the end of 1990, football was becoming badly disrupted. Clubs from neighbouring republics refused to make the dangerous journey into Ağdam to honour their fixtures at Imarat Stadium. Of the twenty league wins the team achieved in 1991, eleven were awarded as technical victories. Qarabağ finished eleventh by dint of having the most dangerous home ground.

Similarly, Dinamo Gandzha, from the city of Ganja – previously known as Kirovabad – roughly 50km from the Nagorno-Karabakh border, came third largely because no other team wanted to travel to a city where there had been a violent pogrom waged against its Armenian population in 1988.

Ağdam finally fell on 23 July 1993. Nine days later, Qarabağ beat FK Khazar Sumgait 1–0 to claim their first national title. Instead of celebrating, the players returned to their shattered homes to search for family and loved ones.

* * *

It's February 2017, and I'm at the Azersun Arena for one of the Azerbaijani Premyer Liqa's many Baku derbies, Qarabağ v. Inter Baku. Of the eight clubs competing in the league this season, five of them are based here in the capital, largely because this is the only part of the country that still has any money.

Since the republic won its independence in 1991, Azerbaijan's football landscape has flip-flopped quite drastically. The ascendency of Neftçi Baku, traditionally the flag-bearers for the country in the Soviet Top League, has come to a sudden and unexpected end, and into the power vacuum has rushed a previously unfashionable and impoverished club from the isolated mountains of Nagorno-Karabakh in the form of Qarabağ.

Neftçi and Qarabağ mimic the two faces of Azerbaijan – one represents the old Soviet order, a team that played for a dominant capital city and took its identity from the thriving energy sector that once powered the USSR; the other epitomises post-Soviet trends – the emergence of regional powers and bellicose nationalism that would have been unthinkable in the Soviet era. This is a sign of the times. Neftçi, which literally means 'petroleum worker', are sweat and industry, and they are on the decline. Qarabağ are the new kings, Azerbaijani martyrs in the country's struggle against Armenia.

In 2014, they became champions for the second time, their first title since 1993 when the league was in its infancy. They won again in 2015, before taking the title by a landslide twenty-two points in 2016 to cement their place as Azerbaijan's top side.

More titles have followed. To date the team have racked up six Azerbaijan championships in a row, but the club has now set its sights on Europe.

In 2014, they matched Neftçi's achievement from two years previously by becoming only the second club from the country to qualify for the group stages of UEFA's Europa League. The holy grail, though, is the Champions League, but first they must take care of the formality of another domestic title, beginning with a win tonight against Inter Baku in the Arena.

Qarabağ have bucked the Premyer Liqa trend of splashing out on big wages for mediocre foreign signings – the chief architects of this ruinous policy have been Neftçi – in favour of buying local. Tonight's starting XI has seven Azeris in it, if you include the Brazilian-born Richard Almeyda, who's been at the club so long he's been granted citizenship and even now plays internationally for Azerbaijan.

The player they love most here is Rashad Sadygov, the captain. No one has played more times for Azerbaijan or for Qarabağ than the classically handsome Sadygov. The 34-year-old, a highly technical central defender, briefly tried his hand in the Turkish Süper Lig before being lured back by the money on offer at Neftçi, though he quickly regretted it – the Azerbaijan football federation switched the date of the country's transfer deadline, and Sadygov spent six months playing professional basketball whilst he waited for his Neftçi registration to clear.

Most of Sadygov's teammates are fellow internationals. Up-front for Qarabağ tonight is the Azerbaijan striker Vüqar Nadirov, a refugee from Ağdam whose father was killed on one of the last days of fighting before the town fell to Armenian forces.

Watching him warm up from the press box, he does not seem to have the right physique for a striker. When he runs he's all elbows and arms. His leap when he goes up to head the ball is weighted and cumbersome, but his touch is clean and true and he looks a fine technical player.

Nadirov was born in June 1987, a few months before the Sumgait pogrom that started the war with Armenia. Since making his debut for Azerbaijan against Israel in 2004, he has become one of the country's most-capped footballers, making his fiftieth appearance for the side during a 0–0 draw with Croatia in 2015.

Nadirov was five years old when Ağdam was destroyed. His memories of home have been made sketchy by time.

He remembers the mosque, though his family was not particularly religious. He remembers the primary school that he attended for just a year. And like anybody who spent time in Ağdam before the occupation, he remembers the town's famous tearoom, Çay Evi, with its spectacular spiral staircase snaking up against the outside towards to a glistening blue minaret. To a child of five, Çay Evi looked otherworldly, as though lifted from the dense volumes of Turkic mythology and planted in mundane suburbia, hinting at the existence of a world more magical.

A child's imagination becomes a crutch when war breaks out. Bombs and gunshots exist without context, with no framework for understanding. Nadirov left Ağdam with his mother and two sisters late in 1992 and started new lives as refugees in Sumgait. He had no grasp of the finality of what was happening.

His father Asif was killed in action on 22 July 1993, hours before Ağdam fell to Armenian occupation.

'There were these shiny sweets my father used to give me,' he tells me when we meet at the Azersun after the Inter Baku game. Nadirov is young and athletic, much more shapely in person than he had seemed from the press box whilst playing for Qarabağ. He has a snappy dress sense, deftly marrying a blend of leather and blue denim. He would look at home amongst the well-to-do aesthetes of the plush Port Baku shopping centre on the Caspian seafront. 'On that last day, when he took us to the lorry, as he was about to say goodbye, I suddenly realised he hadn't left me with any. That was the last thing I said to him before we left.' Nadirov never returned to Ağdam.

A win tonight for Qarabağ would have put them within reach of a fourth title on the spin and another stab at reaching the Champions League, but Inter have come here to wreck the game and try to nick a draw. Playing with an ultra-disciplined five-man defence, they have no interest in trying to attack Qarabağ. Instead they stink the place out with their niggling, diving and hoofing, kicking lumps out of the champions and, in a depressing victory for attritional football, they actually win the game thanks to a late bundled goal from former Blackburn defender, the lanky Georgian Zurab Khizanishvili.

It's hard to see why Qarabağ thought they needed to build the Azersun Arena. It isn't really an arena at all, any more than Morecambe's tiny 6,000-seat Globe Arena is an arena. In fact, the Azersun holds considerably fewer spectators than the Shrimps can get into their seaside home ground for matches in the English fourth division, and their ground is bizarrely missing an entire stand down one side.

Qarabağ moved to the Azersun from the old Tofiq Bahramov national stadium in 2015 – named after the linesman whose flag awarded Geoff Hurst a contentious World Cup final goal at Wembley in 1966. The famous 'Russian linesman' wasn't Russian at all; he was from Baku. The stadium is a gorgeous example of old-world Soviet architecture; an exposed sweeping bowl with ten imposing Corinthian columns standing guard at its entrance hall. On the other hand, the Azersun looks like it came from a job lot, and it wouldn't look particularly out of place in an out-of-town industrial park somewhere in England.

The problem for Qarabağ is that they can't get supporters through the door. There's not many more than 1,000 here to watch them play Inter Baku. Heaven only knows how depressing it must have looked when the same number used to be spread around the 31,000-seater Bahramov stadium. Fans here would rather watch the English Premier League on TV than drive all the way out to ramshackle Surakhani to watch third-rate football.

I'm joined in the press box by Habib Mahmadov, a reporter with the sports newspaper *Futbol+* in Baku and a respected football analyst in Azerbaijan. Inter, he says, have been doing this kind of smash and grab all season, but most visitors to the Azersun have come with a similarly defensive approach. Tonight, remarkably, is Qarabağ's first-ever defeat at their depressing little home, more than two years after they moved in. Pitch-side after the game, Mahmadov and Ibrahimov fall over one another to expound on the national importance of this peculiar football club, which very quickly becomes repetitive so I surreptitiously slip my dictaphone back into my pocket and try to enjoy the sunset over Baku.

Qarabağ is a political chess piece for the government in Baku. Lavished with funding from the energy-rich country's oil boom via a state-backed holding company, Azersun Holding, figures both inside and outside the club make no secret of how Qarabağ is a symbol of Azerbaijan's rightful dominion over Nagorno-Karabakh.

One week before my arrival, five Azerbaijani soldiers were killed on the line of contact between the two territories and their bodies were left to lie in no man's land. To ordinary people, these soldiers are the heirs of those that gave their lives defending Ağdam to the end. The war remains very much alive here.

That in turn informs the poisonous relationship which exists between Azerbaijan and Armenia. The conflict has become political currency for leaders on both sides of the line, with neither government ready to risk losing face over the region by softening its rhetoric. Baku's bizarre response to the extradition of the convicted murderer Ramil Safarov is just the most visible symptom of the damage that has been done to civil society over the politicisation of the Karabakh issue and the demonisation of the enemy.

Iconic Qarabağ FK, meanwhile, benefits immensely from its unique role in the conflict. Intersun Holdings first became attached to the club in 2001 via the holding company Azersun; its logo is ubiquitous around the stadium that bears its name. After almost a decade of financial turmoil, during which time Qarabağ very nearly went under, the club was revived by the vast resources pumped into it by the company's president, an Iranian-born mogul named Abdolbari Gozal.

In Azerbaijan, an uneasy relationship exists between power and society. Transparency International's Corruption Perception Index places the country 123 out of 176 globally, whilst Freedom House scores the state 87 out of 100 (100 being the worst) for press freedom, adding 'the government and political elite use defamation charges as one of many legal means of punishing individual journalists and stifling independent and opposition media'. Reporters Without Borders placed Azerbaijan 162 out of 179 countries on its 2011/12 Press Freedom Index.

This all means that it is difficult to establish the ultimate source of Qarabağ's financial backing. Formally and publicly, Azersun are a food-processing giant, but doubt has been cast over the relationship between Gozal and the country's autocratic President, Ilham Aliyev.

A 2013 report by the International Consortium of Investigative Journalists showed that Gozal and his brother Hasan's business interests have won major contracts from Azerbaijan's state-owned oil company, where Aliyev served as an executive before becoming President. The brothers' various companies, all under the Intersun umbrella, have benefited from $4.5 billion in construction contracts around Baku, which were all financed by the state's vast oil-wealth. Hasan Gozal is also listed as a director of three offshore companies set up in the names of Aliyev's daughters, Arzu and Leyla.

Another of the Gozal companies was shown to be behind the construction of luxury villas for the President and government elite. In January 2017, dissident Baku blogger Mehman Huseynov was arrested and jailed on charges of defamation against the police, weeks after publishing photos of the villas alongside interviews with the construction workers who had built them.

The links between the Gozal brothers and the ruling Aliyev family tie Qarabağ up in a network of secretive groups, which keeps vast sums of money circulating amongst a closed-off elite circle; however, links to the presidency are talked about openly within the club. According to the club's press officer, Nurlan Ibrahimov, it was Azerbaijan's former President, Heydar Aliyev, father of Ilham Aliyev, who gave the green light for Azersun to assume financial responsibility for Qarabağ in 2001.

For the company's part, they list association with Qarabağ as being part of Azersun's programme of 'corporate responsibility'. Of the financial difficulties that threatened the team's existence in the 1990s, a statement reads: 'All these problems were resolved in 2001 after [Azersun] assumed the sponsorship of the team. Azersun Holding, which became famous for its charity deeds not only in Azerbaijan but also in the entire East and the Turkic world, started practical actions for FK Qarabağ not to sink into oblivion.'

The company reference the success that has come with their investment in the club, as well as providing assistance to 'over a million displaced persons' affected by the war (only about 30,000 of these came from Ağdam). 'That's why Azersun Holding is loved by everyone in our country,' I'm told by Reshad Ergun, a reporter for Azerbaijan sports website Komanda.az.

Qarabağ's history can be divided cleanly between pre- and post-conflict. In some senses this is obvious; the uprooting of the club, the massive influx of seemingly limitless wealth, the parade of trophies. But there is a more subtle sense in which Qarabağ has been separated from its past, culturally as well as geographically.

The conflict has turned Qarabağ into a beacon of national hope. In footballing terms, the club has become synonymous with Azerbaijan. It's a world away from the community organisation that meant so much to the people of a provincial town tucked away in the rural hinterlands.

But then so much of the country has been transformed in the years since independence. The government here is highly conscious of its global image, and there is more than enough money in the coffers to paint a convincing picture of a thriving up-and-coming republic in the hyper-rich Western tradition.

Baku Olympic Stadium, a shimmering new arena completed in 2015, is the face of the drive to associate the country with elite sporting events and organisations. Azerbaijan's name has appeared on football shirts from Atlético Madrid in Spain to Sheffield Wednesday in South Yorkshire, and all the stops were pulled out in 2013 in order to secure hosting rights for Baku for a handful of matches at the Euro 2020 championship. The compulsory acquisition and subsequent tearing down of apartment blocks housing low-income families that was necessary to clear space for the stadium is a part of the story that is not told round these parts.

Azerbaijan in the twenty-first century is a country divided by the rich and the poor. The road that leads from Heydar Aliyev International Airport into central Baku is resplendent with ultra-modern feats of architecture, products of multibillion-dollar investments made by the government since the turn of the century, and all financed by the state's vast natural gas reserves.

Glance up, and the skyline is dominated by the Flame Towers, three shimmering glass skyscrapers decked out in LEDs to evoke an image of flickering flames – built by another firm under the control of the Gozal brothers – as well as the recently completed SOCAR Tower, which houses the headquarters of the state oil company.

Port Baku Towers on the seafront host the offices of a raft of foreign companies, most of which are working in the country's buoyant oil trade. Then there is Trump Tower, a still-incomplete construction project involving the US President that is shrouded in mystery and has been the subject of extensive speculation regarding the interests and motives of the scheme's partners and investors.

Foreign visitors can get from Heydar Aliyev Airport to Baku's financial hub and back, sampling the lavish restaurant and retail outlets of Port Baku, without ever catching sight of the crumbling Soviet-era accommodation that provides homes for the bulk of the city's native residents.

In football terms, the money has been a mixed blessing. 'The wages are very good in Azerbaijan,' argues Ibrahimov, 'so that means that players don't really go and play abroad. They are happy to stay here because the conditions are good. This affects the national team. Because very few players go and play abroad, the team doesn't benefit from that experience. That's why Azerbaijan hasn't done so well in international games.'

For Qarabağ, their successes are heavily invested with the raw emotion fuelled by the war. This in turn encourages the investment to keep rolling in, inevitably in a country where sport is seen as a great symbolic pacifier.

It's all highly personal, which is no surprise when one considers the human cost the war continues to have on the country.

Some reports claim as many as 600,000 internally displaced persons (IDPs) resettled in Azerbaijan following the conflict. Baku and Sumgait between them absorbed more than 200,000 refugees fleeing

Nagorno-Karabakh and Armenia, and the ongoing nature of the conflict means that today Azerbaijan has the highest number of IDPs per capita in the world.

Some, like the Qarabağ striker Vuqar Nadirov and his family, were fortunate and found shelter with friends and relatives who were able to take them in and support them financially. Others were forced to rely on makeshift accommodation in schools and other public buildings. The shockwaves from the Nagorno-Karabakh conflict ripped across the whole of Azerbaijan and have left in their wake a legacy that has been difficult to undo; the last tent camps housing refugees from Karabakh weren't taken down until 2007.

'We went to live with an uncle in Sumgait,' explains Nadirov when describing life as a refugee after leaving Ağdam. 'Me and my mother and my sisters all shared one room. We relied on money from our uncle because no one in the family was able to work.

'That's how it was for about ten years. There were massive numbers of refugees like us who moved to Sumgait and to Baku, but where we were, we weren't really part of any community. We were quite isolated.'

Nadirov was lucky. His nascent football talent offered a way out for him and his family, a route to independence and to break free from the cycle of handouts, remittances and unemployment that became life for many refugees.

'When I first started to play football, I had to travel for two hours each day from Sumgait to Baku for training, and then two hours to get home. But people had much bigger problems than that. People came here with no clothes, no possessions. It was hard to find somewhere to live and people struggled to work.

'I was fifteen when I joined up with the first team and began to train with them. My uncle played a big part in helping start my career here. I always felt it was my responsibility to play for Qarabağ.'

That uncle, Adil Nadirov, took over as manager of the club after the previous coach, the heralded Ağdam general Allahverdi Bagirov, was killed days after leading a squadron at the battle for the historic town of Sushi, a decisive moment in the Nagorno-Karabakh war. I'd heard Bagirov's name before. 'He's something of a hero here?' I say to Nurlan Ibrahimov, Qarabağ's press officer, when he drives me from Surakhani back to my hotel in Baku.

He smiles knowingly, as if to say, 'Are you kidding me?'

'We'll take you tomorrow to see,' he promises. 'Then you will know who is Allahverdi Bagirov.'

* * *

Four storeys up in an apartment block just outside the centre of Baku, life goes on as normal for Valide Bagirova and her family. Her small, simple living room is crawling with wide-eyed grandchildren – two boys, one girl – each clamouring for space and attention inside of this cosy domestic tableau. The place has an atmosphere that reflects Valide's long and full life.

Against the wall opposite the door, resting on top of the piano, there is an 8in by 10in framed picture of a man with piercing, yet sunken eyes. His face is covered by a thick black beard from the nose down, and he wears a military camouflage jacket over a black and white striped undershirt. His face is known by every man, woman and child in Azerbaijan.

Allahverdi Bagirov was appointed Qarabağ's first-team coach in 1976. Like most people connected with the club, he was a local, he first joined the club as a player at eighteen years old and went on to captain the side before inheriting the top job.

Bagirov was a coach in the Spartan mould. He could inspire a stubborn loyalty in those who worked for him, regardless of odds or circumstance. He was a coach driven half-mad by the lust for competition and, above all, victory. 'If you don't want to win,' he would tell his players, 'you shouldn't be in Ağdam.'

All conversations about Qarabağ's past sooner or later lead back to Bagirov. His legacy as a coach, and as a man, is felt by everyone I met at the Azersun Arena, and here in this modest apartment far from the stadium and miles away from Ağdam, memories of him are everywhere.

'Once the war began, Allahverdi's priorities changed,' says Valide, his widow. 'They changed from football, to land. His only interest then was to protect Ağdam.'

Upon joining the military in 1988, Bagirov formed his own detachment to help defend what had already become a strategically important town in the nascent conflict. In stepping down from his role at the club, he left a profound missive to the players he was to leave behind. 'I can find 200 soldiers to fight in this war,' he told them, 'but I cannot find eleven players to play football.' So whilst the team played on, winning promotion in 1990, the coach they adored took up arms as a general in defence of the homeland.

I'm meeting Valide and her family on 26 February 2017. This is a poignant date for Azerbaijan, and in particular for the people sitting around this table. But the outpouring of emotion around Valide's living-room table is striking.

Tonight marks the twenty-fifth anniversary of the massacre at Khojaly, a small town at the Karabakh border just a few kilometres from Ağdam, and where, on this night a quarter of a century ago, as many as 600 Azeri villagers were gunned down by Armenian snipers or froze to death in the sub-zero temperatures in the woods. Khojaly was a watershed moment in the history of this country.

'Before Khojaly, Allahverdi knew that there would be a tragedy there,' says Valide. 'But our defence ministers wouldn't allow him to go in there. The Russians, who we relied upon, didn't want for us to go because they never wanted Azerbaijan to be independent. They wanted our lands occupied, so they said no.

'Once the massacre began, Allahverdi didn't wait for orders. He took his men and he went to Khojaly anyway. He did it all himself. He saved 1,300 people from the Armenians at Khojaly, and he brought hundreds of dead bodies from the area back to the mosque at Ağdam. They were frozen from the cold.'

After Khojaly, Bagirov moved on to Shushi, the historic cultural capital of ancient Karabakh, where the next violent struggle for territory was to unfold.

Like Ağdam, Shushi sits in a prime location near Stepanakert, 600 metres up on a mountaintop overlooking the capital. Its capture by Armenian forces on 9 May 1992 was a turning point in the conflict and ceded an initiative to Armenia from which Azerbaijan never recovered. It was the first in a succession of losses that was to end in the occupation of Ağdam.

On 12 June, Bagirov's battalion fought successfully alongside Fred Asif – the lieutenant colonel who banned footballers from joining the army – to regain control of Shushi's surrounding villages, liberating the Azeri populations there. But it was to be his last contribution to the war effort.

Two days later, whilst travelling back to Ağdam after hearing news of the death of his close friend, the military doctor Asif Nizam, his car was hit by an anti-tank mine. Bagirov and his driver were killed instantly.

The general's last wish had been to see the flag of the nascent Azerbaijan republic raised in Stepanakert – or Khankendi (the Azeri name for the city), as I am hastily corrected by everyone in chorus when I repeat this for clarification. It was a wish that was never fulfilled.

'Instead, he was the first person to take the Azerbaijan flag to Ağdam,' recalls Valide's son-in-law, Pashayev. 'Of all the people he saved at Khojaly and at Shushi, for so many years the international peacekeepers cannot save even half of this number.

'Allahverdi's ethics were to never do harm to civilians. He always said that whatever happens on the other side, whatever the Armenians do to our men on their land, that is not what we do. Never commit violence unless necessary. He always commanded that men should be returned alive whenever possible.'

Bagirov was posthumously awarded the rank of National Hero of Azerbaijan, the country's highest military accolade, in recognition of his actions at Khojaly and at Shushi. 'He never wanted to kill,' reflects Pashayev. 'To Allahverdi, every life was valuable, and all life was to be respected.'

It's suddenly clear that the atmosphere in the room has changed. The children's energy has dissipated, absorbed by the tragic story they've heard a thousand times before. They never knew their grandfather, other than through his legend. And yet on this sacred anniversary I cannot shake the feeling that they believe him to be here with us.

Bagirov's death was a collective tragedy for Ağdam. Amongst those hit hardest was Mushfig Huseynov, the Qarabağ striker, who had been spotted by the coach as a seven-year-old and who he made a special effort to nurture, both spiritually and on the football pitch.

'It made an incredible impression on me, at such a young age, to be mentored by a man like that,' says Huseynov. 'He took an interest in me from when I was seven and encouraged me at every opportunity to play.' By the age of fourteen, he was in Bagirov's first team at Imarat Stadium.

'I think I touched the ball four times during that first game, and each time I gave it straight to the other team. I only played for the last fifteen minutes. I was only a child really and I was very nervous and excited. But I adapted after that. I owe my career to Bagirov.'

After the general's death, the crisis in Ağdam continued to deepen.

At the end of 1992, women and children were evacuated to surrounding towns outside of the Karabakh mountains, leaving behind just those men who were fit and able to fight. The players of Qarabağ relocated to the city of Mingachevir, 75km away, returning to play their home fixtures in the newly formed Azerbaijani Top League. By then, their only supporters were the soldiers who had stayed behind to defend the town.

'Those people fought instead of us,' states Huseynov, whose family had been broken up by the evacuation; his sister and elderly parents and he and his elder brother went to Mingachevir, along with the rest of the town's refugees, and a younger brother was left behind in Ağdam. 'They defended our homes on our behalf. And all they asked from us in return is that we play football. That is our legacy.'

Huseynov has never forgotten his last day in Ağdam. There was a bonfire, one evening in July 1993, whilst he was visiting his brother. A missile shot past overhead.

'We could recognise by then exactly where the bomb was going to fall, whose house it was going to hit. We could tell from the sound. I never went back after that.'

III

The journey from Azerbaijan to Armenia is a logistics nightmare. There are a couple of ways that it can be attempted, travelling via either Iran to the south, or Russia and Georgia to the north, but to make it from Baku to Yerevan in anything less than thirty-six hours, the long trek north is the only one that makes sense. The land border between the two countries is resolutely shut down.

The prospect of consecutive nights on a sleeper train, broken by twelve hours in the Georgian capital Tbilisi, had seemed appealing at first. This proved to be a very naïve assessment.

The first red flag was the hammer and sickle motifs stuck to the train windows when I boarded at Baku. Soviet-era transport is not especially well-known for providing consumer-friendly facilities.

I was reminded of an old joke about trains not allowing passengers to use the toilets whilst on the platform because the flush mechanism empties out onto the track below. I had never been able to properly satisfy my curiosity about whether or not this is true. Of Soviet trains, there is no such mystery. The flush pedal simply pulls away the interior of the bowl, leaving a gaping hole down to the track as it races by at 120km/h.

My first experience of Tbilisi passes in a tired haze.

They say the city's design is borrowed half from Moscow and half from Cairo. Georgia is trying desperately hard to forget its Soviet past, but the capital does look mostly Russian, although there is an unmistakable Levantine influence.

Half a mile from the station, the crown jewel of Tbilisi is the Boris Paichadze Dinamo Stadium, named after the country's most famous footballer. It's a wonderful old ground, with its patron Paichadze – a Soviet league star with Dinamo Tbilisi – immortalised in stone in front of the gates. Two plaques commemorating the greatest football moments in the team's history hang from the stadium wall, one for Dinamo's Soviet championship wins of 1964 and 1978, the other for their UEFA Cup Winners' Cup triumph in 1981.

There's a certain sense of Georgian exceptionalism, a hangover from the nation's dissidence to Soviet rule, and it affects football too. Players from the country have worked their way into folklore in some of Europe's biggest leagues.

The winger Georgi Kinkladze made a name for himself that endures today in England at Manchester City and Derby County in the

1990s and early 2000s, whilst the rock-hard central defender and former national captain Kakha Kaladze was a Champions League winner with AC Milan. Kaladze is so widely adored that he was made mayor of Tbilisi in 2017.

The national team, on the other hand, are a constant disappointment. They've never got a sniff of qualifying for a major international tournament, and remain one of the great anomalies in post-Soviet football.

During the 1960s, 1970s and 1980s Georgia produced some of the best footballers, not just in the USSR but in Europe. Players like David Kipiani, Vitaly Daraselia and Vladimir Gutsaev were world-class technicians who were known beyond the Soviet world despite the country's isolation. The English press were dumbfounded by the Georgians when Dinamo Tbilisi thrashed Liverpool 3–0 in the 1979 European Cup, a performance that resonates as one of the all-time masterclasses from a Soviet team.

Dinamo are nothing today to what they were. Club football in Georgia is rudderless and impoverished, with dwindling attendances and financial shortfalls forcing many clubs to the wall. Surviving from one season to the next is the new metric for success.

But the game enjoys relative stability compared to the chaos that reigns over the border in Armenia.

Yerevan is ankle-deep in snow when I step foot off the train from Tbilisi, early one Saturday morning in March 2017.

I've shared a cabin with a young American from Virginia named Oren. Softly spoken with a wispy beard and a sinewy, wiry frame, he'd moved to the Georgian capital from Richmond several years before having been taught Russian by an eccentric high-school teacher. Six months previously he had relocated to Yerevan, where he now worked as a political journalist.

'Whenever I cross these borders, I tell them I'm a tourist,' he tells me in a hushed voice as the checkpoint officials board our train at the

Georgia–Armenia crossing. 'I don't know whether it would cause me problems or not to say otherwise. But because of my work and the way things can sometimes work out here with officials, it's just safer that way.' When the border guards take my passport and ask my reason for entering Armenia, I follow my new friend's example.

'Tbilisi is like Yerevan,' Oren explains as we step out into the freezing pre-dawn darkness and onto a blanket of snow. 'It's beautiful, yes, but it's kind of chaotic.'

And what about Baku, the glass-plated paradise on the shores of the Caspian? He looks at me offended. 'Baku? Soulless. Not a good place.'

Leaving aside the glistening new-builds, which starkly contrast with the parts of the city that are in their pre-financial revolution form, I had found Baku to be somewhat disordered in its body language, so quite what this warning means for Yerevan is not clear. I find out exactly how chaotic around two hours later when, after a frantic hunt, I locate my hostel only to find it has closed down and is abandoned, which leaves me homeless in the snow as I traipse around desperately looking for a cheap hotel.

Welcome to beautiful, chaotic Yerevan.

* * *

The hill of Tsitsernakaberd sits about 3km from Freedom Square and marks the point where the bustling hub of Yerevan gives way to the calm of the city's outskirts. If the traffic is kind, it's no more than fifteen minutes by road from the neoclassical pomp of Yerevan's opera theatre; the cultural epicentre of this ancient metropolis that sits at the meeting point of two continents.

Armenia is the cradle of Christianity. This was the first nation in the world to adopt the doctrine of Christ as its creed in the fourth century, but Armenian heritage as a people stretches even further. The mythical founder of the nation, Hayk the Great – Hayastan is the country's autonym – established the first Armenian state in around 2107 BC, the start of a long and exhausting relationship of co-existence with the Turkic and Persian tribes that shared the Caspian corridor.

In the first week of March, Tsitsernakaberd is still carpeted with snow, and when it catches the early spring sun it glistens. Over to the east, Mother Armenia watches over Yerevan with sword in hand from her plinth amongst the greenery of Victory Park, whilst centrally the national football stadium rises ungainly out of the Hrazdan gorge just near the river.

It was here in October 1973 that 70,000 people watched FC Ararat Yerevan, a provincial football club from tiny Armenia, defeat Russian giants Zenit Leningrad as the side were crowned champions of the Soviet Union. These are a gallant people – Armenia is a state of mind.

The Armenian national consciousness has been forged by huge suffering. At the top of Tsitsernakaberd stands the nation's dedication to the victims of the Armenian Genocide, a murderous crusade inflicted by the Ottoman Turks on 1.5 million ethnic Armenians as the early twentieth-century world was gripped by war. Here, high above the city, the sound of the snow crunching underfoot summons the ghosts of the men, women and children who were led by Ottoman psychopaths from freezing Yerevan on death marches towards the Syrian desert. Older generations of Armenians still casually refer to Azerbaijanis as 'the Turks'.

Between the Hrazdan Stadium and the Tsitsernakaberd monument, there is a small sports complex – three artificial pitches with a few modest stands erected to accommodate a handful of spectators. Like at the Hrazdan, the seating is bedecked with the tricolour of the Armenian flag. Despite the small stature of the place these are good facilities and are especially appreciated on a day like today when the frost would have made any grass pitch unplayable.

It's on these pitches that FC Pyunik – the Armenian Premier League club that in the 2000s won ten consecutive league titles – school their next generation. Whilst clubs in the rest of Armenia are increasingly signing players from overseas, Pyunik have defiantly stuck to a policy of blooding homegrown kids reared on these pitches, even at the expense of their competitiveness in the league.

Pyunik emerged in the first days of independent Armenia. They owe their dominance to the patronage of a notorious Yerevan oligarch named Ruben Hayrapetyan.

Even by the standard of Eastern Europe's murky post-Soviet nouveau riche, Hayrapetyan is something of a specimen. Various media outlets have accused him or his staff of involvement in a selection of crimes, including murder, battery and embezzlement. Were he just another shady Eastern Bloc football club owner looking to ferret away a few million dirty dollars, he might have passed into obscurity. But as well as being the former owner and patron of Pyunik, he is an ex-member of the Armenian Parliament and was the recent president of the Football Federation of Armenia (FFA). People dare not speak out publicly against Hayrapetyan; the extent of the dissidence that I'm able to find is the occasional injurious graffito tagged onto walls and buildings around Yerevan. Hayrapetan has denied the allegations against him, commenting after the dismissal of accusations of possession of illegal guns that it was the latest example of government monkey business.

But I've come to Tsitsernakaberd in pursuit of less murky business. Forty-eight hours after leaving Baku, the Nagorno-Karabakh war is still my object, and for now the hunt for Hayrapetyan will have to wait.

The Pyunik Training Centre on a frozen Saturday marks the end destination for a long personal journey. I began trying to trace Eduard Bagdasaryan, the founder of the previously defunct Yerazank FC, several months earlier via a protracted series of hopeful emails and calls with members of the Armenian diaspora that stretches from Gyumri near the Turkish-Armenian border all the way to New York City. But it was only two days before arriving in Yerevan that I was able to finally confirm his name and where in the world he was.

Yerazank translates as 'dream team'. In the 1980s, the team played in the senior leagues of Soviet Azerbaijan despite being composed only of teenagers. When Armenia and Azerbaijan went to war in 1988, Yerazank found themselves at the epicentre of the conflict.

I almost lose my footing as I make my way down the icy steps that lead from the Tsitsernakaberd highway to the cabin that houses the Pyunik administrative offices. I'm forty-five minutes late.

At the bottom, at the other end of the car park, a blue tracksuited man with a wide nose and grey hair leans up against a concrete bollard, studiously observing a game that's taking place on the complex's synthetic pitch. As I approach, he extends his hand and his lined face fixes me with a smile. 'Eduard Bagdasaryan,' he says gently. Six days of travel and 5,000km from London, this is the man I've been looking for.

'There were so many difficulties in running a football club during war time,' explains Bagdasaryan, as he sits down in the Pyunik clubhouse and places a brown leather satchel on the table between us.

'There were times when the whole team would be staying together at a relative's house, cooking and living on top of each other, or we would be all staying in someone's house close to the stadium. People would say to me, "Why don't you ask for funding for all this stuff?" But the country was in a war. How could I have asked for money for football?'

He suddenly stops flicking through pages and pushes the open book across the table towards me. At the top, etched neatly in red biro, is the word 'ЕРАЗНК' – 'Yerazank' spelled out in Cyrillic script – and beneath it are two black and white photos, each framed by a thin black border.

The defender Loris Grigoryan and the striker Ashot Adamyan were eighteen and nineteen years old respectively when they died on the front line of the Nagorno-Karabakh war.

Adamyan, with his classically striking Armenian brow and deep, dark eyes, was a lithe and technical centre-half, whilst the boyishly handsome Grigoryan led the Yerazank line with an uncompromising brutality.

They had been with Bagdasaryan from the start, helping the club climb from the amateur ranks into the senior leagues. As athletes, they embodied everything the club stood for. As men, they were its ambassadors.

'I received a call from Loris's father on the final day of the battle of Shushi,' recalls Bagdasaryan. 'He asked me to try and persuade his son not to go to the battle. We had already won at Shushi by then and he wanted him to stay away. So I said to him, "If it was you, would you stay away? Or would you go to fight?" He had no answer.'

Grigoryan died at Shushi on 9 May 1992. Later the same day, the last Azeri forces were expelled from the city. Armenia had won the war.

On the pages in Bagdasaryan's book, both Grigoryan and Adamyan look business-like, dressed smartly in suits and ties, gazing just beyond the camera into a future they would never know. The pictures carry a footnote – 'Loris Grigoryan 1973–1992' and 'Ashot Adamyan 1972–1992'. The whole team went off to fight, but only these two failed to return.

In some sense, the young footballers turned soldiers of Yerazank were not any different to their compatriots who they followed to the front line to fight in the Karabakh war. Bagdasaryan, who was once a goalkeeper with FC Ararat but was forced into early retirement by injury, founded Yerazank FC himself in 1982 with the goal of leading the club to the Soviet Top League.

'The team had all the potential, but the war interrupted that,' he states.

Armenia was battered by the war. Somewhere between 25,000 and 35,000 lives were lost and more than a million people displaced. It coincided with the country's awkward transition from a stale but stable form of Communism into the unpredictability of post-Soviet capitalism. By some measures, the republic is still recovering from the trauma.

The outbreak of the war also coincided with a devastating earthquake, which hit near the northern town of Spitak on 7 December 1988. Estimates suggest that the deadly quake took the lives of between 25,000 and 50,000 people. Armenia, already anticipating the shock that was to come from being cut loose from the Soviet state, was rocked harder than at any time since the genocide in 1915.

Levon Mkrtchyan was a teammate of Grigoryan and Adamyan. At sixteen years old, he stood shoulder to shoulder with men in the Azerbaijan leagues, although looking at his dark, leathered face and serious, furrowed brow it's hard to imagine he was ever young.

'It was difficult,' he says. 'It was very hard at first because we were teenagers and our opponents were more developed physically and had been playing for many years. But because of that, we found that we began to play better and better. We had ideas about where in the league we wanted to finish, and I think being so young worked for us.'

When the call to arms came in 1988, most went willingly, including Mkrtchyan. The players of Yerazank were seconded to regiments across the region, and the club ceased its football activities. Bagdasaryan's application to join the armed forces, however, was denied.

'I had five children, and when I went to sign up they said to me "no",' he remembers. 'So I became a conditioning coach for the boys who did go to fight.'

The assignment was a good fit. Bagdasaryan had experience as a father figure in his career as a coach, so it made sense that his skills would be put to use to prepare the young bodies of Karabakh's soldiers for battle.

Playing for Yerazank served as preparation for the wider conflict. The players – young, fit, enthusiastic – had built the club from nothing, and against long odds had flourished in a competitive environment. Their talents then became tools of war, sporting camaraderie re-purposed for conflict.

It's the anecdotes, the flashes of character as told through a haze of time and half-remembered conversations, which bring the Caucasian tragedy to life. Yes, the war was the common denominator in Karabakh. But everyone experienced it differently.

The Yerazank FC squad would regularly fly between Stepanakert and Yerevan on a group ticket with twenty-two paid-up fares that weren't always filled. Grigoryan once questioned Bagdasaryan why, when the plane had empty seats, he never sold the spares on to the black market, and instead allowed people who needed to travel for personal reasons take up the spare places for free. After all, Grigoryan argued, the club could use the money.

It was the most minor disagreement, the calm and collected coach versus the sharp-eyed youth pepped up by Armenia's new barter economy. Thirty years later, it brings the black and white thumbnail of Grigoryan stuck in Bagdasaryan's book to life. His death suddenly feels immediate.

Bagdasaryan reaches inside the back cover and takes out a folded newspaper clipping. It's from the day Grigoryan and Adamyan died. The headline, roughly translated, reads 'The Dream Dies'. For the first time since he introduced himself out in the snow, the old coach goes silent.

In 1993, Yerazank returned to top-flight football, still playing in the Armenian league but based out of Yerevan. There was stability, for a while, until the mess that is Armenian domestic football finally caught up with them.

The government in Stepanakert pulled funding for the club midway through the season in 2003, after its US-based financial backers began to exert pressure for the Nagorno-Karabakh republic to form its own independent league.

Bagdasaryan suspects the real reason lies more in that the backers wanted to focus on their other major sponsorship interest, FC Ararat Yerevan. Either way, Yerazank were on their own.

A year later, the call came from the club's management, the Karabakh Defence Minister Samvel Babayan, that Bagdasaryan – who had been born in Stepanakert – was to be removed from his position as coach in favour of an alternative candidate of full Armenian heritage.

Without their founder, the club limped on for another two years, before folding in 2006. Bagdasaryan, so he says, walked away with his head held high and a wry smile on his face, as his club was picked apart by men who didn't understand the game and whom he was certain would run it into the ground in his absence. He was proved right.

'From then on, Yerazank stayed as a dream,' he states wistfully, closing his book and sliding it back into his satchel.

Today there is no cross-border competition between Armenia and the rogue state Nagorno-Karabakh. An appeal made at the start of the last decade by the football authorities in Azerbaijan made sure of that through FIFA statute, and Karabakh's isolation has been entrenched ever since. In 2018, a new Artsakh football league was established in the republic, but possibilities are limited by lack of contact with the outside world.

Bagdasaryan still works in football, coaching Pyunik's young goalkeepers here at the academy. It seems fitting that a man whose outstanding talents have lain in getting the best out of young players is working at a club where those players will get a decent crack at the first team.

But things are not like they were. Pyunik, for all their titles, will never be Yerazank. That dream has been put to bed.

* * *

The First Armenian Front are rebels with a cause. Speaking out against Armenian football's ruling cartel carries a degree of risk, so the disgruntled rank and file of Yerevan's football scene mostly let off their grievances anonymously in the form of graffiti.

When Ruben Hayrapetyan was elected president of the Football Federation of Armenia in 2002, regulations forced him to give up the presidency of FC Pyunik. But after his son was installed as club president in his place, there were allegations that Hayrapetyan remained the club's puppet master.

In 2012, three Armenian army medics were attacked outside the Harsnakar restaurant – owned by Hayrapetyan – which left one man dead and two more hospitalised. Six of the restaurant's employees were imprisoned for the attack and although Hayrapetyan denied any involvement, he resigned his parliamentary seat following public pressure. However, he continued as president of the football federation – which presumably has its own less exacting ethical handbook – until he was removed in 2018.

In 2015 Hayrapetyan was also accused of beating up the director of Armenia's national airline after he intervened on behalf of a third party over unpaid debts. The airline boss then announced, from his hospital bed, that he wouldn't be filing charges against Hayrapetyan, and that he would instead be seeking a 'reconciliation' deal in the interests of the future of the company.

'You will find very few people in Armenia who are willing to talk openly about Ruben Hayrapetyan,' I was told via text by the First Armenian Front leader, a man who goes only by the name Seroj, the day before I first arrived in Yerevan. 'But we will.'

The group was founded in 2013 as a protest organisation hoping to draw attention to the corruption that has become endemic to football in Armenia since the republic won its independence in 1991.

The football league here is in disarray. In the 2016/17 season, there were only six teams playing in the Armenian Premier League, two fewer than UEFA says is necessary for a league to be classed as professional. In the 2019/20 season there are nine teams competing.

Only once since 2005 has an Armenian club won an aggregate victory in the qualifying rounds of the Champions League, and this occurred when Pyunik eliminated Northern Ireland part-timers Derry City. After this, the Armenian league plummeted down UEFA's country coefficient table, slipping to fifty-first place out of fifty-four member nations in 2015.

The nadir for the sorry state of Armenian football came at 3.50 p.m. on a lush summer afternoon in Yerevan in July 2014. Champions League history was about to be made.

FC Santa Coloma's Marc Puyol took a last look at the neon scoreboard and launched a hopeful 70-yard ball towards the FC Banants penalty box teeming with the blue shirts of the Andorran champions. As he did so, the clock silently indicated that the allotted five minutes of injury time were up. Santa were 3–1 down, facing elimination.

The ball was flicked on and, as it hung in the air, time seemed to slow to a crawl. It landed at the feet of goalkeeper Eloy Casals Rubio who, having joined his team's last-minute onslaught in the opposition area, controlled the ball deftly and fired it into the bottom corner of the goal. Eloy disappeared beneath a stampede of disbelieving teammates, as the part-timers of Santa Coloma celebrated being the first-ever Andorran club to progress in the Champions League.

Yards away, eleven shattered men in white shirts fell to their knees.

The next day, the Armenian press did not hold back. 'Never before have we witnessed such a disgrace,' ran the headline on ArmenianSoccer.com. 'Last night in the pages of our football history was written the most shameful chapter. Unfortunately, however, it is a fair reflection of the state of our national game.'

The humiliation of FC Banants' early exit from Europe was felt throughout the Armenian game. Though the alarm bells had been ringing for years, no one had really been listening.

Twenty years of mechanised failure in continental competitions meant that by 2015 only the amateur leagues of San Marino, Andorra and Gibraltar were ranked lower than the Armenian Premier League. Its score, based on the performances of all clubs in European competition over the previous five seasons, was lower than that of Wales and the tiny Faroe Islands. In 2014, Banants suffered the ignominy of being the only fully professional side made to enter the Champions League at the first qualifying stage. Just 1,500 spectators turned up to watch them lose.

I'm meeting with Seroj and his fellow members of the First Armenian Front on a freezing Saturday evening in Yerevan. Jisnot's, with its wood-panelled interior and alluring selection of spiced teas, provides a welcome respite from the freezing temperatures outside, and inside it's surprisingly quiet given the weather. 'You should have been here three days ago,' says Arsen Zaqaryan, as we take our seats near the window looking out onto the Yerevan Cascade. 'That was when we had real cold.'

The Cascade – a giant stone walkway that rises over 100 metres above Freedom Square – is an analogy for the landscape of modern Armenia. It's built into the remarkably steep contours of the land and offers a sweeping panorama of the city from its summit. But it's also only half finished. The foundations were laid in the 1970s as part of a museum dedicated to the Armenian Genocide, but after the land was prepared the plans were abandoned, leaving behind a haunting mesh of steel and rubble that is slowly being overrun up by nature.

The meeting with the Front nearly didn't happen. Whilst in Baku, I had been contacted by Seroj to say that he had been made aware of my association with FK Qarabağ – 'that self-declared football club built on oil money' – and that their continued cooperation was contingent on my being able to justify my involvement with their great rivals.

The tone and language had become frosty, in cold contrast to the reception they had promised as we'd made our arrangements days earlier. If I'd been in doubt about the seething distrust the countries felt for each other, this had made things clear.

The 'association' that Seroj had referred to was a few photos I had posted on social media of me standing besides the Qarabağ logo at the Azersun Arena, and a few platitudes about Azeri hospitality. In the climate of hate that exists between Armenia and Azerbaijan, this got Seroj's back up, and it was only after I grossly underplayed my understanding of the situation and feigned naïvety that he relented. The meeting was still on.

'Azerbaijan has always tried to claim Karabakh as their territory,' declares Seroj. He is a young, fresh-faced man, not nearly so militant looking as his activities would suggest. He is well dressed and has tidy hair, and though our conversation proceeds through a translator he looks me in the eye and delivers his message calmly but forcefully. 'But because there is no historical background and no historical proof for Azerbaijan in Karabakh, they're always trying to find some justification.

'In this case they use the creation of a football club sponsored by the government, and they call the football club Karabakh. It's in order that they can have some association with the name of Karabakh.'

'Football fans don't know history,' adds fellow member Zaqaryan.

'People hear that Qarabağ plays in Azerbaijan, so then they would never think that Karabakh is Armenian. It's like a political project. They just need some way to communicate to Europe that Karabakh is Azerbaijan.'

To that end, a Europa League tie against Tottenham Hotspur in 2015 provided fertile ground. When Qarabağ visited White Hart Lane for an otherwise routine group-stage fixture, pamphlets were distributed by the club amongst journalists outlining the details of the Ağdam occupation and subsequent refugee crisis the conflict created. 'The history they gave was the Azerbaijani interpretation of history,' argues Zaqaryan.

Seroj cites the advertising deals that the state of Azerbaijan has cut in European football – from shirt sponsorships with Atlético Madrid and Sheffield Wednesday, to Baku United FC, the London-based Futsal team funded by the Azerbaijani NGO, Odlar Yurdu Organisation, who are the only professional and by far the most successful Futsal outfit in the UK. In Baku, they call it brand awareness. Here, in Yerevan, it's more like reputation laundering.

According to the Front, the government in Baku use Qarabağ as a way of covering up their role in a brutal conflict. Zaqaryan says that foreign journalists and UEFA delegates are a soft target, and that disseminating literature that skews the story of the war in Azerbaijan's favour is just another example of Baku's aggression over the Karabakh mountains. 'They tell the history they want to tell,' he says. 'It's a small part of the wider propaganda game. They name the club Karabakh and then promote it as being Azerbaijan. It's psychological.

'But to us in Armenia, as football fans, it is hurtful. We don't have a team that bears the name Artsakh [the Armenian name for Nagorno-Karabakh] in Armenia because of FIFA and UEFA rules.' The one team that does take the region's name, Lernayin Artsakh, plays its games in the city of Stepanakert.

'Maybe that's because we don't have the same money in Armenia as they do in Baku. They have their oil money and because of that they have a successful team that makes their fans happy. But we are hurting.'

The standoff over Artsakh is like rubbing salt in the wound for many Armenians. Seroj believes that Hayrapetyan's controversial involvement with the FFA, with FC Pyunik and with professional football in Armenia has been a major turn-off to investors. But mistrust has spread deeper into football here, and can also be found around a number of the individuals that own the clubs.

Pyunik are formally owned by Samuel Aleksanyan, a business mogul who in 2007 was accused by retail industry reps of causing a nationwide sugar shortage to his own advantage, and he has since established a monopoly over imports.

The 2014 Champions League flops Banants (now known as FC Urartu) are part-owned by the country's wealthiest man, Oleg Mkrtchyan, who has been accused of being part of a major tax evasion network in Ukraine and who was at the centre of a third-party ownership debacle that derailed a proposed transfer for national team captain Henrikh Mkhitaryan from Shakhtar Donetsk to Liverpool. He was also charged with embezzlement in Russia in 2018, whilst he was owner of Russian Premier League side Kuban Krasnodar.

The owner of Yerevan-based FC Mika, Mikhail Bagdasarov, was hit with a lawsuit for $22 million by the Russian bank VTB over outstanding debts in 2013, shortly before the company filed for bankruptcy leaving the debt un-serviced, yet Bagdasarov's MIKA Group continues to control the country's aviation fuel and diesel imports.

Even FC Shirak chairman, Arman Sahakyan, who was awarded the city of Gyumri's Man of the Year award in 2010, was responsible for attempting to block a film festival organised by the Caucasus Centre of Peacemaking Initiatives to promote solidarity with Azerbaijan.

These are the men who pull the strings Armenian football. 'Investors don't invest in football because it is so corrupt,' states Seroj.

In 2008, Pyunik played FC Ararat in a title decider that some supporters believed was fixed. A goal in the last minute of extra time from the striker Albert Tadevosyan won the game for Hayrapetyan's team, but the repercussions from that match can still be felt today.

'People were really disappointed after that result against Ararat,' explains Zaqaryan. 'Afterwards, the financial investments stopped. People saw the unjust situation.

'The referees' decisions helped Pyunik to win that match. From that game, everybody in Armenia understands that you don't beat Pyunik. The referees often help them and Pyunik will win because of the wrong decisions.'

Even Pyunik's policy of utilising homegrown players is tainted. Club officials are accused by the Front of putting pressure on the football federation to select the team's players for the Armenia national youth teams, and for scooping up financial rewards intended as an incentive for clubs to invest in youth development.

The First Armenian Front blame the lack of interest in the game on the toxic atmosphere created by Hayrapetyan, which they say means that outside parties are reluctant to deal with him. Football here, at least in the eyes of those who would pay for it, is the plaything of the apparatchiks.

It's no wonder they look across the border at the success of Qarabağ and feel a longing to overthrow the old order. The First Armenian Front give everything to their country, sending parties of up to 100 supporters to every away game the national team plays. Their performative displays in foreign cities and stadiums are colourful and wild. The fact that Armenia have never qualified for a major international tournament doesn't deter them.

The country approached international football in the same way that it embraced independence: nervously. Armenia played its first match in 1992 but spent the next fifteen years sitting deep, packing its defence and trying not to lose by a hatful. Occasionally the side would come up against another frightened team of similarly muted ambition and narrowly scrape a cherished win, but this was attritional football by and large where the majority of victories came in not being walloped.

In some ways, independence shattered the confidence of the former Soviet republics. Armenia had produced a football team capable of winning the Soviet Top League less than twenty years earlier, but after 1991 the Armenian team was handicapped by the country's small status. This directly reflected how these nations saw their new position – politically, economically, culturally – in a post-Soviet world.

At some point amidst the stagnation, the FFA opted in to the Eastern European trend of hiring foreign coaches to try and shock their workmanlike squads into life. An Argentine, a Romanian, a Frenchman and a Dutchman all took a turn at the helm, before the unlikely appointment of an FA Cup final-winning goal scorer from the Firth of Forth.

Ian Porterfield's goal for Sunderland at Wembley against Leeds in 1973 – a game better remembered for a save by Sunderland goalkeeper Jim Montgomery from Leeds' Peter Lorimer that seemed to defy the laws of physics – gave the FA Cup its biggest underdog story. But when Porterfield was appointed by the Football Federation of Armenia as the national coach in 2006, he'd never faced such a challenge.

Porterfield attained the country's first-ever back-to-back wins in June 2007, which included a memorable 1–0 victory over Poland in Yerevan, and the team followed this up with draws against

Cristiano Ronaldo's Portugal and a Serbia side managed by the former Spain coach Javier Clemente.

Under Porterfield, the team's playing style radically altered, switching from a deep-lying reactive game to one that kept the play high up the pitch and pressurised teams into forced errors. It was a watershed moment for the timid Armenia team.

Of all the stories I've gratefully collected from Eastern Europe, and of all the portraits of footballers and managers my friends and colleagues have generously painted for me, the most numinous came in a dirty Swindon pub on a rainy afternoon.

Tom Jones, an ex-Chelsea trainee who made a journeyman career in England's lower leagues, played under Porterfield years before, but a chance meeting catapulted him into a role as the Scotsman's number two in a job in South Korea at Busan IPark. The pair developed a professional and personal bond. When Porterfield was diagnosed with cancer of the colon in 2007, there was only one person who could take over the reins in Yerevan.

'Ian gave me the tapes to look at of his first few games in charge and asked me what I thought,' Jones recounted. 'In those tapes I don't think I saw the opposition goalkeeper once.'

Armenia, new to the international football scene, had developed a complex. 'I spoke to Vardan [Minasyan, the first-team coach] and he said the team were frightened of losing by six or seven and embarrassing the nation. So, they just sat back and defended. I said that mentality would have to change.'

Before then, Armenia had won just three games in three years. 'Vardan was a fantastic organiser and administrator, but on the pitch his teams never had a shot on goal. So I came in and brought a different mindset – set up training sessions to be high pressing, high tempo. I don't care who we're playing, just don't let them play.

'Until then all these guys had thought about was keeping the score down. So I worked to change the mentality, to get men forward and occupy the opposition back line. There wasn't to be any more of just letting the opposition have the ball. Once the players bought into that mindset, we started to see a change.'

Armenia still bobbled along near the bottom of their qualifying group for Euro 2008, but there was no doubting that something had changed. The team fought gamely in narrow defeats against Belgium and Poland, but it was during a week in June 2007 that things finally clicked.

'What Tom brought to Armenia when he came, he said that we were playing much too defensive,' says Minasyan. 'He said all our tactics had to change to become more offensive. He was the one that did that work in training. Then all of a sudden, game by game, the team started to improve, and the result came.'

The team won back-to-back games for the first time in years, winning 2–1 away in Almaty against Kazakhstan before beating group-leaders Poland 1–0 in Yerevan.

'I had people coming up to me in the park in Yerevan saying, "Coach, coach – fantastic,"' recalls Jones. 'It was surreal. It completely changed how they saw the team. After that they thought they could beat anyone.'

'The team was used to playing without belief,' says Minasyan. 'But Porterfield influenced the minds of the players.' But things would take a tragic turn.

'Ian's health was deteriorating all the time,' says Jones. 'He wasn't getting better. Then he phoned me when he was in Brompton Hospital in a very bad way and he said that the only game he wanted to see through was the Portugal game [in Yerevan on 22 August 2007]. That was his only target.

'Two days before the game they flew him out there. I'd been doing all the coaching up to that point, assisted by Vardan.

'It was the day before the Portugal game, we'd just finished our training session for the day at the stadium. All the media were there and everyone could see that Ian was struggling. He had a colostomy bag and God knows what else. He could barely stand.

'Then he got everybody together in the middle of the pitch and he said, "Link hands." He got everybody with their hands up in the air and he said, "This. This is for us. Together."'

It was a night unlike anything they'd seen in Yerevan. Fifteen thousand people packed into the Vazgen Sargsyan Stadium to see if their buoyant team could topple Portugal's world stars, a team led by Cristiano Ronaldo and coached by the Brazilian World Cup winner Luiz Filipe Scolari.

As the national anthem was belted out, Armenia's three coaches stood side by side on the touchline, Minasyan and Jones in training jerseys and Porterfield in suit and tie. It's likely that he knew this would be his last match.

His blazer barely concealed the medical apparatus that was plugged into his body, and his grey hair was receding and thinning. His once full and ruddy cheeks were now bony and yellow, and the angle of his jawline was so pronounced it cast a shadow beneath the stadium floodlights.

In the first few minutes of the game, the midfielder Levon Pachajyan showed just how confident this new Armenia team was; after collecting the ball in the Portugal half he literally ran circles around three defenders before delivering a devilish cross that nearly led to a goal. It recalled the days when FC Ararat Yerevan dazzled the USSR with their crafty, technical football en route to winning the Soviet title.

And so it went on – Samvel Melkonyan danced inside from the touchline and fizzed a shot narrowly over the bar; Hamlet Mkhitaryan jinked and teased and tied Portugal's Raul Meireles in such a knot that he hacked him down in frustration. Portugal spluttered and wheezed, whilst trying to keep track of Armenia's electric passing and ghost-like movement.

Robert Arzumanyan connected his head with a cross from a free-kick to nod the hosts in front after ten minutes, and the Sargsyan stadium erupted. Ruben Hayrapetyan, surrounded by balding and burly henchmen in the VIP box, punched the air in delight. Porterfield dragged himself painfully to the touchline to call for calm amongst his players.

Armenia didn't get the win they craved as an equalising goal from Ronaldo saw to it that Portugal escaped Yerevan with a draw. The hero of the north-east at Wembley in 1973 didn't get to taste one last giant-killing in his final act. But he had touched a nation.

It was three weeks later on 11 September, whilst the team were preparing for a friendly against Malta, that the news came through. Armenia had ironically been scheduled to play a qualifier against Azerbaijan the next day, but the game was cancelled after Baku stated that they would refuse to allow the Armenia players into the country.

'We were told on the morning of the game,' remembers Jones. 'Vardan and I had to call a team meeting with the whole committee and the president [Ruben Hayrapetyan] present and we had to break the news to the players. There were a lot of tears. A lot of tears.

'The players really didn't want to play the game, but I just thought it was what Ian would have wanted. But no one's mind was on the game, we lost 1–0 [to Malta] and it was horrible. Afterwards we had a meeting and I just said, "Look, we can't allow that to happen again. All that we've built together is going to be lost."'

The chance for redemption came a few weeks later, when qualifying matches resumed with a home game in Yerevan against Serbia. By now, Jones and Minasyan were in sole charge of the team.

'I make a point of never trying to copy anybody. But I got them all out on the pitch before kick-off, we got together in a circle and we raised our hands together and we said, "This is for us." The stadium went absolutely berserk. Everyone in that ground was completely together, behind us and in memory of Ian. It was incredible. We drew 0–0 but it should have been 10–0.'

Armenia played Serbia off the park in Yerevan, peppering the visitors' goal with shots but failing to find the breakthrough. Within weeks, the team's coach Clemente was sacked, such was the superiority of the Armenians as they played for the memory of a manager they had loved.

Jones shows me two slightly battered and worn photographs. They show Porterfield near the end of his life, thin and unsteady, but brimming with pride as he celebrates with his players in the back rooms of the stadium after the Poland victory. They are the last pictures that Jones owns depicting his friend alive.

When he returned to England, Minasyan took on the top job alone, and the high-press, fast-tempo approach he had learned from his mentors became the new blueprint for his team. He's never sought to change the legacy that Porterfield left behind.

'I was just starting my coach career,' states Minasyan. 'I was looking to learn about tactics, technique, fitness. But the most important things I learned from Ian were courage, team spirit, belief in yourself, discipline, character. These I learned from not only a great coach, but mostly from a great man.'

Under Minasyan's guidance, Armenia had a great run in the qualifying games for the 2014 World Cup. The team won 4–0 away in Denmark and 2–1 in the Czech Republic, before drawing 2–2 with Italy in Naples having twice taken the lead. Two years earlier, he took them to within a game of reaching the Euro 2012 play-offs, winning 4–0 against Slovakia – conquerors of world champions Italy in the previous World Cup – in Zilina, before losing out 2–1 on the final day of qualifying to the Republic of Ireland in Dublin. By the end of 2014, the team had risen to thirtieth in the FIFA world rankings, up from seventy-ninth when Jones and Porterfield had first touched down in Yerevan.

Time hasn't diminished the affections felt towards these two British coaches. 'Every year on what would have been Porterfield's birthday we hold a small celebration,' says Seroj. 'People still love him here for what he did for our country.'

The day after meeting Seroj in Yerevan, I get a glimpse first-hand of just how far Armenia has fallen since the glory years of Porterfield and Jones.

This weekend in March sees the first football played in the country since November, with the resumption of the domestic league at the end of a long winter break. There have been a couple of changes in the Armenian Premier League since a ball was last kicked.

One of those changes has been the temporary relocation of FC Gandzasar Kapan from the south-eastern city of Kapan to the capital, meaning that seven of the eight teams in the division are now based here in Yerevan. The reason given by the club is that there are no facilities in Kapan for playing football in the cold weather; a miserly indictment of the shoddy state of infrastructure. The arrangement leaves Gyumri as the only city in Armenia outside of the capital that hosts top-flight football.

I'm at the Yerevan Football Academy in Avan in the city's northeast to watch Gandzasar play Pyunik as the Armenian Premier League resumes after its hiatus. Technically this is a home fixture for the side from Kapan, but since the academy traditionally hosts Pyunik's fixtures, any sense of there being a home and away side is lost.

In fact, nothing about this match is like top-flight football. The academy's grass pitch is out of action due to the weather, so the game is taking place on the adjacent synthetic surface. There are no terraces, so the supporters – I count thirty-five of them – stand just back from the touchline.

The press box is a small wicker table standing near one corner flag, at which is sat one cold-looking woman with a notepad. She doesn't write a single thing down for the entirety of the match. I notice later that she has no pen.

Towards the end of game, the meagre crowd is joined by the players and staff of FC Banants who are due to play next on this pitch. The set-up is more like a five-a-side league or pub football than a game that could affect who qualifies for the Champions League.

I watch the game with Pyunik's press officer, an early-twenty-something girl named Anush, who I'd met for the first time the previous day on the Tsitsernakaberd hill in town. Anush is a complete football anorak. She follows the national team to the farthest corners of Europe as part of the First Armenian Front, and knows all there is to know about football behind the old Iron Curtain.

Wide-eyed and with a wicked grasp of casual English, she was born during the last months of the Nagorno-Karabakh conflict.

'There were periods during the war and in the years afterwards where we didn't have access to electricity because the country was so poor,' she tells me as we half-watch Gandzasar defeat Pyunik 2–0.

In Anush, I see someone in the mould of the Western millennial. She would seem just as at home in London or Paris as in Yerevan or Gyumri. To hear her speak about the turmoil surrounding the Karabakh war and how this affected her life and shaped her upbringing makes the conflict real. She's not like the lined, greying men who were hardened on the front line of battle. She's young, optimistic and wide-eyed. Paradoxically, speaking to her is the closest I have felt to the war.

After the final whistle, Anush coordinates the post-match press conference inside one of the academy's dingy dressing rooms. The Pyunik coach fields two questions from the floor – which is composed of only three reporters, all of whom look like interns – though this at least trumps the awkward silence that greets the Gandzasar boss as he takes his seat to face no questions at all.

Watching the empty press conference, my mind drifts, and I can't help but think back to some of Minasyan's reflections on the good times. I wonder whether the spirit of Ian Porterfield can yet save Armenian football from its hole.

'In the last part of Ian's life, when the illness had become torture for the great man, that was when the big results came,' he told me.

'In my opinion, the players saw his great spirit, willpower and aspiration. And they started to play with double excitement. The players understood that if you play with spirit, then with courage you can achieve anything.'

IV

The drive from Yerevan to Stepanakert is deftly allegorical of the politics that divides these two cities; they are aching to be close but are divided by circumstances.

To reach Stepanakert from the Armenian capital means a gruelling six-hour bus ride through the winding mountains of the Lesser Caucasus.

The roads cling to the steep hillside and spiral up for what seems an eternity, until finally snow-topped peaks give way to the lush greenery of Karabakh as the capital reveals itself some 800 metres up. For all its natural beauty, the journey only emphasises just how isolated this contested region is.

High up in these mountains, I am invited to meet with Samuel

Karapetyan, the head of the Artsakh Football Federation (AFF), in his Stepanakert office. I am, he says, the first foreign journalist to have come here to ask him about his work in Karabakh football, and he wastes little time in outlining his ambitions to lead the republic to UEFA membership.

'All this war and conflict is temporary,' he declares, whilst lighting a cigarette and planting two meaty elbows on his desk. 'One day soon, the Artsakh national team will participate in the World Cup or European Championship.'

Karapetyan is a swaggering brick wall of a man. Draped in combats, he sits behind an oak desk the size of a small tennis court, and the domineering wingspan of Artsakh's eagle coat of arms rises up over his shoulder from where it is pinned to the back wall.

During the Karabakh war, he was one of Artsakh's celebrated military leaders. Alongside being president of the AFF, at the time he was also Artsakh's deputy Defence Minister, a not insignificant posting for a region that is still engaged in active conflict.

Here in these mountains, football imitates real life.

'We are hopeful,' says Karapetyan. 'We are convinced that recognition will come soon, because all the world is interested in establishing peace in this region. Sooner or later Azerbaijan will recognise Artsakh, then we will participate not just in football but in every aspect of international life.

'The process is underway. We are confident that the Artsakh team will participate in international tournaments, and that it is coming soon. If we were not confident in our success, then we wouldn't live here.'

I was fortunate enough in my student days to be tutored by the bulldog ex-*Independent* journalist Jonathan Foster, a smooth-headed maverick who was a correspondent in South Africa when Nelson Mandela was released from prison. His famous maxim about the journalistic trade was: 'If one person tells you it's raining outside and another says it's sunny, your job as a journalist isn't to report both; it's to stick your head out the fucking window and find out which is true.'

In the spirit of Jonathan's philosophy, it's worth stating that Artsakh are not about to be recognised by UEFA, and I can't imagine why Karapetyan thinks I would believe they are. The governing body stipulated some years ago that membership is open only to recognised sovereign states, and since not even Armenia recognises the country's self-declared independence, the chances of opening a conversation with UEFA are slim to nil.

After we've talked, Karapetyan brings out a bottle of fine Armenian cognac, and over the next twenty minutes we toast everything from Armenia, to English football, to the dead of the Karabakh war. Armenians are well known for their brandies, but as exquisite as this one is, it's completely deadly. It nicks the back of the throat like razor wire, and as I have been fighting off a cold for most of my time in the Caucasus, I feel particularly vulnerable to the effects of the liquor as I stumble out of Karapetyan's office.

The Stepanakert Republican Stadium sits at the bottom of a procession of steps, which lead down almost from the door of the Presidential Palace.

On this cold spring morning in March 2017, there is a game taking place between the under-fifteen side of local club FC Artsakh and a development squad sent over from Yerevan by the Football Federation of Armenia.

The stadium is a classic Soviet-style concrete bowl, with seats decked out in the red, blue and amber of the Armenian flag, save for one corner of the ground where Artsakh's white chevron motif has been painted. The stadium's low roof means the jagged green hills of the Caucasus are strikingly visible behind the ground.

The game itself is a dull 0–0, the only highlight a red card for the young Armenian goalkeeper for a thrilling dash from his goal that leads to a spectacular foul. Football here is not of a good standard.

For Stepanakert's young footballers, this has been a rare chance to test themselves against opposition from outside the republic's borders. Since watching Armenia's greatest football export, Henrikh Mkhitaryan, transform into a world star at Manchester United, many kids dream of making careers in Europe. But they face multiple obstacles.

At the start of the last decade, the Association of Football Federations of Azerbaijan (AFFA) appealed to FIFA against the involvement of teams from Artsakh in competitions organised by the Football Federation of Armenia and vice versa. This means that any cross-border football interaction is limited to occasional friendly games against sides that are hardy enough to make the long trek.

'Before 2006 there was no organised football in Artsakh,' states Slava Gabrielyan, the UEFA Pro Licence coach with responsibility for selecting the emerging Artsakh national team, when he meets me in stadium's clubhouse after the game.

As we walk its corridors, my attention is caught by two neatly framed pictures hanging on the wall near the entrance. I recognise the faces instantly but can't place them.

The boyish good looks, the smart but serious demeanours, the hopeful glint in the eyes as the two men stare beyond the lens. It's not until we're outside that it clicks.

Loris Grigoryan and Ashot Adamyan were the two Yerazank FC teenagers killed in the Nagorno-Karabakh war. It's only right that they should be immortalised here at their former home ground, in the heart of the city that they gave their lives to defend.

'They were great guys, real patriots both of them,' former Yerazank teammate Levon Mkrtchyan fondly remembers. 'Both great players too. Loris died in an attack at Shushi of course, on the last day there. Shushi was such an important city for us, being so close to Stepanakert, and Loris died to defend it.

'Because of that and because of the war, neither of them ever became the great footballers that they should have been. They both had good football brains, both very self-confident.'

Mkrtchyan and Gabrielyan didn't go into battle with Adamyan or Grigoryan. But they did fight on the front line with some of their other teammates. Mkrtchyan was just seventeen years old when he took up arms.

'There is nothing else in the world like war,' describes Gabrielyan. 'War is loss. And when you lose someone, you cannot be happy. That is why war is the worst thing.

'Imagine the situation between England and Scotland. Now imagine that after the referendum in your country [the 2014 vote on Scottish independence] that your central government has sent soldiers to kill the people who voted not to be members of the United Kingdom.

Because people in Karabakh didn't want to be a part of Azerbaijan, they were killed. As Armenians and as football players, we understood that this was our homeland. We didn't want to be an Azerbaijan team, we wanted to be a Karabakh team. That is what we wanted to be a part of; Karabakh football. This war was about our will, about what we wanted as a nation. Like I said, there is nothing like war.'

Both men lost family and friends in the war. No one in Karabakh was left untouched on some level. Both are at pains to emphasise that Grigoryan, Adamyan and every other player from Yerazank who went to fight did so not out of compulsion, but willingly. 'They chose to go,' states Gabrielyan. 'We all did.'

Before there was war, there was football, and in football terms the relationships between Yerazank and their Azerbaijani rivals were strained. League matches between the club and teams from Azerbaijan became part of a wider narrative of nationalist hate. For ninety minutes every week, the political war came to the football pitch. These were fractious and fraught games, and they gave a licence for the free expression of the irrational dislike between the two nations.

In February 1988, in response to a loosening of central Soviet authority by Mikhail Gorbachev's government in Moscow, the Supreme Soviet of Nagorno-Karabakh in Stepanakert passed a vote calling for the detachment of the Karabakh Autonomous Oblast from Azerbaijan and its absorption into Armenia. The motion was rejected out of hand, both in Moscow and by the authorities in Baku, which led to a mass public demonstration in Stepanakert's Lenin Square. The protests were condemned by the Moscow government and in the Soviet state press, but it was in Baku where the ire was felt most strongly.

The anti-Armenian rhetoric, some of it voiced by senior members of Azerbaijan's republican government, was vitriolic. In mid-February, the head of the Central Committee of the Communist Party of Azerbaijan Oqtay Asadov exclaimed, 'A hundred thousand Azerbaijanis are ready to storm Artsakh at any time and organise a slaughter there,' if the demonstrations didn't stop.

Two weeks later on 27 February, the ticking time bomb finally exploded. A pogrom in the eastern Azerbaijani town of Sumgait led to the deaths of thirty-two Armenians at the hands of rioting Azeris. However, this figure accounts only for those whose bodies were identified, most observers believe the actual figure was much higher, and is likely to have been in the hundreds.

Men, women and children were killed and homes were looted and destroyed. The crimes were perpetrated by neighbours, against neighbours. The Communist Party of Azerbaijan representative

Hidayat Orujov's warning to Sumgait's Armenians that '100,000 Azeris from neighbouring districts will break into your houses, torch your apartments, rape your women, and kill your children' if the demonstrations over Karabakh's unification with Armenia didn't stop, was brutally borne out.

'Yerazank had been due to play an away game in Sumgait against FK Khazar the day after the massacres,' recalls Gabrielyan. 'After what happened, all of the mothers of the players and all the team's coaches came together and said that we could not go to Sumgait to play. Can you imagine? It wouldn't be safe for Armenian footballers there after what had happened.' Once that decision had been taken, there was very little room left for manoeuvre. 'After Sumgait, we knew we couldn't continue to play football against teams from Azerbaijan.'

For Yerazank, it was checkmate. To allow the game to go ahead would require parents to send their sons into a city where Armenians were being killed in the streets. Refuse, and it would be the end of football in the region, the end of the club that had built their sons up into men from boys. It was no choice at all.

Yerazank closed its operations in Stepanakert and withdrew from the Azerbaijani league. Meanwhile, a new incarnation of the club was formed in Yerevan to compete in the Armenian leagues. A handful of the original squad went with them. The rest stayed in Stepanakert to fight the war that had been started at Sumgait.

It's interesting to watch these young footballers play this morning at the city stadium in light of what happened here thirty years ago.

In 2006 footballers in Stepanakert founded FC Artsakh, the republic's only organised club, but there has never been a national championship in the country for the team to play in. 'We have some friendly games against teams from Armenia and sometimes from Georgia,' Gabrielyan says. 'But we never have competitive games.

It's not possible for us.' A new league was finally formed in the republic in 2018. But it could be years before the damaging effects of years of isolation are undone.

'In Crimea, UEFA have recognised that the territory is neither part of Russia nor Ukraine' says Gabrielyan. 'They have put measures in place to allow football there to prosper. We hope and expect that UEFA will do the same here in Artsakh.'

The armed conflict between Armenia and Azerbaijan is a long way from being resolved. The ceasefire is regularly broken on both sides of the line of contact, which often leads to the deaths of dozens of soldiers and civilians. In April 2016, the situation deteriorated into a six-day war that many feared would reignite full-scale hostilities between the countries.

At the same time, the AFA's general secretary Karen Vanyan was in the final stages of organising a series of games in Stepanakert between the Artsakh team and other unrecognised territories. Those plans had to be cancelled due to the fighting.

'The problem is that we don't have the means to show the world that we can play,' says Mkrtchyan. 'We only play here for ourselves, but our aim is to show outsiders what we can do. We want the world to know about Karabakh and Karabakh footballers.'

One of the realities of living in a region stalked by conflict is that security measures trump most other considerations. When Artsakh men reach eighteen years old, they are whisked away for two years of military national service. Gabrielyan and Mkrtchyan believe footballers should be exempt from the rule but the status quo holds, meaning FC Artsakh's players have their development interrupted at a delicate stage.

The AFF does what it can to limit the disruption. Much of the funding it receives from the Ministry for Sport is reinvested in training up local coaches to international standard. Mkrtchyan currently holds a UEFA B Licence and plans to match his colleague's Pro Licence soon. With Artsakh a non-entity in world football, both coaches are registered with UEFA via the Football Federation of Armenia in Yerevan.

'We take coaching seriously here,' says Karapetyan, head of the AFF, back in his office. 'This year we will have some international coaches from other countries coming to Stepanakert to work with our players. However, we mostly have to use retired coaches so as not to cause problems for other national football associations.'

Internationally, the AFF's work continues largely under the radar. In 2010, FC Artsakh competed in a tournament in France organised by the Armenian diaspora, which was followed in 2017 by a visit to Catalonia as part of a similar arrangement.

For Gabrielyan's national team, their most conspicuous foray into the international scene remains the 2014 CONIFA World Cup (a tournament for unrecognised states and nations) in Ostersund, Sweden, where defeats to the County of Nice and the Isle of Man's team Ellan Vannin saw them eliminated in the first round. A formal protest made to CONIFA by the AFFA in Baku over Karabakh's involvement went unheeded by the organisers.

After more than an hour of being surrounded by muddy kit and boots, Mkrtchyan, Gabrielyan and I head back out of the clubhouse and onto the pitch, to continue our conversation against the more pleasing backdrop of the glorious Karabakh mountains.

As Karabakh struggles for internal solutions, success over the border in Azerbaijan continues to barb. FK Qarabağ's resurgence under the Azersun regime has brought the struggles being felt in and around Stepanakert into sharp contrast. Like in Yerevan, there is no affection felt here for the exiles in Baku, especially since figures both inside and outside the club make no secret of Qarabağ being a symbol of Azerbaijan's rightful dominion over Nagorno-Karabakh.

In the middle of it all, the AFF quietly continues its work, its future bound up in the throes of forces over which it exercises no control.

'We'd all like to think that football is separate from politics,' ruminates Vanyan. 'Azerbaijan does not have the right to decide for our children whether or not they play football.'

* * *

The story appeared about three weeks after I returned to the UK.

The Ministry of Foreign Affairs of the Republic of Azerbaijan had published a news article via the country's state news agency. Some of the language was alarming.

> During his illegal visit, Robert O'Connor, by politicising football and sports in general, is trying to promote the regime created in the occupied Azerbaijani territories.
>
> The article openly demonstrates the one-sided and biased position of the author. It is clear that the author prepared his article for the order of Armenian lobbyists.
>
> Regarding the author's attempt to politicise sports... such international football governing bodies as FIFA and UEFA in their activities are guided by the norms and principles of international law and respect the territorial integrity and sovereignty of states.
>
> It is regrettable that *The Independent* newspaper published such an article of propaganda nature.
>
> The author of the article will be added to the Azerbaijani Foreign Ministry's list of undesirable persons.

If that wasn't concerning enough, worse was to follow. The following day, I received the following note from the Foreign Ministry in Baku:

> Robert, you illegally visited occupied territories of Azerbaijan in defiance of our laws, and regulations and UK Foreign Office advice. Your name automatically will be put in the list of undesirable persons.
>
> It is considered violation of sovereignty and territorial integrity of Azerbaijan, as such laws and regulations of my country. We have opened criminal files against foreign nationals who are engaged in actions undermining territorial integrity of Azerbaijan and promoting the illegal regime established therein.

Naturally, the words 'criminal files' were enough to make me sit up, especially as I was now in the crosshairs of a state with a less than exemplary record on human rights.

I was also invited to write a letter of apology to the President of Azerbaijan, detailing my naïvety and ignorance of the sensitive nature of the relationship between Azerbaijan and the separatist territories. The letter was written and sent, but a response is yet to arrive, and I am resigned to the fact that my relationship with the country is over.

The result of this development was that I was unable to continue following the story as it unfolded in Baku. In September 2017, six months after I returned from the South Caucasus, FK Qarabağ made history by becoming the first Azerbaijani team to qualify for the group stages of the Champions League. They went on to play huge games with the other teams in their group, which included Chelsea, Atlético Madrid and Roma.

To my disappointment, I watched all three of the legs of these matches that were played in Azerbaijan from home. Likewise, I wasn't present when the stadium hosted the Europa League final between Arsenal and Chelsea in 2019, nor will I be when Baku hosts matches at the postponed 2020 European Championships. This seems to me more than a little absurd, although I concede I'm biased in my own favour.

Azerbaijan desperately seeks favour via sport in Western Europe, and I am one of a small number of reporters from Europe that has spent time with Qarabağ on their own patch since the beginning of their new era. Therefore, for the country to turn its paranoia against me is ridiculous.

It isn't clear how Azerbaijan can have the kind of future it wants until the conflict with Armenia over Nagorno-Karabakh is settled. The Europa League final in 2019 was overshadowed by the withdrawal of Arsenal's Henrikh Mkhitaryan ahead of the game, citing fears that his safety could not be guaranteed in Baku, despite the government offering to waive legislation that bars all Armenians from entering the country. For a nation that is desperate to present an image of prosperous modernity to the rest of the world, this was an embarrassment that could have easily been avoided.

PART THREE

BREATHING CORPSES: GEORGIA, ABKHAZIA AND SOUTH OSSETIA

Life is not the property which we have to defend
But the gift, which we have to share with other people
ENGRAVING AT SUKHUMI BAY

© Ssolbergj & creator of source map / CC BY-SA

I

The Enguri River hypnotises. Its water washes between twin civilisations, and as it snakes its way through the aching valleys formed by the dramatic Lesser Caucasus, its gentle current forms a perfect foil for the harsh, never-ending rock.

From the east bank in Georgia, they gaze across the gaping Enguri towards rebels and hellraisers, an illegal commune cloaked in the plausible robes of a peaceful existence. From the other side in Abkhazia, they see invaders who waged an unholy war and withdrew their guns only after inflicting the most heinous suffering in the bellicose name of conquest.

History craves the stubbornness of certainty. The Enguri cuts between two versions of the same story. Neither is, nor could hope to be, as righteous as its foe.

Once, tanks rolled over this bridge. Now, only horsemen cross, hauling rickety improvised carriages back and forth in a daily Sisyphean ritual.

The little Georgian town of Zugdidi, tucked away in the country's north-west, once fed into the mouth of hell. There is not really any other way to describe the depravity that ensued when the newly formed Georgian republic went to war with gun-toting Abkhaz separatists in 1992.

I came here in early 2018 – my second time in Georgia, but my first beneath its mountains – just as an unusually mild winter was preparing to give way to a warm and welcome spring.

After stepping off the train following a six-hour journey from Tbilisi, most passengers arriving at Zugdidi are heading onwards to the towns and villages that pepper the country's rural, mountainous north, a world away from the bustling metropolis of the capital. Some are collected by friends or family, embraced by familiar arms and welcomed with kisses and smiles. Others drop themselves wearily into cabs to be ferried along on the last leg of a long and tiring trip up through the hills and into the hearth of home.

I'm almost the last person off the train. In fact, almost nobody has alighted the service since we left the capital at a little before 7 a.m. We collected a handful of stragglers about one hour into the journey as we passed through the town of Gori, the birthplace of Stalin. Somehow, even this unique faultline along the unyielding terrain of Eastern European history felt quaint and insignificant when set in the context of a peaceful, temperate Georgia.

My throat is dry as I prepare for the guttural task of hailing a cab. The further from the capital of a country one travels, the more accents seem to matter. I can see only one driver not already loading luggage into his car. 'Abkhaz?' I offer in a rasping voice that sounds nothing like my own. The compound sound 'kh' has no equivalent for those used to languages in the Roman script, and so to effect it in a way that sounds passing to Transcaucasians requires sticky airways. 'Abkhaz,' the driver parrots back, and opens the back door of his car for me.

It's supposed to be twenty minutes from Zugdidi to the military checkpoint. So it's disquieting when a couple of minutes along the road the car pulls over and the driver steps out, beckoning me to do the same. Stepping out of the car, there's not a khaki jacket or semi-automatic weapon in sight.

The driver is already on his way towards a steep embankment, set back ten or fifteen metres from the roadside. I follow after him, cautiously but curiously. By the time I've clambered up the hillside, he is already stood some distance off, gazing across the steppe at what looks like a military memorial.

He talks emotively about the stones in front of us, a few yards away across what would have once been a green lawn; now there are only a few blades of verdant grass amongst the dry dirt. He knows only that I am a foreigner, probably a Westerner, and that I plan to cross the border from Georgia into Abkhazia, so this must be some attempt at an explanation of the history I'm about to encounter. I relax into the moment. Whatever this ritual, I decide it is for his benefit rather than mine, the gifting of some textural essence of what it means to travel on this road.

When he is finished, he turns to me with a kind of sad smile, places his hand on my shoulder then returns silently down the hill to his car, leaving me standing alone with just the birds chirruping overhead. I take a last look around, still not knowing quite what I've been brought here to observe. We don't speak again until arriving at our destination.

A lonely police cabin marks the last point of contact with the Georgian authorities. At the window, I surrender the signed, stamped and sealed letter of invitation issued to me days earlier by the Ministry of Foreign Affairs of the Republic of Abkhazia. To these officials, the document is meaningless, confirming only that I will not be turned back by the soldiers I meet when I cross the bridge.

I've been told to prepare for difficult questions at this stage in the crossing, especially since my passport contains a visa issued by another of Eurasia's 'illegal' regimes, the Nagorno-Karabakh republic sandwiched between Armenia and Azerbaijan. Both officers study my passport.

'English?' asks the first.

'Yes.'

'So,' says the other purposefully. 'Who will win today? Manchester United, or Chelsea?'

A phone call is made in Russian to tell the officers on the other side that they can expect me, then there's one final question before I'm allowed to pass.

'And Tottenham? They will beat Crystal Palace?'

II

Georgia, the country of Josef Jughashvili – or Stalin – and his trusted Politburo aides Lavrentiy Beria and Sergo Ordzhonikidze, was special to the USSR. The Georgian language, with its ornate curling script, enjoyed privileges not seen elsewhere in the union, and the subtropical, reviving Black Sea climate made it a longed-for haven in the stolid grey imagination of the Soviet Union. Its fertile soil and lush warm waters produced fruits, wine and caviar that were the envy of Europe. But the country also has a dark, destructive streak. Tbilisi berthed a strong, anti-Soviet dissident class that was loyal to ancient ideas about Georgia's glorious past; a movement that harnessed such popular support that, by the late 1980s, it had become powerful enough to pull the ailing Soviet Union to its knees from below, before the newly independent republic then turned both barrels of the revolutionary shotgun on itself.

Certainly this was once a great civilisation. Beginning with the eleventh-century reign of David the Builder, the Kingdom of Georgia – known to natives by its indigenous name Sakartvelo – was a melting pot of different peoples who were unified under the umbrella of Orthodox Christianity and the Georgian language, most prominent amongst them the Mingrelians, Kartvelians and Svards. During the twelfth century, the kingdom collapsed under the strain of Mongol invasion, and for the following centuries the region was passed back and forth between Ottoman and Persian ownership, until an appeal was made for the Russian Empire to absorb Georgia as a vassal in the early nineteenth century as protection against threats from Turkey. Thus began a 200-year relationship between Tbilisi and Moscow that continues to hang over the politics of the South Caucasus like a cloud.

Tbilisi carries its patchwork history in its curiously diverse architectural bones. An Iranian shah sacked the town in 1795, virtually razing it to the ground, after which a new Russian viceroy began the long process of re-imagining the old city in a new European style. On the wreckage of the pre-urbanised Persian town, a new Western-styled metropolis rose up centred on the grand sprawling Rustaveli Avenue. In 1989 and again in 2003, Rustaveli would become the site of huge popular revolutions, as twice Georgia rejected Russia and turned its head west.

Georgian exceptionalism defined its experience as a Soviet republic, and the people of Tbilisi bullishly rejected the economic realities of Communism. In no other corner of the USSR did the illegal shadow economy play such a central role in the lives of ordinary people. The black market in fruit, wine and caviar created wealthy criminal clans that owed their status to extra-legal activity and their loyalty to the system. This, coupled with old Caucasian traditions that made family and kinship rather than state institutions the backbone of public life, in turn bred a political class that traded in favours and backhanders, where senior posts within the Communist Party were bought and sold and where the criminal world became indistinguishable from the political.

Mafia-like bosses enjoyed huge popular respect. When the entrepreneur Evgrapi Shevardnadze – brother of Soviet Minister of Foreign Affairs and latterly President of independent Georgia Eduard Shevardnadze – took control of the tiny provincial football club Guria Lanchkuti on Georgia's western Black Sea coast in the 1980s, he was lauded as a hero for bankrolling their rapid rise into the Soviet Top League, where they competed shoulder to shoulder with the giants of the Soviet empire – Dynamo Kyiv, Spartak Moscow, Zenit Leningrad and, as we shall see, their compatriots in the Georgian capital, Dinamo Tbilisi. No one seemed bothered that Shevardnadze's vast fortune would have been completely impossible to accumulate legally within still-Communist Georgia.

The result was that, by the time independence was achieved, civic society had been eaten away from the inside. The economy served the narrow interests of a parasitic elite, whilst the republic's infrastructure had been propped up by subsidies from Moscow, and these were suddenly taken away. No one in the country had any experience in economic planning – quite the reverse, in 1989 the Georgian economy was little better than an embezzlement racket – and there were no security forces of which to speak. Without the tools to build a functioning state, Georgia simply collapsed into civil war.

The crisis, sparked when the independent republic's first President – the Shakespearean scholar and super-nationalist Zviad Gamsakhurdia – was driven at gunpoint out of his office and out of the country by a self-proclaimed military council of opposition paramilitaries in December 1991, made Georgia a lawless failed state before most of the world had even noticed its existence. For most of the next year, towns and villages were divided up by small-time militia into personal fiefdoms, some partisan, others merely opportunistic, and the authority of the government extended little further than the central districts of Tbilisi.

Dinamo Tbilisi, the football club of the Georgian Interior Ministry, became a bastion for the country's sense of self-expression during Soviet times. The people had good reason to feel invested – Dinamo produced some of the finest teams and individuals to come out of the union. League champions twice in 1964 and 1978, the team of David Kipiani, Vitaly Daraselia and Vladimir Gutsaev also became the first Soviet team to win European honours, lifting the Cup Winners' Cup in 1981 in the final in Dusseldorf. The team was also a reminder of Georgia's ethnic pluralism – Daraselia, who scored the winner in the final, was an ethnic Abkhazian from the town of Ochamchire, whilst Gutsaev, who got the assist for Daraselia's goal, was an Ossetian born in Tbilisi.

But like Georgia itself, Dinamo was a caged animal. Three times they came second in the league and three times third. There was a barely disguised policy within the Communist Party that only Moscow and Kyiv should produce Soviet champions – Beria even expressed as much in a furious outburst to the Dinamo star Boris Paichadze after he voiced the possibility of creating a more level playing field for Tbilisi. Transfers were often held up or hijacked altogether by the more powerful clubs, usually on the say of the Communist Party, and players failed to win the international honours their talents deserved. Two of the USSR's best players, Dinamo's Kipiani and Gutsaev, were left out of the USSR squad for the 1982 World Cup in Spain because the four Georgians already selected for the team were considered enough. Georgian football, like the rest of the country, was primed to break free.

The work to make football independent of the USSR authorities began in July 1989. One day, Mamuka Kvaratskhelia, a 23-year-old student at Tbilisi State University, read an article in the local Communist newspaper that asked the question: 'Do we need football separation from the Soviet Union?' In the context of the rapidly growing independence movement, there could be only one answer.

'When you're young, you're crazy, you know?' Kvaratskhelia explains to me, whilst reflecting on the bloody-mindedness of rebelling against the Soviet centre. 'Maybe I was brave too. I gathered football players, veterans, students. I met with hundreds of them and explained why Georgia needed independence in football. Imagine it – a national team for Georgia! The national anthem, the flag, Georgia playing in the World Cup.'

The first meeting was held in July at the Dinamo Lenin Stadium, a gathering of twenty-one stakeholders and interested parties who would begin the task of preparing Georgian football for independence. 'The USSR was weak economically at that time,' explains Kvaratskhelia. 'In Georgia, we had people like Gamsakhurdia and

[Merab] Kostava who were well-known dissidents, who had been in prison for the cause. There was only one direction the country was moving.' Two months earlier in April, twenty-one pro-independence protesters had been killed by Soviet troops at a huge rally on Tbilisi's Rustaveli Avenue, which fatally undermined central authority and set the republic irreversibly on the path to separation from Moscow.

Preparation for the new Georgian league lasted from July to December, during which time Gamsakhurdia turned up the temperature nationally with a decree, which declared that the Bolshevik invasion of 1921 had been an illegal annexation, with a conference to be held on 15 February 1990 to vote on the next move.

There were two questions on the ballot: 'Should Georgian football clubs leave the Soviet championship?' and 'Who will be president of the new Georgian Football Federation?' But the conference itself did not go smoothly. A clutch of older, established players fought the case for staying with Moscow – 'a bigger problem for us than the KGB, the players didn't understand the importance of independence for Georgia at that stage', explains Kvaratskhelia – the lure of the glitzy fixtures against Dynamo Kyiv and Spartak Moscow was still strong. But they were against a larger, more committed faction that wished to follow Kostava, Gamsakhurdia and the crowds on Rustaveli Avenue in breaking with the inertia of everything Soviet.

The reformists won the vote comfortably, before Dinamo Tbilisi's 1981 Cup Winners' Cup-winning coach Nodar Akhalkatsi was elected as the new federation's president. A letter of protest in the local Communist daily appeared the following day signed by the core of the Dinamo team, but the die was cast. Kvaratskhelia delivered the news to the USSR football chief Vyacheslav Koloskov personally.

'It was a huge shock to them in the USSR,' he describes. 'I believe I had my phone tapped by the KGB authorities, and I heard some rumours that they wanted to throw me out of the university for my role. But by then, the USSR was realising Georgia was slipping away.' The remaining dissenters in Tbilisi were pacified with senior appointments within the new football federation and the arch-tactician Akhalkatsi showed he would be just as skilled a functionary as he had been a coach.

The shock to the Soviet system was undeniable. Georgian footballers and particularly Dinamo Tbilisi had been, if not at the centre of the USSR's football story, key characters in it. But to the people of Georgia, Dinamo had been virtually the only legal means by which to demonstrate resistance to the centre in Moscow. 'Dinamo Tbilisi was the best and the biggest weapon in our hands against the Soviet Union,' states Kvaratskhelia. 'We had no possibility to beat the Russians who had been in Georgia for 200 years. Only in football did we have the chance. And we beat them all – Dinamo Moscow, Spartak Moscow, Torpedo Moscow, Zenit Leningrad. We beat them again and again.'

The importance of Dinamo to the people of Georgia, or more accurately to Communist Party officials, had been demonstrated most glaringly in 1987. The team spent the season flirting with relegation, and by the summer there was a real possibility that the club might drop out of the Soviet Top League altogether. Worse still, their closest rivals for survival were FC Guria, the provincial upstarts from the Black Sea village of Lanchkuti, propped up by the millions of Eduard Shevardnadze's brother Evgrapi.

Football under Communism meant that there were no privately owned clubs. Instead, teams were administered by various branches of the state – this explains why familiar names can still be recognised across the countries that were once affiliated with the Soviet Union. Dinamo (or Dynamo) was the sports club of the internal security services, whilst CSKA (which stands for 'central sports club of the army' in Russian) was run by the army and Spartak (after the Roman gladiator Spartacus) was the people's club. The industries were represented too, usually by Lokomotiv (for the rail industry), Torpedo (for the automotive industry), Shakhtar (for the mining industry) and even the Pakhtakor cotton farms of the Uzbek capital Tashkent. In this way the military–industrial complex of the USSR was mirrored through the make-up and identities of the country's football clubs.

Legally, pumping money into a football club was banned. But as in every other walk of life in Georgia, the not so invisible hand of the black market found a way. Guria shot from the fourth tier to the Top League in a matter of seasons. The team from Lanchkuti, a village of 9,000 inhabitants with a single main thoroughfare and no hotel, took their place alongside the Soviet football elite, backed by the mightiest powerbrokers in the Communist world.

Sergey Gerasimets, a Belarusian player who had been working in his native republic, claimed to have been offered a salary of between 2,600 and 3,400 roubles per month if he accepted the manager's job at Guria – he had earned just 250 roubles in his role playing at Dinamo Minsk, which was the leading club in the Byelorussian Soviet Socialist Republic. Even Georgia's top club Dinamo Tbilisi paid their players a fraction of the money at Guria. 'We got about 300 roubles per month,' Vladimir Gutsaev tells me. 'That was not at all enough for the hard work we were putting in.'

Not that he was alone in his consternation. Legend has it that Dynamo Kyiv's Oleg Blokhin hit the roof when he learned that his Soviet teammate Merab Jordania was earning three times his salary playing in this poxy, provincial backwater.

Another Guria player, the Ukrainian striker Viktor Khlus, claimed that the players would receive win bonuses of up to 800 roubles per victory, compared with just fifty roubles that was paid by Dynamo Kyiv. 'When my wife went out to the market, she would return with full baskets having not paid a penny,' said Khlus in a 2017 interview with *UA-Football*. 'The Georgians found opportunities to make additional payments. We felt like kings there.'

Not everybody felt so warmly towards Guria, particularly the players of Dinamo Tbilisi, who were waking up to the reality that they were no longer the only show in town. 'Everything they were paying to the players was unofficial,' exclaims Gutsaev derisively. 'It was under the table, illegal, and everyone knew it. But because we at Dinamo were controlled by the internal affairs ministry, we couldn't afford what they could. We did things by the book, we were official.'

Matchdays in 1987 brought Lanchkuti to a standstill. Shevardnadze's new stadium, which could hold more than double the population of the town and was the first in the USSR to be built without a running track, was improbably filled to capacity, and the single main road was so jammed with cars that visiting teams had to arrive hours before kick-off in order to access the stadium. Away fans spoke of paradise in the streets and hell in the stadium. When CSKA Moscow came to Lanchkuti, the brave handful of visitors that made the long trek south from the capital were lavished with food and Georgian wine by locals in the build-up, then pelted with stones and glass bottles during the game. There was no away fans enclosure inside the stadium, which rendered it a Colosseum for those supporters hardy enough to enter through its gates in visiting colours.

'It's insane,' remarks Kvaratskhelia. 'Can you imagine how much money they spent? Even now, Evgrapi is a hero in Lanchkuti. He was a mafia figure, yes, but you must remember that in Georgia in the 1980s it wasn't possible to live within your salary. One hundred and twenty roubles a month, that's maybe $100. So it became about how well you worked the black market. Everybody relied on it. Everybody traded privately, everybody wrote the wrong figures in their books.'

The shadow economy's role in football didn't begin with Evgrapi Shevardnadze and Guria. As far back as the 1960s, Dinamo Tbilisi had relied on the city's more successful racketeers to bring USSR international Slava Metreveli back to Georgia from Torpedo Moscow. 'They could never have afforded it otherwise,' explains Kvaratskhelia. 'The mafia were basically paying his salary.' This weakens Gutsaev's insistence that Dinamo were in some way above the shenanigans that permeated Georgian society, and the fact is the club were never unwilling to play dirty when circumstances required.

Dinamo and Guria occupied the bottom two places in the division with a few games to go in the 1987 Top League season. In October, they met at the giant Boris Paichadze National Stadium, now called Boris Paichadze Dinamo Arena, in Tbilisi. According to testimony from Guria players, the team from Lanchkuti were suspected of coming under heavy Communist Party pressure to produce the result that the party bosses wanted.

Most of the ageing Ukrainian players brought in by the manager and ex-Dynamo Kyiv star Mykhaylo Fomenko were left out of the team in favour of their Georgian teammates. According to Khlus, 'Georgians agreed with Georgians', as the apparatchiks of the Central Committee trusted in their countrymen to uphold their end of the deal. In any event Dinamo won 2–0 and Guria's goose was cooked.

The following week, FC Metalist arrived in Lanchkhuti from the Ukrainian city of Kharkiv. 'We were instructed to lie down,' explains Khlus. 'Lanchkhuti is a small town, and rumours spread to the people quickly about what was happening. You could tell when the game started that everyone in the crowd knew.'

Metalist won 1–0 and Guria were condemned to relegation, which sparked a riot the like of which tiny Lanchkhuti had never seen. At the final whistle, the players of both teams were attacked by the supporters, and they cowered in the tunnel that connected the pitch with the dressing rooms for four hours under heavy police protection whilst irate fans sacked the dressing rooms and destroyed parts of the ground.

'The next day a delegation from Moscow arrived in Guria,' describes Khlus. 'It was arranged for the stadium to be restored and the broken glass to be replaced. The official line was that nothing at all had happened.' Two weeks later, Metalist threw their game against Dinamo at the Paichadze Stadium, losing 3–1 to allow the team to pull clear of Guria and towards eventual safety. Guria finished last and were relegated.

'There was match-fixing all over the Soviet championship,' claims Kvaratskhelia, and it's likely that Guria was also involved. The Lithuanian striker Arminas Narbekovas years later claimed that Guria officials had offered his team Žalgiris Vilnius 25,000 roubles to throw a league match in Lanchkuti that season. 'You had five teams from Moscow, five teams from Ukraine, and they were all run by the Communist Party, all run by the same people. All it takes is one order – "Dynamo Kyiv need two points today, make sure it happens."'

I wonder whether thirty years later, Gutsaev might be more reflective on what happened the year Georgia's football dons were nearly relegated by Evgrapi Shevardnadze's vanity project. 'The Communist Party helped us, of course,' begins Gutsaev, stopping short of an outright admission. 'They helped the development of football. Georgia was the main talent source for Soviet football. We were beating Liverpool, Inter Milan, Napoli. We won the Cup Winners' Cup in 1981. That was with all local Georgian players. We were supported by the party in our activities – infrastructure, pre-season tours, travel.' No mention of brown paper envelopes or clandestine meetings with match officials. The son of another Dinamo star, the late Vitaly Daraselia, is more of a realist: 'Of course the party helped Dinamo, because they were the best team in the country,' Vitaly Junior tells me. 'There was a lot of help. A lot.'

Guria v. Dinamo pitted the power of the shadow economy against the might of the Communist Party, the twin pillars that had propped up Georgia for decades. In the end, the party prevailed. Dinamo could not be allowed to fail. If they did, then little Georgia might be crushed under the steel boot of the Soviet dictatorship. The republic was Dinamo, Dinamo was the republic, and their status was to be protected whatever the cost. As Kvaratskhelia put it, 'Dinamo was the light in the darkness for Georgian independence.'

During the 1970s, Georgian nationalism appeared as a political force for the first time, led by the dissident Zviad Gamsakhurdia. On 9 April 1989, twenty-one mostly young Georgian women were killed after Soviet soldiers attempted to put down a huge pro-independence rally on Rustaveli Avenue using shovels and tear gas. Kremlin officials were disgusted by the heavy-handed response, which paralysed Moscow's capacity to resist what was now a popular wave powerful enough to bring tens of thousands of protesters onto the streets.

Following years of popular risings and failed military put-downs, by 1991 Soviet authority had simply withered away, leaving behind an independent Georgia riven by violent factionalism. In December 1991, the first President of independent Georgia, Gamsakhurdia, was thrown out of office in a violent coup d'état that saw Rustaveli Avenue smashed to bits, and Georgia was plunged into civil war. These were the circumstances in which Kvaratskhelia and the new Georgian Football Federation sought to build their new championship.

Dinamo Tbilisi won the first league title of independent Georgia by six points from their old rivals Guria, even though the stars of the golden 1980s, Kipiani, Gutsaev and the rest, had now retired to desk jobs in the football federation. The team went on to win the next nine league championships. The lack of competition was a concern, but the real story was that the football league survived at all. 'Even during the civil war, everything was put on hold for football,' explains Kvaratskhelia. 'There were borders going up all over the country – roadblocks, checkpoints – between Mingrelia and Ajaria and Gali and all the different regions. But when a football team bus arrived at a checkpoint, whether it said Torpedo Kutaisi or Samtredia or Dinamo Batumi, they were allowed past. All roads opened immediately. The football league functioned better than the state itself.

'My position as a football reporter travelling around the country during the civil war was very sensitive. I am Mingrelian by heritage, where Gamsakhurdia is from. During the civil war, the Zviadists were very strong in that region, and so when I had been there to report from Zugdidi and Ochamchire and so on, I was accused in Tbilisi of being a Zviadist.'

Through the disorder, Georgia's football clubs doubled down on breaking ties with their Russian past. At the start of 1990, Dinamo Tbilisi ditched the name they had taken from the Soviet Interior Ministry and became FC Iberia, after the ancient Georgian kingdom that, at its second-century peak, covered most of the territory of the South Caucasus. Meanwhile Lokomotiv, Torpedo and Spartak were all abandoned in favour of less political names. The players also got in on the re-writing of history: Dinamo's Omari Osipov became Omari Tetradze (he went on to play for Russia at the 1994 World Cup and Euro 1996, prior to which he tried unsuccessfully to Russify his name once again), whilst the former USSR international Alan Kulumbegov took the name Kantidze.

FC Iberia quickly passed out of public ownership and fell into the hands of Jaba Ioseliani's paramilitaries, who allegedly turned the business into an effective front for smuggling and tax evasion operations that funded the club's league success. When, around the turn of the millennium, President Shevardnadze began to weed out the more flagrantly criminal influences in Georgian society, Dinamo came under forensic investigation from its former patron the Interior Ministry. The club became the subject of investment from a chain of what might loosely be termed 'entrepreneurs' with connections to the oligarchic clans of Russia's infamous 'Davos Pact' – the team that bankrolled Boris Yeltsin's 1996 re-election in the Kremlin – and for all of Shevardnadze's work to sanitise the country, the shadow economy continued to be the lifeblood of football and society at large.

In Tbilisi, they talk about seventy years of occupation, such is the unjustness with which they view the period between 1921 and 1991 when their nation was swallowed by Bolshevism and the Communist Party. The Red Army rolled into Tbilisi in February 1921 and crushed a nascent independent Georgian republic with ease, bringing to an end a brief experiment with social democracy.

All three Transcaucasian republics between the Black and Caspian Seas – Armenia and Azerbaijan included – had briefly been independent following the collapse of the Russian Empire in 1917. However, none resisted Soviet expansion as Lenin's tanks moved south in order to both grow and protect the October Revolution.

Tucked in amongst this drama and inextricably bound with the region's fortunes, the tiny seaside nation of Abkhazia found itself swallowed; not Georgian nor Russian, just separate, but now unwillingly shackled to both by waves of political change outside of its remit to control.

Today, Georgians see Russia's presence in Abkhazia as being a result of the 1921 invasion. On a wall at the Georgian National Museum in Tbilisi, a map of the country shows Abkhazia and South Ossetia coloured blood red, beneath it the words: 'Occupation Continues'. The spectre of Mother Russia – with its troops permanently stationed on Abkhazia's seaside coast and its roubles rolling into the capital, Sukhumi, still looms large over beleaguered Georgia.

* * *

An open, watery chasm separating irreconcilable foes. The Enguri is a gentle ogre of a river.

There's a sharp bend just past the Georgian checkpoint, which in my anxious state takes what feels like an age to pass. When the road straightens out, there is an unbroken stretch of road that leads straight into mountainous Abkhazia.

A giant revolver, four metres high and forged in iron, aims its sights down the mile-long road towards the border. The barrel has been tied off and points to the sky; a memorial to the ceasefire that made the guns fall silent. It's a reminder that, for Georgia at least, peace manifestly does not equal reconciliation.

From this vantage point, in the distance it's just possible to make out the Abkhaz flag hoisted high on the hill, a wash of green, white and red with its infamous open palm firmly raised in one corner. Georgians call it the hidden hand of Moscow.

To some, the flag's open hand is a sign of welcome. To others, it is a warning: back off. Abkhazians have good reason to exercise caution. It was via the bridge over the Enguri that Georgian tanks came rolling into their country in August 1992, shattering the sunny tranquillity that had made this stretch of Black Sea coast the envy of the Soviet world.

Two features characterised the war. The first was the extreme appetite for human cruelty exhibited on both sides. The second was the irrefutable impact of Russian influence on the outcome – the hidden hand of Moscow at work.

Beslan Gubliya spent most of 1993 making hand grenades and donating blood, though he would rather have still been doing his day job, marshalling the midfield for Dinamo Sukhumi in the football league of Abkhazia. Instead, his days were spent flitting between munitions workshops and the local morgue in the Abkhazian town of Gudauta, transporting bodies and helping identify the dead.

'That was the role Gudauta played in the war,' recalls Gubliya, a beast of a man whose physique, now that he's in his forties, is more rugby player than footballer. He has small thick ears, a prominent mouth and nose and efficient buzz-cut hair. He looks like he could consume a pint of ale in a single breath, but he betrays a manly gentility. Our first interview is postponed as he's taking care of his new-born baby son.

'Our town was the only part of Abkhazia that was never occupied by Georgian soldiers, so we became a stronghold for the resistance. I played with Dinamo Sukhumi up until the Georgians invaded. Before that, I played for Ritsa Gudauta, but I moved to Dinamo when I was sixteen.'

Dinamo Sukhumi were the little brother of their namesakes in Tbilisi. Never rising higher than the Soviet First League, they'd spent most of their seventy years' existence coasting by, always preceded by a reputation that placed a good time before a hard game. 'There's always a wedding or a funeral to attend for Abkhazian players,' says Inal Khashig, a respected Sukhumi journalist who witnessed the relative rise and fall of the club. 'Footballers in Abkhazia have always been more technical than they are athletic. They like to relax and drink more than to work. It's a chronic disease for the people of the south.'

Sukhumi gets short shrift in the long history of Soviet football, though the town's reputation for its laid-back atmosphere – one visiting Western journalist summed the place up as 'Communism on the beach; a kind of Eastern European Cuba' – is not necessarily earned. Nikita Simonyan, arguably the USSR's greatest-ever player, was raised and learned to play football here, which in itself warrants Sukhumi a star on the Soviet football walk of fame.

Simonyan's first coach and mentor, the great Georgian midfielder Shota Lominadze, was himself a football aesthete. In the 1940s, he encouraged Simonyan and the boys he found idling with a ball at their feet on Sukhumi's streets to become expressive practitioners of stylish, artistic football. There were no exhausting training exercises or ultra-disciplined routines for which the USSR's football schools became notorious. Instead, Lominadze preached samba football with a Soviet twist, just as he himself had been weaned by his Dinamo elders on a doctrine of total soccer. Khashig claims that Lavrentiy Beria, Stalin's right-hand man, tried to block Simonyan from leaving Dinamo for Krylya Sovetov Moscow in 1947, and it is widely known that the Communist Party of Georgia arrested his father as part of an attempt to pressure him into signing for Dinamo Tbilisi.

'The best Abkhazian players had traditionally gone to play for Georgian teams,' explains Khashig. 'That's why we never had a team in the Top League. The general trajectory was from Sukhumi to Tbilisi, then from Tbilisi to Moscow. But it meant we never had a strong Dinamo Sukhumi team until the 1990s.'

The first people to play football in the city were students. In 1908, members of the Sukhumi high school, who hailed from Greece, Armenia, Russia and Georgia as well as Abkhaz natives, began playing friendly matches against teams from Batumi in Ajaria and Poti in Mingrelia on the Georgian coast, and later after the First World War in Gali and Ochamchire. The first formal team that appeared in Sukhumi called themselves *Veni Vidi Vici* – 'I came, I saw, I conquered' – a sad portent of what was to come nearly a century later.

After the arrival of the Bolsheviks in Abkhazia in 1921, football became more organised. A team comprising English sailors played a Sukhumi select side in 1923, the first 'international' fixture to take place on these shores. Legend has it that the English team walked off in disgust after going 4–0 down to the locals. After that, Sukhumi's reputation as a football centre of the Caucasus only grew. In July 1936, a Dinamo Sukhumi junior team beat their Dinamo Tbilisi counterparts 5–0 in the Georgian capital to win the right to represent Georgia at the all-Soviet youth championships that same summer.

After watching their performance at the Moscow finals, the Russian sports daily *Krasny Sport* hailed the Sukhumi youngsters as the most technical players at the tournament, with a reputation for guile, craft and sumptuous ball skills.

The win against Tbilisi and success in Moscow represented the high point for football and for life in general in Soviet Abkhazia. Until then, the republic had largely dodged the worst excesses of Stalinism, owing to the favoured status of the head of the local Soviet, Nestor Lakoba. As a personal friend of the dictator, Lakoba negotiated autonomous republic status for Abkhazia and kept the region outside of Stalin's deadly collectivisation programme that spread starvation across the USSR. In the end, it was not Stalin but the jealous Beria who took it into his own hands to erase Lakoba. On a visit to Tbilisi in December 1936 Beria poisoned Lakoba, and thereafter Abkhazia was hit with a brutal scheme of repressive Georgianisation. As a result, the region's political and cultural significance within the USSR dwindled, and eventually it received a reputation as being the 'Soviet Florida'.

Former Dinamo Sukhumi midfielder Gubliya remembers the day war began. It was 14 August 1992 – 'before lunchtime'. The Georgian offensive was intended to knock out the Abkhazian volunteers who had taken over government buildings, but it did not work out that way.

Gubliya was booked that day for a fitness test at the Abkhazia State University. He'd borrowed a pair of trainers from a teammate, promising to return them later in the day. The hotel the team were staying in was near Queen Tamar's Bridge, an ancient relic built during the reign of the twelfth-century Georgian empress, which made it 'a target for the Georgians when the war started', according to Gubliya.

'When we got back from the university, it was like hell had opened up. Tanks, helicopters, bullets. People were screaming and crying. I never made it to the hotel. It had basically already been destroyed.' He would never return his teammate's trainers.

'When we made it back to Gudauta, we were treated as messengers. Everyone was asking, "Is it true what we hear about what's happened in Sukhumi?"'

In the end, the war provided Gubliya with a way to continue his football career. The fighting lasted thirteen months. When it was done, he left Abkhazia.

There was a football coach from Russia who fought with a volunteer unit of the Confederation of Mountain Peoples of the Caucasus, who travelled south from the mountains to fight on the side of the rebels. Gubliya never knew his real name, only that on the battlefield they called him *'Gumilla'*, which means 'the one who operates the machine gun'. A friend of Gumilla mentioned that there was a talented midfielder working in the war effort in Gudauta. When the conflict was over, he went with Gumilla to the city of Cherkessk in Russia's north Caucasus to resume his football career and begin a new life.

'I left Dinamo and Abkhazia after the war because it was clear the country wasn't going anywhere,' describes Gubliya. 'All professional players had to leave in order to save their careers.' The USSR football system was dissolved in 1991. As Dinamo Sukhumi were unable to join either the new Russian league that succeeded it or the breakaway Georgian league, they were left marooned in the no man's land of the amateur Abkhaz division.

Two brothers, Ruslan and Beslan Ajinjal, became the faces of Abkhazia's collapsed football ecosystem. Like Gubliya, they also left Dinamo Sukhumi, and headed for the southern Russian town of Maykop where they reached a Russian Cup semi-final with FC Druzhba. Beslan, who scored the day the club played its final game as a professional team, a typically swaggering 6–0 win against Stavropol

Krai from across the Caucasian mountains, conveys something of the brothers' pain in leaving home and family behind amidst the deteriorating security situation. 'They told us straight away that we could no longer be a part of the USSR structure,' he tells me. 'It was pretty clear that Dinamo were only going to be able to play in the Abkhazian league. We were both ambitious, and still young. We needed to leave for our careers.'

The collapse of the USSR footballing ecosystem at the end of the 1991 season meant that everything changed for all of the teams throughout the region. However, it completeley snookered the already struggling Dinamo Sukhumi. Two years earlier, as clubs throughout Georgia had resigned from the Soviet league to form their own championship, the team had been torn in half by the exodus of its Georgian core, who left to form a new club, Tskhumi Sukhumi. A rump Dinamo team remained briefly in the Soviet First League, the holes in its squad papered over by emergency recruits from clubs in Moscow who made fringe players available for emergency transfer, but the chasm it left in Abkhazian football was already irreversible.

'We had our best moment in football at the same time that we started to have ethnic problems,' explains Inal Khashig diagnostically. 'Dinamo Sukhumi was half Georgian, half Abkhaz. So as you see, that was going to be a problem.'

'The Abkhazian players were desperate to stay with the Soviet Union,' says Kvaratskhelia. 'When the Georgian players of Dinamo Sukhumi left, everybody cried and kissed each other. Everybody. Then they separated. The Abkhazians and the Russians were desperate for them not to go.'

But go they did. The new Georgian club, Tskhumi Sukhumi, was founded at the behest of one of the most tragic figures in the conflict, a former Dinamo player and Soviet football referee named

Guram Gabiskaria. He was backed by the club's most senior Georgian player, the defender Giorgi Chikhradze – who years later could be spotted ducking out of the path of an Alan Shearer free-kick as Georgia lost 2–0 to England in front of 70,000 fans at Wembley in 1997 – a player who played for years on both sides of the divide for three Dinamo teams – Tbilisi, Sukhumi and Gagra – and who was reportedly deeply troubled by the need to separate. He went on to enjoy a fine international career in independent Georgia. His mentor Gabiskaria was not so fortunate.

'Gabiskaria was a brave patriot,' remarks Kvaratskhelia. He was also a scheming pragmatist. The team were scheduled to play away against Mertskhali Ozurgeti in 1993, during the chaos of the civil war. As kick-off approached, the Mertskhali players were out on the pitch waiting, but there was no sign of the Tskhumi team, who were still living in the same hotel as their former Abkhazian teammates at Queen Tamar's Bridge – 'We lived on the twelfth floor, them on the thirteenth,' says Gubliya – and who it was presumed had been held up by the dozens of roadblocks and checkpoints that dotted the war-torn countryside. Just as the referee was about to call the game off, the sound of spinning blades could be heard overhead, and a helicopter descended and came to rest in the centre circle. Out ran the Tskhumi players, in full kit ready to start the game. Gabiskiria, slightly abusing his new position as mayor of Sukhumi, had commandeered the aircraft from the local administration. The game went ahead as planned.

'I knew Gabiskiria well,' recalls Kvaratskhelia. 'I was with him in Sukhumi in August 1993 working on plans to build a new stadium. Can you imagine? During a war and the mayor is planning on building a football stadium! I took the last picture of him alive. I travelled back to Tbilisi to write my article, and within two or three days I heard the news.'

On 27 September 1993, a successful offensive by Abkhazian rebels ran the ill-disciplined and ravaged Georgian National Guard and the remaining civilian administration out of Sukhumi. In the capital, Gabiskaria was dragged from his office in the government building by Abkhaz militia out into the town square. Alongside fellow members of the committee, he was ordered to kneel. '*Nekagda v zhizniy!*' he cried out in defiance – 'Never in my life!' These were his final words before he was executed by a single bullet to the head. Footage survives of jubilant Abkhaz militia celebrating in the square as the bodies of Gabiskiria and his colleagues lie motionless yards away, the thirteen-storey headquarters of the Supreme Soviet can be seen burning behind them. Tskhumi Sukhumi, a side that had run Dinamo Tbilisi to within two points of the title the previous year, were dissolved weeks later, taking Abkhazian sides FC Amirani Ochamchire and DC Mziuri Gali with them.

Why were the Abkhazians so eager to leave Georgia? How did the conflict become so infected with bloodlust and hate? And what was the relationship between Abkhaz nationalism and the collapsing Soviet state?

War in Abkhazia was not inevitable. The two populations had lived in relative harmony in and around Sukhumi since the 1860s. Georgia's first President, the hard-line and unpredictable nationalist Zviad Gamsakhurdia, had even proposed a power-sharing compromise between Tbilisi and Sukhumi in 1989, which would have allowed a good degree of autonomy for the country's Abkhazian minority after Georgia separated from Moscow.

From 1864 through to the end of the nineteenth century, imperial Russia fought to put down a series of rebellions in the South Caucasus, waged first by the Abkhazians' local and ethnic cousins, the Muslim Circassians, and latterly by the Abkhaz themselves. In reprisal, the tsarist regime in Saint Petersburg punitively deported huge numbers of tribal Islamic Caucasians to Ottoman Turkey, leaving the remaining Orthodox Abkhaz a minority people in their own nation and huge swathes of fertile land unoccupied. Colonisation from western and central Georgia was encouraged to occupy the empty land, until Georgian-speaking Mingrelian and Kartvelian tribes greatly outnumbered the Abkhaz all along the Black Sea coast. Though in the twentieth century it only intermittently caused violence at the local level, in the political sphere the Abkhazian psyche became generally distrustful of the Georgian leadership in Tbilisi.

The Abkhaz Autonomous Soviet Socialist Republic, a constituent part of the Georgia Soviet Socialist Republic, lobbied Moscow repeatedly to be allowed to separate from Tbilisi or become part of Russia. As Georgian nationalism seeped into the political centre through the 1970s and 1980s, the Abkhaz grew frantic that their own national heritage and ethnic rights would be compromised as more political autonomy was achieved in Tbilisi. In 1978, the Sukhumi government made a successful appeal for increased political and cultural autonomy, but it only postponed the inevitable. Desperate to be uncoupled before Georgia's inevitable secession, Abkhaz nationalists met at Lykhny, the former capital of the medieval kingdom of Abkhazia, to demand the Kremlin either absorb the republic or free it from Tbilisi's control. It was this demonstration that led directly to the 9 April tragedy in Tbilisi weeks later, as counter-demonstrations and competing nationalist ambitions pushed both communities deeper into mutual bloodshed.

Today, little remains of the kinship that once existed between the two communities. The most famous link between Georgia and Abkhazia was the Abkhaz-born USSR international Vitaly Daraselia, from Ochamchire near the Enguri border, who scored Georgian football's most famous goal when he slotted home the winner for Dinamo Tbilisi in the 1981 UEFA Cup Winners' Cup final against Carl Zeiss Jena of East Germany. Daraselia was killed in a road accident just a year after winning the cup for Dinamo, but the legacy he left across Georgian and Abkhaz football is profound. 'For a man to have lived only twenty-five years and left a legacy across the whole country, that tells you he must have been pretty special,' proudly states Daraselia's youngest son, Vitaly Jr. 'Not just as a footballer but as a man.'

The Enguri frontier has remained a battleground ever since the 1994 ceasefire. In 2009, Daraselia's childhood home was looted and burned down by Abkhaz vandals, a reminder that the spirit of the struggle still lives, but also that the striker is often erroneously remembered as being Georgian. The house, in the town of Ochamchire not far from Gali, had been renovated and turned into a public museum by Daraselia's mother, a tribute to her son who was killed at the height of his powers. 'The attack was made by someone from outside of the area,' says Vitaly Jr. 'It wasn't a local of Ochamchire. My father's legacy in the town and in Abkhazia as a whole is still cherished here. People still appreciate Vitaly Daraselia in Abkhazia.' He died aged twenty-five, just months after winning the cup for Dinamo. His goal in the Dusseldorf final, scored when he danced onto a deft pass from teammate David Kipiani and planted the ball into the bottom corner, is his legacy, but he is also the most visible point of connection between the Abkhaz and Georgian banks of the river Enguri, a celebration of a time when footballers from the Black Sea ruled the Soviet Union with their skill and flair and no one asked if their heritage was Mingrelian or Circassian.

'Abkhazians and Georgians are like brothers,' says Vitaly Jr. 'We always had a good relationship before the war. Nowadays, legacies like my father's are one of the few areas of common ground where people can remember the good times. It helps relieve the tension.'

Georgian commander Tengiz Kitovani's raid on Abkhazia proved that there is no honour amongst thieves. The behaviour of the Georgian National Guard in Sukhumi was not that of an army but of a posse of drunken vandals. They allegedly looted the city, burned the Abkhaz national archives and introduced the permanent, lurking threat of torture and sexual violence. The 1992 attack on Sukhumi, launched without the consent of the Georgian President Eduard Shevardnadze, introduced a new factor to what had hitherto been a low-level nationalist movement between competing ethnic groups – the 'entrepreneurs of violence'. Both Georgian soldiers and fighters from the Confederation of Mountain Peoples of the Caucasus – freelance volunteers from the north of the Caucasian chain loyal to the abstract idea of a federal union between the mountain tribes – exploited the pretext of war to rob and pillage from private homes and government buildings, a depressing pattern that was repeated across the post-Soviet wars. During the thirteen months that the Georgian National Guard held Sukhumi, the tense relationship between the two groups disintegrated into hatred.

Abkhazia had been a popular destination for training camps for teams all over Georgia. Although Georgians outnumbered the Abkhaz by more than two to one, families and friends lived on either side of the Enguri and travelled back and forth frequently, and football was one amongst many common languages. 'I was in Sukhumi when Dinamo Tbilisi became the first Georgian team to play in the European Cup,' remembers Kvaratskhelia fondly. It was 18 August 1993, and the opposition were the Irish team Linfield. 'Our hotel was situated on high ground, and I saw the positions of the Abkhazians. They were all watching the Dinamo game on TV! It was the middle of the night because of the time difference, but still everyone in Abkhazia watched that Dinamo Tbilisi game. Even in Abkhazia, even at war, they were adored.' Less than a month later, using heavy weaponry acquired from Russia, Abkhazian volunteers launched an intensive campaign to retake Sukhumi from the Georgian National Guard. The city was smashed to pieces, and the Supreme Soviet building was burned. Those that remained of the Tbilisi government were dragged out and shot, whilst Georgian civilians were either chased over the Enguri or murdered in their homes by marauding North Caucasus bandits. Abkhazia's war was over.

'There was still a bond between Georgia and Abkhazia until those final days,' recalls Kvaratskhelia. 'Dinamo against Linfield in the European Cup was our last moment of connection. After that, it was finished. We were separated, probably for ever.' Dinamo were thrown out of the tournament days later for attempting to bribe the match referee, a further reminder that the South Caucasus wasn't ready to be absorbed into the civilised world.

* * *

The Abkhazian military checkpoint at Enguri is staffed by two kinds of soldier; those who offer smiles and welcomes, and those who relish in the power bestowed by the uniform. The atmosphere at the checkpoint is made more intense by the stifling heat; it is moist and heavy air and sticks to the lungs like grease, which makes drawing breath an uncomfortable process. Stepping off the bridge over the Enguri, I am now past the natural border between Georgia and Abkhazia. Now comes the hard part.

For my fellow travellers, the crossing is relatively painless. The majority carry Russian passports and the soldiers therefore take little notice of them, other than to make a brief glance at their documents before sending them on their way.

There are Organisation for Security and Cooperation in Europe peacekeeping vehicles travelling back and forth over the bridge, but they too receive little attention at the blockade, just a cursory glance beneath the bonnets of their trucks and a look in the back seat. One gets a poke around beneath its undercarriage with a long stick, presumably in an attempt to check for contraband, but then the barrier is lifted and the brief security check is done. Today, there is only one traveller that this little regiment seems to be taking a sincere security interest in.

The first soldier is friendly and speaks conversational English. He asks about my plans in Abkhazia. I tell him I will spend five days zin Sukhumi before returning this way. He seems offended by the briefness of my stay. 'Why would you stay in only Sukhumi?' he complains, as he unzips my bag and begins to rifle through my belongings. 'You can take a taxi for just 200 roubles to Gagra. It is beautiful there.'

Gagra. Shit. My body tenses, and I feel a weakness in the knees. I have been sweating since Zugdidi on account of the baking Transcaucasian sun roasting me alive inside my thick black leather jacket, but now I'm dripping with it, as my new tour guide rummages his long, tanned fingers through my bag. Had he not mentioned it – Gagra – it probably wouldn't have even occurred to me. Certainly it hadn't when I'd packed up my things this morning at the dodgy backpackers' hostel in Tbilisi I'd called home for the previous three days.

'Be careful what you try and take over the border.' I'd been given variations on that advice more times than I could count since arriving here from London.

Now I fear my adventure in Abkhazia may be over before it has begun.

III

Stalin loved Gagra and it isn't hard to see why. Palm trees surrounded by unbroken blue skies give the place a tropical air, which is made all the more dramatic by the luscious green mountains that cover the surrounding landscape almost the entire way to the sandy coast. Towards the end of his life the Soviet leader increasingly spent his summers recuperating here at his purpose-built Cold River dacha at Lake Ritsa, complete with toilets shipped from Germany as trophies from the Second World War and billiard tables specially adjusted to account for his short stature. The dreamy climate of this place was, apparently, a grateful tonic to the dictator's troublesome arthritis and other ailments.

I first became aware about the significance of Gagra whilst sat in an uncomfortable press box seat at the David Petriashvili Stadium on the extreme outskirts of Tbilisi, just before I set out for Abkhazia.

It's late February 2018 and the first day of a new football season in Georgia. The Super Cup is a fixture that serves as the curtain raiser for almost every football season in Europe. Today, with the ugly relics of old industrial-era Soviet Tbilisi looming intrusively over the stadium's shallow main stand, it's last season's league champions Torpedo Kutaisi against cup winners Chikhura Sachkhere.

There is a heavy armed police presence, owing to a rivalry between the cities of Kutaisi and Tbilisi that has festered since the early 1990s. Kutaisi claims to have birthed Georgia's punk rock and indie scene and exported it to the rest of the country, whilst the enlightened aesthetes in the capital deride the music culture created in Kutaisi as variously inconsequential and a national disgrace. The two cities' football supporters, eager to stake a claim to the bad blood, have made a frequent habit of kicking seven shades out of each other inside and outside stadiums ever since.

Today, the air carries all the violent energy of an afternoon at the beach. Although it's well past noon the sun is still high above us, turning the bare stone of the terrace into a baking-hot walkway that reflects the heat like steel.

Far in the distance, there is a church on high ground, whilst a little nearer, bent and broken steel machines quietly go rusty in the sun, and the twin arches of Georgia's Orthodox and Communist pasts line up in a singular neat frame.

I'm here to meet with Goderdzi Chikhradze, the founder of second division club FC Gagra. He arrives late, just as Kutaisi score the second of two late goals on a lightning-quick counter-attack to beat Chikhura to rapturous appreciation from the small crowd.

Chikhradze was born in 1960 in the town of Racha in western Georgia's Rioni Valley. As a footballer, he was talented enough to impress the great Dinamo Tbilisi star Mikheil Meskhi, who arranged for his new protégé to move to the capital at the age of fourteen, where he was billeted with another of the Dinamo glitterati, the gliding winger Slava Metreveli. Meskhi and Metreveli – Soviet internationals and USSR championship title winners in 1964 – became fathers to Chikhradze, mentoring him both as an athlete and as a young man.

He spent the summers of his youth staying with family in Gagra, which he remembers as 'a tranquil seaside paradise', and through the prism of nostalgia for the Soviet 1960s and 1970s, he recalls that ethnic differences between Georgians and Abkhazians went unobserved and neighbours lived as neighbours. All that changed when the National Guard landed on the shores beneath Stalin's Cold River in August 1992.

Gagra was strategically important because whoever held it controlled the only road north from Abkhazia over the Psou River into Russia. As Kitovani's first advance captured Sukhumi, an amphibious force landed in Gagra to cut off the Abkhaz from Russian and North Caucasian support, penning them in around the town of Gudauta. The Georgians held the town for ten days amidst intermittent fighting, until on 2 October the Chechen warlord Shamil Basayev took advantage of confusion over a ceasefire and simply walked his men into the town to take it back for the Abkhaz. Locals who believed this would mark the restoration of order in Gagra were quickly proved tragically mistaken.

The details are disputed, but it is alleged on the Georgian side that

Basayev turned the local Dinamo Gagra Stadium into an execution yard. 'They beheaded Georgians in the stadium and played football with the heads,' claims Chikhradze. 'That used to be the legacy of football in Gagra.'

Reports about the Gagra stadium massacre vary and are rejected altogether by most Abkhazians. As with all wartime atrocities, our knowledge of them is sourced from survivor testimonies. The most dependable account comes from a Russian army observer who reported that Basayev's battalion entered the city late on the afternoon of 2 October, before rounding up between 1,000 and 1,500 Georgian civilians inside the stadium. According to this report the captives were kept there for five days, as drunken Abkhaz militia tortured and taunted their captives. Some of the prisoners suffered execution by being hanged from power lines outside the ground. Most of the rest were shot and buried in mass graves. Though the myth remains, it has never been settled as to whether Basayev's butchers really played football with the desecrated remains of Georgian prisoners.

Chikhradze's face is lined and creased from a combination of subtropical sunshine and the passing of time, and his hair shines silver. He hasn't been back to Gagra in nearly three decades.

Instead, he keeps the memory of the town alive as founder of FC Gagra, a football club in exile that represents one of the many prongs of Georgia's efforts to reach out to its territories that were lost in the war.

'The internally displaced persons from the war all follow FC Gagra,' proudly states Chikhradze. 'The name plays a huge role. We have won support from the locals through our football too.'

The silver-haired coach has drawn up plans for a football academy for young players to be built on the picturesque shores of the Black Sea in Gagra. But they sit dormant in his archives, ignored for years. It's likely they will never see the light of day.

'Sometimes,' he ponders, 'when I go through my documents, I see those papers. And it is very difficult for me when I remember those times in Abkhazia, and what now will never be.'

Chikhradze isn't bluffing about the team's supporter base. In 2011, they caused a minor sensation in Georgia when they won the David Kipiani Cup, the country's national knock-out competition, beating Torpedo Kutaisi 1–0 after extra time in the final. Chikhradze estimates that three quarters of the 12,000 fans in attendance at the Boris Paichadze Stadium were supporting Gagra. 'We feel and receive support from people living in the different regions of Georgia because of what we represent.' Cup glory meant qualification for the UEFA Europa League and a chance to advertise Georgia's prerogative over Abkhazia to the world.

Fate paired them with the Cypriot team Anorthosis, themselves exiles from their country's conflict with Turkey, which has left their former home city Famagusta a ghost town trapped inside a UN buffer zone. As Gagra play in Tbilisi, Anorthosis play in Larnaca, and it was there that Chikhradze's team received boisterous support from Cyprus's large Abkhaz expat community, who are descendants of the Muslims expelled from the Black Sea when Russia crushed the Circassian rebellion of 1864. Chikhradze believes this is a clear signal of the Abkhaz–Georgian kinship that is the natural status quo.

'We feel ready now to go to Gagra to rejoin with our Abkhaz friends who wish to cooperate and create something new with us,' he preaches. 'Because this club has existed for fourteen years, and we've had some success. We are ready to find our friends in Abkhazia and create a much bigger club, much stronger.'

Later on, I raised the matter of FC Gagra in an interview with the chief of Abkhazia's Olympic Committee, Valery Arshba. Whilst I hadn't expected Arshba to give a formal endorsement, there is a tendency for spokespeople in Eastern Europe when speaking on the record to at least pay lip service to the idea that sport is transcendental of politics. There was none of that from Arshba, who spat his condemnation of Gagra at me like chewed gum.

'They do this a lot in Georgia,' he said peevishly. They appropriate Abkhazian names for factories, businesses and sports teams. They're trying to rebuild small pieces of Abkhazia in Georgia.

'I don't understand why they are doing this. Maybe just to support the internally displaced persons and to help their adjustment somehow. But we lost thousands of Abkhazians through this conflict. We want to leave behind what went before, not preserve it.

'You should ask that club how many Abkhazians play in their team. I think the answer will be zero. So they'll take our name, but it's not about us.'

Arshba isn't far wrong. A handful of Abkhaz have worn Gagra's white and sky-blue stripes since they were founded in 2004, but the demographic reality makes any ambition to create a team representative of the old Gagra unrealistic. At first, the squad was made up of former youth players from Lokomotiv Tbilisi, who found themselves without a team to play for when the Georgian railway withdrew its backing for the club. Chikhradze's cousin Besik, a semi-successful exporter who made a modest fortune flogging cheap Georgian wine and vodka in Ukraine, put up the money for the team to join the Georgian league in the second division. After a slow start that took them a month to score their first goal, they finished third in their debut season, missing out on promotion via the play-offs against another exile club, FC Tskhinvali from South Ossetia. They finally reached the Erovnuli Liga on their third attempt and have bounced between the two leagues ever since.

Some of the team members are refugees from Abkhazia. Irakli Khutchua, who is from Gali, took advantage of Besik's relationship with Dynamo Kyiv and won an eighteen-month contract with the Ukrainians, before eventually returning to play for Gagra. Defender

Tornike Okriashvili, though not from Abkhazia, began his career at the club and later became a mainstay of the Georgian national team.

Two Abkhaz players were invited from Gagra itself to join up with the team in 2015, but their attitude was poor, and they failed to take the opportunity to play professional football in Georgia seriously. But that wasn't the only obstacle. 'It's so hard for us to meet with them in Abkhazia,' says Chikhradze. 'Because if people there find out that they are trying to meet with us, they will have problems in their communities. So we have had meetings in Russia and Georgia and some other places for the sake of their safety. This is a very political gesture.'

It's one point on which Chikhradze and the testy apparatchik Arshba seem able to agree. 'World sport is all about politics today,' he grumbles. 'And that is very bad news for Abkhazia.'

Like Sukhumi, Gagra's football community was split in half by Georgia's secession from the USSR. The first club to form here were Dinamo Gagra, who played in the lower reaches of the Soviet league system, but in 1990 the Georgian-Abkhaz social division led to the creation of a new club called FC Sikharuli – which means 'happiness' in Georgian. Their president was Sergo Abashidze, a friend and colleague of Mamuka Kvaratskhelia and whose son later became the chief of the Tbilisi-backed Abkhazian administration in exile, based in the Upper Kodori Gorge.

At the beginning of August 1992, Kvaratskhelia and Abashidze were together at Gagra Stadium to meet with two Chechen players interested in signing for Sikharuli. Also on the agenda was a delivery of new adidas-manufactured kits for the club, a Western luxury almost unheard of in the South Caucasus. 'When war began, those new kits were hidden in the cellar of my colleague's house, under the ground in wine cases,' recalls Kvaratskhelia. 'They had to stay out of sight because they were of the Georgian team. The house was later destroyed by the Abkhazians, and as far as I know the Sikharuli shirts are still there in the wine barrels, thirty years later. I sometimes think about how a few weeks later, it was the same place where Abkhaz militia cut the heads off Georgian civilians.'

'Late in the Soviet period, a third party began to infiltrate both societies in Gagra,' describes Chikhradze. 'These societies started to separate from each other, became more closed-off within. Then, pretty much immediately, the war broke out. It seems to me that this third party played the crucial role in turning the Abkhazians and Georgians against each other.'

And that third party is Russia.

* * *

There is no wildlife here, at least nothing visible. Only the occasional overly friendly, grotesque little insect. Amongst all this untamed greenery, surely there should be some creature zipping through the sky overhead or something shaking the grass as it scurries away. Instead there's nothing, just stillness and heat, neither of which are softened by the dank breeze. I find myself wondering what these soldiers get up to during the long hours when there are no travellers to process.

I can see Russian pendants hanging from the cabins all around the camp, which is a reminder that without Russia, there could be no Abkhazia. All roads here lead to Moscow. Russian aid accounts for around half of the republic's annual budget, but because the two countries' economies are so closely tied, and since international sanctions have left Abkhazia isolated amongst would-be trading partners, the state is almost entirely dependent on Russian roubles.

Abkhazia emerged from the war in 1993 with its freedom, but at a confounding cost. By some estimates, the war effort exceeded $20 million. Approximately 4,000 Abkhazians were killed in the fighting. Large areas of Sukhumi were razed to the ground.

When the war ended, Abkhazia's problems began. The second half of the 1990s saw Tbilisi impose trade embargos on the separatists, which fatally undermined early attempts at state building. In 2004, following a period of détente, Georgia imposed a sea blockade on Sukhumi, which reinforced Abkhazia's economic dependence on Russia.

The soldier has been searching my bag now for more than twenty seconds. The item that I fear being pulled out is a sweatshirt I was given at the David Petriashvili Stadium by Goderdzi Chikhradze the day before, a souvenir for the story he had told. It bears an incendiary message:

FC GAGRA
GEORGIA UNITED

'Be careful what you try and take over the border,' is the advice I hear rumbling around my head.

This is propaganda of the most inflammatory kind. Gagra's capture by Abkhaz separatists in October 1992 laid the foundations of their state, and it is sacrosanct. It represents the birth pains and convulsions of the modern republic after years of being led around by Tbilisi's bloodless bureaucrats. It assumes a confessional significance in the broader testament of Abkhazia's liberation.

And here am I cheerfully attempting to smuggle in a clarion call for its repatriation.

The soldier doesn't spot the sweatshirt. His hands pass over it, but he doesn't lift it out and read the text on its front – if he had, I would have been going nowhere but back to Zugdidi, or to a prison cell. My unzipped bag is thrust back at me, and before I can hoist it onto my shoulder a Russian soldier in full fatigues with a revolver tucked into his holster drags me by my jacket and leads me off the path towards the woods and into one of the cabins.

'Close the door,' he orders, foregoing the indignity of actually prodding me with the tip of his weapon.

The interrogation proceeds in an awkward kind of Anglo-Russian. My custodian, a youngish man with robotic eyes, leaves confusing pauses between questions. He wants to know my reason for travel, my occupation, the address of my employer and invasive details about my family. Once he has extracted my responses, he enters them slowly into his computer as though using a keyboard for the first time.

After nearly an hour, I'm shooed back outside, and the fear that I'm about to be beaten or shot lifts slightly. The guards then leave me to roast in the sun, with the steep slopes of the hypnotising Lesser Caucasus mountains rising up on all sides, and I watch with envy as every other traveller passes through the militarised checkpoint with minimal hassle.

By the time my passport is handed back, I've had time to reconsider this ritual, and I have a new theory. This isn't tactical, and it's not a game. Rather, the crossing at the river Enguri is a performance space, a perverse theatre constructed to communicate to roaming Westerners that they've wandered into the Russian world. Here in the mountains, military authority is the only currency, and it is controlled by the hidden hand of Moscow.

On the road from Gali to Sukhumi, every third house has been burned, looted and stripped down to its bare bones. I've spent the last three days with a survivor of Abkhazia's blitzkrieg against its Georgian population. His name is Zurab, and he has been my fixer during my stay in Tbilisi. Zurab and his family lived here in Gali, the closest Abkhaz town to the Enguri border.

'The day we decided to leave, we were very lucky,' he told me the previous evening as we drove through the twinkling evening twilight of Tbilisi after a late dinner. 'The Abkhazians broke into our house with weapons just a few minutes after we had left. We made it out by maybe twenty minutes. We crossed the Enguri Bridge and down into the rest of Georgia. There were great columns of refugees escaping south over the bridge.

'Honestly, we thought we'd be going back soon. And many Georgians did go back to Gali after that. The Abkhazian state was very weak to begin with. They only really had control of the centre of Gali. Out in the villages where we lived, there were just a few police patrols.'

Zurab left Gali with his family three days after the fall of Sukhumi. Georgians made up around 45 per cent of the Abkhazian population before 1992, compared to just 17 per cent who were Abkhaz. The war left an estimated 250,000 Georgians homeless. Old sanatoriums, holiday camps and crumbling hostels were pressed into use as emergency housing. In some towns, three generations of Georgians are still living in improvised, supposedly temporary housing. Government handouts remain the principal source of income for those families, leaving refugees entrenched in their status as permanent outsiders in Georgia.

Driving north from Gali through the ruins of old neighbourhoods, the grand peaks of Enguri province yield to the raw flatlands of Transcaucasia's hazy outback. My next stop is the Abkhazian capital.

* * *

With its jarring dissonance between destruction and design, I have not seen a more dramatically beautiful city than Sukhumi.

The town is working through its grief, not just collectively but privately in its houses, its schools and its Orthodox churches. Apartments and government departments sit a few yards along on the same streets as the scorched and hollow shells of buildings that didn't survive the shelling, bomb blasts and fires started when Abkhaz fighters successfully re-captured the town from the Georgian National Guard in September 1993.

Branches of trees reach out from empty windows of derelict apartment blocks, and nature has begun to claim back the wreck of a city that looks half alive and half dead. It would be easy to be down on Sukhumi. The place is full of breathing corpses.

The ruined headquarters of the Supreme Soviet, which burned the day the city was re-captured, has been allowed to remain. Towering thirteen brutal storeys high in the centre of town, the damage caused by the blaze has over the years sunken deep into the stone fascia, and the carcass has roasted in the Black Sea sun, which has left a Constructivist cadaver glazed in a golden tan.

The drama of the green and red Abkhaz flag fluttering from its roof is lost when viewed from the ground, but when I see it later from my hotel room window the picture acquires a theatrical brilliance, exaggerated by the tropical rain and ocean winds that pound the city for much of my stay.

Top Communist Party officials once holidayed here. When Trotsky was exiled from the Soviet Union to Turkey in 1929, he set up his residence on Büyükada in the Sea of Marmara to mimic the Black Sea dacha he'd cherished at Sukhumi years before.

Sukhumi isn't like a lot of ex-Soviet towns that are still creaking back to life after years trapped beneath a layer of grey dust. The seaside culture that has thrived here for 2,500 years, since this was a flourishing port city at the meeting point of East and West and still known by its Greek name Dioscurias, has not been eroded by the Stalinism that sterilised the town for a number of decades.

Sukhumi's wide-open boulevards and clean ocean air give it a holiday feel – close your eyes to the Cyrillic lettering on the fronts of cafés and your ears to the clunk-clunk of clapped-out Ladas rumbling through the streets and you could be in Valletta, Thessaloniki or Palma. The palm trees that sprout up on the roadsides provide a visual respite from the city's bombed-out buildings, whose dead and empty windows blindly stare out over the old city.

Leonid Dzapshba, a swaggering old-style Communist Party apparatchik, was the president of the Football Federation of Abkhazia from 2007 to 2012. Before we have even sat down to talk, he boasts about how he personally oversaw the construction of thirteen gleaming new football training centres for young people in the republic, accelerating the game's recovery in the period after the war.

With his eyes hidden behind huge dark shades, he is an icon of authority, unflinching in his perceived destiny as a man ordained with irrevocable influence.

What he doesn't mention are the criminal charges of which he was accused. In 2012, Dzapshba was arraigned over the embezzlement of state money totalling nearly 8 million roubles allegedly pilfered during the construction of the new training centres. The indictment claimed the ex-president wrote off massive expenses against travel to Russia and Europe for 'official' meetings, as well as on cars and other personal items for himself and his family.

In his defence, he argued that special dispensation had been issued by the republic's then President, Sergei Bagapsh, for him to cover the football federation's losses with government funds. However, by the time the charges were brought Bagapsh was no longer alive to corroborate or deny the claim, and the prosecutor's office was unable to proceed with the case.

As for the thirteen football training centres, the authorities alleged that they had been paid for without the drawing up of the necessary legal documents, so a second investigation was launched into whether the contracts presented by the football federation matched the market value of the work carried out.

Dzapshba himself, meanwhile, grunted nonchalantly in the local press with the swagger of a man who knows he is nevertheless beyond recrimination: 'What can they give me [as punishment]?' he retorted. 'Let them figure out how the money was spent.'

Dzapshba holds that a deputy of the Russian parliamentary Duma named Otari Arshba financed the centres with 30 million roubles of his own personal funds. Like Dzapshba, Sukhumi-born Arshba is a graduate of the Soviet security service. He served as a political adviser to the inaugural President of Abkhazia, Vladislav Ardzinba, whose rule is associated with the devastating austerity the Abkhazians suffered through the 1990s.

Arshba also heads up the Moscow Duma's commission on ethics, though he has never commented publicly on the millions of roubles that were claimed to have gone missing from the coffers of the Football Federation of Abkhazia on Dzapshba's watch. He is reported to have been one of the biggest private donors to the Abkhaz separatist fighters during the conflict in 1992, and his association – not to mention his deep financial entanglement – with the football federation indicates the extent to which Abkhazia depends on its Russian patronage, as well as of the general unaccountability with which the gears of the machine turn.

Dzapshba was eventually acquitted, and the Abkhazian President felt secure enough in his innocence to appoint him as his minister for internal affairs.

Yet controversy still plagued the 55-year-old. In April 2016, an angry crowd of 1,500 protesters, dissatisfied with Dzapshba's record on crime statistics in his new role, broke down the gates to the interior ministry to demand his resignation. President Raul Khajimba, recognising that his minister had become a liability, promptly removed him the following morning.

'Don't misunderstand me,' begins Dzapshba, reclining in the sun and cutting the figure of a man entirely beyond reproach. Despite myself, I like Dzapshba. He seems to me a kind of Soviet iteration of

Shakespeare's Falstaff, and I can only imagine what kind of stories about KGB hijinks both real and fantastical might sputter forth if he were suitably inebriated.

'It isn't possible to just take money coming from Russia and spend it on football,' he argues, anticipating my line of questioning, though surely Dzapshba's own easy reallocation of football federation money means there is at least some freedom in the system. 'There is no direct spending from Russia on Abkhazian football. The Russian money that is in Abkhazia is being spent on schools, infrastructure. There is a very clear plan in Russia for Abkhazia. There is a programme.

'There are businesses and private firms who make sponsorship deals with clubs individually. That provides some income for teams. But eight clubs [there are now ten clubs in Abkhazia] is a lot for such a small country. Some of them don't have sufficient sponsorship, so there is a special mechanism for clubs to receive government money.'

Today, Dzapshba keeps a lower profile in public life – wisely, considering that he was practically dragged from his last public post by rioters. He retains the nominal role of secretary of Dinamo sports club, the famous old Soviet-era society that represented the recreational pursuits of the internal security services, including Dinamo Sukhumi.

He is also a child of the tangled miscellany that is Sukhumi's DNA. The city is a patchwork of tribal principals of the Circassian mountain peoples that were the ancestors of modern Abkhazians, intertwined with facets of the shadow economy so skilfully gamed by Soviet party apparatchiks. In some ways, the city seems to be in a battle with its own past. There's a tension in the way local people here interact with the past, a cautious reluctance to get too cosy with their own history.

'The day the Georgians invaded, I was at the ministry,' recalls Dzapshba, who was then a junior employee of the security services. 'News came through that tanks had been seen coming from the south into Abkhazia. When the news came, we all ran to the headquarters of the Soviet government in Sukhumi. We had an emergency session to decide what was going to be done.

'The day the tanks came, everything moved so fast. We had no time to gather our things, we literally ran to the headquarters to make our plan. When that meeting was over, we went straight into combat. Immediately.'

I heard a similar story when I interviewed Valery Arshba, the head of Abkhazia's Olympic Committee, a few days previously: 'I was in the fight from the first day,' he told me. 'When there are soldiers coming into your city who can kill your family and your friends, there is no way you are going to step away from it. You have to take part. You have to fight.'

The fighting between Georgia and Abkhazia came to an end in 1993. But the year also marked the start of a period of great hardship. The economy in any recognisable form had collapsed under the pressure of infrastructural damage from the fighting and heavy sanctions imposed by member states of the Commonwealth of Independent States (the pan-national body set up by Russia after the fall of the Soviet Union) against the rebel government in Sukhumi. Abkhazia, effectively now an independent republic but unable to trade with its immediate neighbours or receive aid, became at once a pariah state and an economic basket case.

'The blockade and the sanctions that followed destroyed Abkhazian football,' argues the journalist Inal Khashig when we meet at Sukhumi Bay. 'There is no continuity between football in the Soviet time and now. It is a crisis now compared to then. We are excluded today from world football.'

Abkhazia's football federation is not recognised by FIFA or UEFA, which leaves it without funding and unable to take part in international competition for its clubs or national team.

'We have been excluded since the 1990s. If you have only a small environment in which to work, inevitably the quality will be very low. We can't have games against Russian teams. We can't even make transfers legally.

'We can't legally sell players to Russian teams in a way that financially benefits our clubs.'

The game struggled by on a strictly amateur basis during the 1990s and early 2000s, with a local league that was dominated by Nart Sukhumi and FC Gagra, and Dinamo Sukhumi were liquidated shortly after winning the inaugural title in 1994.

Yet, football has a rich heritage in Abkhazia. In 2013, the republic held a celebration to mark 100 years since the game was first played here. 'It isn't simple,' begins Dzapshba. 'This is massive football country. Anyone who doesn't play it watches it.' When Sukhumi hosted the final of the CONIFA in 2016, it was Dzapshba's call to allow many thousands of spectators over capacity to cram into the brand new Dinamo Stadium to watch the final between Abkhazia and a team representing the Indian Punjab.

A day later, I pay a visit to the stadium to meet Astamur Adleiba, the chairman and founder of a re-booted Dinamo Sukhumi. Tall, charming and impeccably dressed, there is no more prominent character in Abkhazian football today than Adleiba. His broad grin seems to swallow his whole face when he smiles, and the brotherly way in which he embraces and engages me is illustrative of his eagerness to sell Sukhumi and Dinamo to the foreign press.

I start by asking for his opinion of Goderdzi Chikhradze's work with another phoenix team, FC Gagra in Tbilisi. 'Everybody likes nostalgia,' he says with genuine sympathy. 'It's natural, human.'

Built in 2015 with financial backing from Moscow, the new stadium is a slightly soulless identikit job standing a couple of hundred metres from the seafront. For Adleiba, as for most Abkhazians, it is a reminder that it is Russia and not Georgia that is the republic's natural ally. 'This place was made possible by Russian money,' he states, spreading his arms wide. 'The war cost us everything we had. Without this money from Russia, we couldn't survive.'

Adleiba joined the old Dinamo as a youth player in 1986, though his build now is more like that of a rugby front row. A promising prospect in the Soviet youth ranks, his development was halted when he was called up for national service, and the realisation soon dawned that a life in Sukhumi's brand new private economy offered a brighter future than a career in football.

'It was a great time for Abkhazia,' says Adleiba of the age of Soviet perestroika that liberalised the state monopoly of commerce. 'The economy had grown so much in a short space of time. We were a tourist state and there was a lot of investment coming in. And of course Dinamo Sukhumi had just been promoted to the First League of the Soviet Union and probably would eventually have gone to the top division but for the conflict.'

As of 2020, Russia formally provides around half of the republic's annual budget, the rest is made up via Sukhumi's almost total trade dependence on Moscow. Even tourism, the republic's most buoyant trade, is propped up by Russian holidaymakers. When in 2004 Moscow threatened to suspend its financial assistance to the republic if Parliament removed its Russian-favoured President Raul Khajimba, it communicated loudly what observers had known since the guns first went quiet in 1993 – if Abkhazia wishes to avoid sliding back towards Tbilisi's sphere of influence, it must dance enthusiastically to Moscow's song.

'Can you understand what I'm telling you?' questions Adleiba insistently. The seating at Dinamo Stadium is well covered, but because of the gale the rain is beginning to reach us from where we are seated at the back of the arena's east stand. 'Abkhazia was a very advanced, high-level society in 1991. And it's not just sport. This was a big cultural city. We had theatres here and festivals. And at the same time, we had Dinamo Sukhumi playing at a very high level. Everything was improving. And then Georgia destroyed everything. Destroyed Abkhazia, destroyed Dinamo Sukhumi. Destroyed football, too.'

FIFA put a block on the only measure that could have kept Abkhazia's football clubs alive in the early 1990s, barring them from joining the Russian Football Union (RFU) and keeping them from competing against teams from the Upper Caucasus in the federation's southern zone. By isolating Dinamo from the RFU, FIFA effectively issued a winding-up order against seventy years of professional football in Abkhazia, one that dates back to the masterclass given by Dinamo Sukhumi's youth players to their counterparts in Tbilisi that earned them the respect of the Soviet world.

'In the 1950s and 1960s, there were never any spaces inside football stadiums on matchdays,' explains Adleiba. 'It was the same throughout Georgia. Football was a celebration when clubs from Abkhazia played Georgian teams.' But just as Dinamo has been revived in the twenty-first century, so too has the team that splintered off and joined the Georgian league in 1990. FC Tskhumi Sukhumi, who left the Soviet league but continued to live in the same hotel as their old teammates at Queen Tamar's Bridge in Abkhazia, have also been brought back to life and now stake a claim to the original club's legacy.

I'd met the team's coach back in Tbilisi. David Taktakishvili was twenty-three years old but he didn't look a day younger than forty. 'That's the Georgian environment,' he says when I express my surprise. 'You can look at a ten-year-old boy and you will think he looks thirty. It's especially true when you work in football.'

Taktakishvili started in football as a player in the Georgian second division for local Tbilisi side, FC Olimpi, until the country's ruling United National Movement Party erected new government buildings on the club's facilities in 2012. 'The party ruined the club,' he says convincingly.

Olimpi have since followed a familiar narrative consisting of bankruptcy, closures and mergers that is common to many football clubs in Georgia, where limited spectator interest means that the game has virtually no commercial value.

Olimpi, together with four other lower-division clubs, now nominally form some part of Erovnuli Liga club FC Rustavi, after a succession of mergers during the 2000s created one relatively stable club out of a clutch of failing ones. It is, therefore, part of the fabric of Georgian football that the question of legacy becomes obfuscated and murky, as is the case with Tskhumi and Dinamo.

'Can you imagine if London declared independence from England?' asked Taktakishvili. 'And you had two teams called Arsenal? Imagine the nonsense of them playing against each other.'

Sixteen out of Taktakishvili's twenty-two players are the sons of refugees from Abkhazia. 'These are young people who have suffered unimaginably,' he explains. 'They've had tragic lives. They lost all their belongings, houses. Some of them lived with their families on the streets, constantly looking for shelter. Right now, we've decided to give them some small salary. It's not much. Maybe $250 per month. In order to have a personal income and to feel like men.'

Maybe some things are more important than legacy after all. Regardless of abstract disputes over who owns the past, the communities of Tbilisi and Sukhumi are using a part of history that they both share to build a future for the young people of their cities.

'We are the same people as Englishmen,' says Adleiba back on the terrace at Dinamo Stadium. 'We have the same dreams and wishes and hopes. Football should be without borders, without politics.'

Today the Abkhaz domestic championship comprises ten clubs, each of them running between two and five youth teams. Young people and sport are taken seriously in the republic. This is a young country that is planning for the future, but not forgetting to take time to indulge in and live for the present. 'Come to any football pitch in Abkhazia at 10 p.m. or midnight,' says Dzapshba. 'I guarantee you will see young people playing football there.'

That evening, when I venture from my hotel at around 10 p.m. to sniff out a late beer, I decide to take Dzapshba up on his challenge, and take a detour up to the caged concrete football pitches that sit near Dinamo Stadium.

Sure enough, the unmistakable clatter of children thumping a ball against the interior of a steel fence greets me as I round the corner, and the din of their harrying, chasing and cheering carries down the street and away into the night.

IV

Ashkar Sanakoyev squints to keep the sun out of his eyes. Every few minutes, when the ball goes out of play here at the David Petriashvili Stadium, he takes his eyes off the pitch and turns to address me directly. 'We wanted to show people that there is a possibility here to play football and develop in another direction,' he explains. 'The club is part of a much larger picture.' Then his attention is drawn back to the Torpedo Kutaisi v. Chikhura Sachkhere game, and I momentarily lose him again.

That club is FC Tskhinvali, and the picture is of a united Georgia. To that end, he is supported in his work by powerful forces.

On 26 June 2007, Sanakoyev's father Dimitry stood before a committee of the European Parliament in Brussels and addressed the chamber in a language it had never before heard. Ossetic is an eastern Iranian dialect. To the uninitiated, it may just as well be Russian or any other obscure language from beyond Eurasia's intercontinental hinterland.

The decision to address the committee in his native language was hugely symbolic. It was the first time that a representative from the Georgian breakaway republic of South Ossetia, which seceded illegally with Russian support after a brief war of independence in 1992, had appeared before the EU's committee on the settlement of the border disagreements between Georgia and its separatist territories.

Sanakoyev's message was clear. The people of South Ossetia were ready to live in peaceful accord with their Georgian cousins after fifteen years of frozen conflict and separatist rule. It was a rallying message of fraternity; not a white flag of surrender, but rather a clarion call for peace and cooperation.

The South Ossetian people were, after all the bloodshed, brothers to Georgia across a barricade that had brought more harm than good. His speech was received by enthusiastic applause, and the chamber patted itself on the back in recognition of a step towards securing long-term peace in Georgia, a highly sensitive region in the proxy struggle between Russia and the European–American alliance.

There was just one problem. Sanakoyev, Head of the Provisional Administrative Entity of South Ossetia, held absolutely no power in the de facto republic. Indeed, the leader of the separatist regime, Eduard Kokoity, had previously denounced Sanakoyev as a 'traitor to his homeland and a traitor to the South Ossetian people', and the organisation that he fronted, the People of South Ossetia for Peace, had been outlawed in the state, a denouncement that had led to both official and vigilante attacks on the group's members, including Sanakoyev.

The Brussels address toed the line of the EU's position on Georgia's sovereignty, reflecting the feelings of those ethnic Georgians still living in the large Tbilisi-controlled areas of South Ossetia, of which there were significant numbers.

But to committed Ossetians living in isolation from the world in the rest of Tskhinvali's unrecognised pariah state, Sanakoyev's proclamations were meaningless, serving only to highlight that the disparity between Georgian and Ossetian interests that had caused the war in the first place hadn't gone away. On the standoff between Tbilisi and the South Ossetian capital Tskhinvali, it made no impact.

Sanakoyev had formerly served as Prime Minister in the de facto government in Tskhinvali, before a change of heart turned him away from the consolidation of independent rule and towards a federal coexistence with Georgia. The People of South Ossetia for Peace was established in 2006 with the intention of bringing such an alternative to the people in the form of a public referendum. Politically hamstrung and exiled almost from the start, the group sought to disseminate its creed amongst the wider cultural fabric of the country. Sanakoyev turned to his energetic son.

Ashkar sits with his hood up perched on the edge of his seat, half keeping an eye on the opening game of the Georgian football season between Torpedo Kutaisi and Chikhura Sachkhere, of which the second half has just begun. He is the sporting director of FC Tskhinvali, and his youthful looks belie the responsibilities that weigh heavy on his shoulders.

A lot of Ossetian men look as though they've had their nose broken several times. It declares a kind of wily authority, but it also serves as a remindful of the guileful practicality that has been inherited over centuries of being conquered and shunted by hostile outsiders. Ashkar has this same look, but at the same time he is fair-faced and athletic in his baggy sportswear, and he possesses the aura of being a willing novice amongst veteran hooligans. He is doleful as he sets the scene.

'FC Tskhinvali are a symbol of common purpose between Georgians and South Ossetians,' he claims. But the truth is that the two peoples are too firmly divided by the passage of history. So much so that Ashkar no longer feels safe returning home. A visible champion for a unified Georgia, his safety cannot be guaranteed. 'I prefer not to show up in South Ossetia these days,' he says. 'I don't think I would have problems with the law necessarily, but there will be people who would not like to see me back there. You never know what could happen, especially when people know who you are.'

FC Tskhinvali were founded in 2007. Funding for the club came from Dmitry Sanakoyev's government in exile. At its peak, the group was receiving around $7 million from the Georgian state per year. The football club – then called FC Spartak – was the jewel in its crown.

'Before 2008, there was a lot of investment from the Georgian government going into the parts of Ossetia that were still under its control,' describes Ashkar. 'In Tskhinvali region, only the capital was under Ossetian rule, but the Georgian-held regions had a lot of European investment. They were building schools and sports facilities, to prove to people that life was improving here. Football was a big part of it.'

As a result, after the club's founding they were parachuted directly into the Erovnuli Liga, the country's top flight, on the say-so of the Georgian government, bypassing a potentially long and drawn-out route up through the divisions (coincidentally, it was after the two teams that we're watching today, Kutaisi and Sachkhere, were denied a licence to compete, that space opened up for Spartak to play in the Erovnuli Liga).

'That was a political decision,' claims Ashkar. 'That first season was very, very tough. We started the club in July and our season began in August.'

The team wore the fierce red and black stripes of the old Tskhinvali team of the 1930s that had played in the Georgian regional leagues during the Soviet era, in homage to the collective Georgian nation. But the colours also served as a reminder that Spartak, under the patronage of the Tbilisi administration, were a political prop in an international proxy war between Moscow and the new Georgian republic backed by Europe and the United States.

Spartak Tskhinvali did survive that season, just. It took a relegation play-off against the third-place team from the First League FC Gagra to hold on to their top-flight status, which they secured with a tense 1–0 win in May 2008, three months before Tbilisi began shelling Tskhinvali in a doomed attempt to bring South Ossetia back under its control.

But things have gotten harder for the football club in recent years. The budget provided by the South Ossetian government in exile, headed by Ashkar's father Dmitry, has been slashed since the project was first established in the run-up to the war of 2008, which is a trend the sporting director attributes to a waning interest in the club's affairs as the possibility of reconciliation has dwindled. In 2016 a re-christened FC Tskhinvali, rudderless and cash-strapped, were relegated from the Erovnuli Liga altogether.

The Ossetians' ethnic ancestors, an Iranian tribespeople known as the Alans, were forced south out of the Upper Caucasus by Mongol invaders in the thirteenth century, settling in Gori in modern Georgia. Pushed back by the Georgians into the north in the fourteenth century, the Ossetians began to trickle back down from their historical northern home 400 years later into the territory they currently occupy, ushering in a period of conciliation between the different nations.

The Kingdom of Kartli-Kakheti – a brief eighteenth-century monarchy that occupied much of the central part of modern Georgia, including the disputed Republic of South Ossetia – was thus home to large numbers of Ossetian communities by the time it was absorbed into the Russian Empire in 1801, and more joined them from north of the Caucasus over the course of the nineteenth century.

The collapse of relations in the twentieth century took the essential character of the schism in the Russian world as it was torn apart by civil war, between the Bolsheviks (supported by the landless Ossetian peasants who were wooed by Lenin's pledge of peace, bread and land) and the Mensheviks, who had seized control in the new social democratic republic of Georgia following the collapse of Tsarism.

The political and economic struggle soon took on the character of an ethnic war, with Ossetians occupying the city administration in Tskhinvali and holding it until Georgia fell to the Soviet invasion in 1921, after which the South Ossetian Autonomous Oblast was created within the apparatus of the USSR.

The current territorial struggle in Georgia takes the form of a proxy war between Moscow and the Western alliance of NATO and the EU. Tbilisi entered into an association agreement with Brussels in 2014 and has expressed its intention to apply for full EU membership. It has been a signatory to NATO's Partnership for Peace since 1994, and has lent its forces to a number of the organisation's military campaigns in Europe and beyond. For Moscow, maintaining an armed presence on the internationally recognised territory of Georgia is not only desirable, but essential, as the political, economic and military apparatus of Europe inches ever further into the Russian sphere.

My conversation at the stadium with Ashkar keeps being interrupted by the roar of the crowd inside the ground. The Super Cup match has been a slow burner, which after a sluggish first half where the players were shaking off the dust of the season hiatus, has come to life after the underdogs Chikhura in their bright gold shirts took the lead.

The stadium has been filling up steadily throughout the game, and with a shock result up for grabs the place is suddenly alive with expectant energy.

Georgian football, when it finds its voice, is a fabulous celebration of culture and local pride. But for the depressing cycle of bankruptcies, mergers and liquidations that leaves teams impoverished and uncertain, the spirit of the great Dinamo Tbilisi side of the 1970s and 1980s would have carried this wonderful country into the annals of the football mainstream.

Ashkar's team have suffered more than most. The year 2018 marks ten years since the blitzkrieg conflict between Georgia and Moscow that razed FC Tskhinvali's hometown of Tamarasheni, forcing them out of South Ossetia into Tbilisi, thus further undermining the cause of Georgian sovereignty and rendering the team permanently homeless.

There is not much positive light that has penetrated the fog. Diplomatic efforts on the Georgian side of the militarised South Ossetian border to find a peaceful settlement have, after early optimism, petered out. FC Tskhinvali, though, have kept up the fight; an unyielding symbol of unity as belligerence reigns.

Another football club, FC Liakhvi-Tskhinvali, was founded in Stalin's Gori, just south of the barbed wire and gunmen stationed on the militarised border, in 2014 by a former captain of the old Tskhinvali team in 1936, Zaz Romelashvili, who fled the region during the 1991 struggle.

The club's stated aim was to build a mixed team of players from Georgia, Tskhinvali and Vladikavkaz, the capital city of the Russian Republic of North Ossetia-Alania across the Caucasus. To mark the club's foundation, a team of government ministers, including the former Prime Minister Irakli Garibashvili, travelled to Gori to play an exhibition game against a side made up of former Georgian professionals, amongst them Kakha Kaladze, the former Energy Minister and AC Milan star.

Yet, in a 2014 interview with the *Caucasian Echo*, Romelashvili insisted that he saw no political conurbation in the activities of FC Liakhvi, despite the fact that it was the club's stated aim to fill its squad with players of Ossetian birth and that the team's fans were almost exclusively drawn from Gori's extensive network of Ossetian refugees.

'This team was created to show that we are not enemies,' Romelashvili protested. 'We are not strangers. I repeat once again, we are of one blood.'

It's one of the great enigmas of football in Europe's disputed regions that those who have worked hardest to counteract the destructive synergy of politics and sport tend to also be those who subscribe to the idea that there was never a link between them in the first place.

A political culture amongst figureheads pervades in Transcaucasia, which means that ex-pros often get shunted to the front of political movements as a reassuring face, whilst chaos reigns over their shoulder.

In 2012, former AC Milan defender and Georgian national team captain Kaladze was appointed Energy Minister in the Cabinet of billionaire Prime Minister Bidzina Ivanishvili, just as Ivanishvili was recovering his reputation after being hit with a record $90 million fine for breaching party funding rules in the run-up to his election (Kaladze is now the mayor of Tbilisi).

The Ossetian question has inevitably been sucked into this drama. In March 2004, the former Dinamo Tbilisi striker Vladimir Gutsaev, whose equalising goal in Dusseldorf set the team on their way to their historic victory in the 1981 UEFA Cup Winners' Cup final, was elected to Parliament as a representative of President Mikheil Saakashvili's ruling United National Movement Party. Gutsaev was born in Tbilisi, but he has never made any secret of his Ossetian heritage.

That following July in 2004, the leader of the de facto Republic of

South Ossetia, Eduard Kokoity, made the allegation that the Georgian hero Gutsaev had visited him with an offer of a $20 million fund plus the position of Vice-President of Georgia in order to 'resolve the South Ossetia conflict as quickly as possible', in short, to reintegrate Tskhinvali peacefully into Georgia proper.

Gutsaev very firmly denied that any such conversation with Kokoity had taken place, and claimed at the time he had met with Tskhinvali's leader only to persuade him to allow a South Ossetian team to participate in the Erovnuli Liga, but that story seemed to have changed somewhat when I spoke to him.

'These were just rumours,' Gutsaev tells me. 'I have never even met Kokoity. I was working in Russia at the time, yes. But this is just people looking to cause trouble. I'm not a politician [though he was at the time]. I am an Ossetian, born in Tbilisi. I still live there. I can only regret what has happened between Georgia and Ossetia. But it's down to the politicians to sort out, not footballers.'

Gutsaev's reputation has since attracted controversy on both sides of the border. In 2012, he was unexpectedly appointed sporting director of Russian Premier League side FC Alania Vladikavkaz. Alania, the traditional name for the Ossetians' ancestral home, is a national myth that unites the people of North Ossetia – an autonomous republic within the Russian Federation – with the south.

To Ossetians, the international border that runs between Russia and Georgia is an aberration that arbitrarily divides their nation in half, and FC Alania – who shocked the nation by winning the Russian championship in 1995, but achieved very little else before being relegated a decade later – are a focal point for the cause for a united Ossetia (North Ossetia, despite being planted amongst the volatile republics of Chechnya, Dagestan and Ingushetia in the separatist minefield of Russia's North Caucasus, has never made a fuss of breaking away from Moscow, largely because the Russian

Federation represents its best hope of eventually being reunited with the south).

As a result, Gutsaev's appointment at FC Alania raised eyebrows.

Reports in Tskhinvali noted correctly that the sixty-year-old hadn't held a job in football for over eleven years, implying the appointment had been made as a means of installing an influential figure with Georgian sympathies – and a known associate of the presidency in Tbilisi – in a senior role at Ossetia's most prominent sports club.

'It wasn't at all strange,' Gutsaev insists when I mention the criticism. 'I had worked in football my whole life. I had known [Spartak president] Valery Gazzaev more than fifty years. When he became director of Alania, it was only normal that he would ask me to come.'

With relations between Tbilisi and the regime of South Ossetia's military leader Eduard Kokoity worse than ever, what chance is there one day of Georgian league matches once again taking place again in Tskhinvali? For now, virtually zero.

In June 2019, the players of Lokomotiv Tbilisi and FC Rustavi caused a media backlash in Russia when they warmed up for an Erovnuli Liga meeting wearing t-shirts condemning the Russian presence in South Ossetia and Abkhazia.

The shirts featured a map of the Georgian borders coloured with the red and white Saint George's cross of the national flag, accompanied by the words 'We are from Georgia – our country is being occupied by Russia'. The players of Torpedo Kutaisi also wore the shirts for their game against FC Bolnisi Sioni the same day, which led to calls in Russia for sanctions to be levied against the Football Federation of Georgia for allowing its teams to breach FIFA rules on political slogans.

If a solution is to be found to the problems in the South Caucasus, it likely lies not in the settlement of South Ossetia and Abkhazia's disputed status but in the decisive construction of some apparatus of peace that will keep the belligerent forces of Moscow, Brussels and Washington feuding somewhere far from the Caucasus.

This would allow the people of Tskhinvali, Sukhumi, Tbilisi and the communities of these troubled mountains the space to work out their futures in whatever way suits their unique situation and history. In the meantime, football will continue, retaining its broad shape, but buffeted by the political long waves of a territorial struggle that is nowhere near from finished.

In the final minutes at the David Petriashvili Stadium, the black-shirted players of Torpedo score two quick goals to turn the game around and snatch the cup away from Chikhura.

Twice in a few seconds, the stadium explodes with a roar of excitement and noise that continues well after the final whistle has sounded and Torpedo have lifted the cup amidst a fountain of confetti.

Then, just as suddenly, it stops, and the crowd drifts quietly away into the evening in muted anticipation of another uncertain football season nestled amongst these ancient mountains.

PART FOUR

BAPTISED IN THE RIVER: MOLDOVA AND TRANSNISTRIA

I love you
But why I love you
I never know
GRAFFITI FOUND IN TIRASPOL

© TUBS / CC BY-SA

I

Victor Daghi wears a freshly pressed, baby-blue cotton shirt. He doesn't button it quite to the top, but thanks to a tailored blazer that clings snuggly to his broad shoulders, he doesn't need to.

He speaks in a soft but professional tone that contains just the right infusion of authority and enquiry. He smiles in earnest, laughs from the belly and plays the diplomat with quick and ready instinct.

I like Victor. More than just like, I trust him. Thousands of miles from home in a land percolating with the unknown, trust is a currency far more valuable to me than the fistful of Moldovan lei idly scrunched up in my back trouser pocket. As head attaché in the Moldovan Football Federation (MFF) press section, he plays the perfect host. So it is understandable, then, that Victor's next words, delivered with that dependable warmth, chill my veins and quicken my heart.

'You seem like a nice guy,' he croons. 'But if you ask the wrong questions over there, anything that criticises Russia or Putin, they will kill you. They will look at the ring through your nose, they will think maybe this guy is not heterosexual. It will not go well for you.'

Cue an awkward, sickly silence. I watch the corners of Victor's mouth, waiting for them to crack into a laugh, and then scan up to his eyes hoping to find a glimmer of a smile in them, but there is none.

Ion Buga, Victor's colleague who has been seated in a corner of the office here at the headquarters of the MFF, is stony-faced when I glance to him for reassurance that his boss's words may have been meant in clumsy jest. In the two days since my work began here, I have not yet seen Ion's po-faced grimace break into a smile. I can only assume then, that Victor is deadly serious about the political and social climate in store for me when I leave the Moldovan capital, Chișinău, and head east over the militarised border into the de facto proto-state, Transnistria. I suppose it's my fault for asking, whether he is indeed serious.

It's April 2019, and I have been in Moldova, one of the poorest countries on the world's richest continent, for six days, attempting to make sense of its unique and multifarious contradictions. Impoverished and ignored, this may not be the very cliff edge of civilisation, but when the sun slinks down behind the Nativity Cathedral's glorious zinc dome on Ștefan cel Mare și Sfânt Boulevard, illuminating the horizon in a deep and seductive orange haze, I think I can see it from here. Nowhere across the breadth of the former Soviet Union did its dissolution bring such hardship.

The convulsions endured as Moldova's free market was born were prolonged, as the collapse of trade networks inside the former USSR bled the country dry. For most people here, the dawn of capitalism meant dragging surplus useless junk from their unheated homes out into the streets to lay on improvised market stalls, with a hope that someone would be interested in buying it. Independence brought an almost instant rise in the rates of alcoholism, unemployment, poverty and suicide.

But not only the poor were poor. When the Welsh football team came here for a European Championship qualifier in 1994 shortly after the country had gained independence, the team's Premier League stars returned with stories of having been made to sleep on damp, mouldy mattresses in cockroach-infested hotels where the gas was rationed and the water that ran from the taps was brown. This was the best accommodation the country could provide.

Not that life in Chișinău today gives much indication of how hard the first thirty years after Communism have been for the country. The centre of the city has all the vital signs of a thriving European capital. Ștefan cel Mare și Sfânt Boulevard is as gloriously sweeping as anything in Haussmann's Paris, and offers up almost all of the city's architectural treasures, right down to the modern beauty of the Presidential Palace; the post-Soviet welfare system, like its Communist predecessor, has a tendency to care greatest for those nearer the top. Raggedy, tatty markets dot the city beyond Ștefan cel Mare; functional dispensers of cheap essentials and cheaper thrills. To say that people make do here would not be damning with faint praise. Chișinău is a working machine, which represents incalculable progress from the dark ages of the 1990s.

Tomorrow, I leave here, and head for Moldova's unknown eastern frontier. Beyond that, Transnistria awaits, a 'Russian-sponsored black hole of organised crime', somewhere more generous critics have called the most lawless place in Europe. You can prove anything with hyperbole. Chișinău has spent much of the last thirty years working to convince foreign observers that the Pridnestrovian Moldavian Republic (Transnistria's official name), which broke loose from Moldova as the Soviet Union was collapsing and certified its independence in 1992 via a short but decisive military conflict, harbours Europe's worst villains and operates as a mechanised network of criminal enterprises masquerading as honest state builders.

In Transnistria the streets are emblazoned with Soviet iconography, and the wind whistles through Russian flags; a gesture of kinship, or maybe a mercenary nod of thanks for the free gas, pensions and $150 million in state aid that flows from Moscow into the capital Tiraspol each year.

The village of Rîbnița in Transnistria's north houses a Soviet-era weapons dump that is almost certainly the largest concentration of ammunition and explosives in Europe. Some believe the arsenal is half the reason Russia consented to its army assisting the separatists in their 1992 war of independence in the first place.

Experts say that if the Rîbnița stores were detonated, it would equate to the power of the A-bombs over Hiroshima and Nagasaki combined, and would presumably wipe out human life the length of the Dniester River – the wending natural border that separates Transnistria from Moldova proper – and beyond. As for what awaits me in Transnistria, I have been unable to shake the image conjured by the words of a former Organisation for Security and Cooperation in Europe diplomat Donald Johnson, uttered during the months the pseudo-republic was putting down its roots in the obfuscating aftermath of the Soviet collapse: 'Whatever it is that exists over there, it's not a subject of international law; it's some kind of nightmarish Disneyland.'

Perhaps I will do better to take my chances with the assassins, and pray that there are more sexually and politically deviant terrorists than me entering Tiraspol in the coming days.

II

Alexandru Guzun speaks to me with a kind of glazed detachment, as if these events happened to somebody else and in another lifetime. 'Can you imagine the shock of arriving in a city you know well and seeing it suddenly at war? There were bombs exploding in the streets.' It is April 2019 and I am meeting Guzun in the plush offices of the Moldovan Football Federation in Chişinău.

On the morning of 2 March 1992, Guzun stepped off a train in the city of Bendery on the quiet, sleepy banks of Moldova's river Dniester. Back then he was a leggy midfielder for local side FC Tighina, an unremarkable little club that had gone a generation unobserved in the hinterland of the Soviet Union's regional leagues.

He arrived in town from the Ukrainian city of Vinnytsia, where the previous day he had turned out for another club, FC Nyva, his dual registration made possible by the chaotic administrative legacy of Soviet record keeping.

This was an historic day in Moldova. Guzun had travelled to Bendery, a fifteenth-century market town first settled as a trading post between the medieval Moldavian principality and the Crimean Tartars, to meet up with his Tighina teammates for the very first game on the very first day of the republic's new Divizia Națională, a fresh football start for the country after nearly fifty years under the Communist super-system. The game would take place at the city's Dinamo Stadium against Constructorul from the city of Leova. The team had arranged to meet at the city's Hotel Nistru, before travelling on together to the stadium for the game.

Guzun made it to the hotel. Then life in the fledgling Republic of Moldova changed for ever.

'The Hotel Nistru was right on the river,' recalls Guzun. He speaks to me in a hushed voice, and sometimes his words seem to disappear into the silence. 'Because of where it is located, with Tiraspol only a few kilometres one way and the Moldovan soldiers coming from the other, we were trapped. We were physically in the middle of the war.'

The war broke out between forces of the Moldovan capital, Chișinău, and Russian-backed separatists on the country's eastern border, who despite the Soviet Union's collapse ached to remain constitutionally and economically bound to the Russian world.

The separatists fought for their right to form a new state, with its capital in Moldova's second city, Tiraspol. That state would be called Transnistria, and the river Dniester would be the natural frontier marking the border between the two republics. This made Bendery the epicentre of a pitched battle over the most strategic patch of land in the dispute.

'Once inside the hotel, we became trapped,' says Guzun. 'We had nowhere to go but underground. We spent three days under the ground in the hotel, sheltering from the bombs.'

The Nistru had become isolated in the line of fire. At the front of the hotel, two tanks were positioned, firing shells across the river towards the forces of the separatists. The Transnistrian militia, backed by the Russian Fourteenth Army, replied in kind. The Nistru was struck again and again in the crossfire. Bullets and shells shattered the windows of the rooms on the upper floors where Guzun and his teammates should have been sleeping, turning the building into a towering death-trap. 'The hotel had five floors, as I remember,' describes Guzun. 'We took everything we could from the rooms on the upper floors and took them to the basement. Everything we needed to live.

'I had one teammate, who was completely crazy, who went up to the first floor so he could see what was going on. He knew how dangerous it was, but he was crazy.' That teammate was Gheorghe Harea, who a few months previously had made history as a goal scorer in the Moldovan national team's first-ever match, a 4–2 defeat to Georgia in Chișinău. 'Harea made a joke that he could either die underground or he could die up there in the sky. As if it didn't matter.'

Meanwhile, in the basement, the players of FC Tighina scavenged to stay alive. 'We would take it in turns between us to run up to the first floor to the hotel restaurant to get supplies to take back down for everyone,' says Guzun. 'On the second day of the siege, some pacifists, who were on neither the Moldovan nor the Transnistrian side, came to the hotel. They erected a white flag from the top floor. These guys came and lived underground with us. For those days, we didn't think about eating or drinking. We only thought about how to survive.'

The war caught Bendery on the hop. Transnistria had been

effectively independent since first proclaiming its separation in 1990, but the fighting on the Dniester's muddy banks blew up quite suddenly.

The rebels sought separation because they feared, legitimately, that post-Soviet Moldova would seek unification with Romania, itself recently liberated from the Stalinist paranoia of Nikolai Ceaușescu's ludicrous regime.

The Dniester region was two thirds ethnic Slav, which gave it a unique ethnic make-up inside Moldova. By the start of 1992 Chișinău had already passed laws that marginalised the country's non-Romanian speakers, and the Russian and Ukrainian speakers in the east feared an accelerated descent towards secondary status inside an enlarged greater Romania ruled over by Bucharest.

On the west bank, meanwhile, Moldovan loyalists fiercely resisted the break-up of their new state, with officials fearful of the economic grenade that would explode if the Dniester republic, peppered multifariously with factories and arable land, abandoned the young country.

Unlike other conflicts that accompanied the collapse of the one-party state, this was not a war fought along the lines of narrow nationalist interests.

On the third day of the siege, word reached the Tighina players in the basement that a temporary ceasefire had been agreed, which was sufficient to allow the siege to be lifted and for the players to flee. Guzun believes the truce could never have been possible without the white flag that had been erected from the hotel roof.

'But we still had to make it from the hotel over the bridge,' he corrects me when I express relief that his tale is reaching its resolution. 'Just because a ceasefire has been agreed, it doesn't mean no one will shoot at you. Nobody would have investigated if anyone had shot at us on the bridge. The bridge was full of bullet holes.

We got to the bridge and ran. We ran for our lives. That bus ride to Chişinău was horrifying. We saw so much destruction. Bombs and bullets. They had attacked the bridge over the Dniester. We were driven south because it was too dangerous to go near Tiraspol.'

On 19 June, the worst atrocities of the war took place in Bendery. Dozens of civilian casualties were recorded as violent clashes broke out. Many of the bodies of the victims were left out in the streets for days, as it wasn't safe for anyone to venture out to recover them. The same day, the Russian news agency TASS reported that thousands of Russian-speaking civilians had assembled at a local Soviet army base demanding weapons to defend the town against Moldovan soldiers. Bendery was trooping its colour, and it seemed to be emphatically the tricolour of the Russian Federation.

More than twenty-five years later, the city has retained its physical scars. On the drive to Dinamo Stadium, the roads are lined with buildings that are pockmarked by bullet holes and shell damage.

The stadium itself sits unassumingly in a quiet residential part of town, though recent cash injections from the government have made this neighbourhood unrecognisable from how Guzun and Harea knew it when they played here in 1992.

A military roadblock manned by Khaki-clad Russian peacekeeping soldiers beckons our car to a crawl as we enter the town's limits. Just off the road, a Russian tank mounted high on a plinth bears a triumphant call to arms along one side: 'За Родину!', which translate as 'For the homeland!'

The tank is a T-72, a souvenir from the Second World War (known in the Russian world as the Great Patriotic War), and helps commemorate the 1992 tragedy of Bendery and marks the holy threshold where the Western world ends and a militarised incubation zone of Soviet life begins.

Over near the river, the sixteenth-century Bendery fortress, built to defend the city against rampaging Tartar raiders storming westwards into Europe from the Black Sea, watches over the town, silently pleading for tranquillity.

Bendery's war lasted for four months, claiming the lives of approximately 600 people (the numbers vary between reports). When it was over, Transnistria had seceded as a de facto independent state. But to this day, the international community does not recognise it as such.

In a triumph of the will, the twelve teams of Moldova's first Divizia Națională season saw the job out. Travelling between Tiraspol, Bendery and the cities in Moldova proper remained hazardous. Delays, detours and military escorts for teams were necessary to mitigate the threat of gunfire and shelling near the conflict zones.

Four days after the June attack on Bendery, the championship was concluded.

The first title was won, controversially, by FC Zimbru from Chișinău, who were awarded the win after rivals FC Tiligul Tiraspol refused to participate in a play-off tie-breaker, as they were angered by the decision made by the authorities to cancel their final two games of the league season due to the fighting.

Tighina themselves finished a respectable fourth, though they struggled all season for goals, and only last-placed Constructorul scored fewer. The livewire midfielder Harea, the nihilist who had diced with death in the Hotel Nistru siege, was top scorer with six goals from midfield, a mark of the inadequacy of the team's strikers. Had they scored goals like they defended them, they would likely have challenged Zimbru and Tiligul for the title, a fine achievement for a team that had finished a lowly ninth in the final edition of the Soviet third tier in 1991.

By the end of the season, the security situation on the Dniester had become dire enough to convince most of the Tighina team to prioritise personal safety and seek a life elsewhere. Most of Bendery's 130,000 inhabitants fled. Guzun himself relocated to Nyva permanently in July 1992, accompanied by his teammate Harea. The following season, a decimated Tighina team finished eleventh.

'I went back to my apartment in Bendery a few weeks after the war was finished,' describes Guzun. 'I was surprised to find that other people were now living in it. They'd found it unoccupied, so they'd moved in. During the war, there was a lot of this behaviour. There was a lot of crime and theft.'

The other FC Tighina players left Bendery in March, and relocated to the town of Anenii Noi on the Moldovan side of the Dniester, roughly equidistant between Chişinău and Tiraspol. Not every player, though, made personal safety a priority.

Yuri Khodykin was the team's goalkeeper in 1992. When his hometown was attacked, he thought of only one thing: the plight of the people. 'People suffered a lot,' states Khodykin, his skin weather-beaten, his eyes shrunken under his brow. There are features observable amongst the generation that lived through the violent breakup of the Communist world that serve as a looking glass into unresolved emotional injury, and there is no doubting that Khodykin is a damaged man.

'I was a participant in these military actions. And I saw a lot. I defended the city. I took arms into my hands.' He sits forward in the sky-blue plastic seat he's taken on the Dinamo Stadium terrace, but he doesn't make eye contact with me, instead he alternates his gaze between the ground and the dry greenery of the middle distance.

'I saw children with tears in their eyes. The women of the city said to us, "You must stop this conflict. You must stop the bloodshed." We didn't go there to kill Moldovans. We went to stop the bloodshed.'

He suddenly snaps. 'But you should be very careful with these questions. These are political matters. We should talk about football.'

My fixer in Transnistria, Andriy, warned me on the drive to Bendery about the reticence of the older generation. He is already finding it hard to keep an increasingly abrupt Khodykin onside.

'I think we need to move on from this now,' he nudges. I try and mitigate the awkwardness by explaining that any outsider would find it impossible to understand the history of Tighina without hearing first-hand about how the club and the city survived the conflict.

'Very well,' says Khodykin, giving in briefly. 'My message to you is this. The war separated, but football united. All I wanted was to stop the conflict. I defended this city, not for a political ideal or a national idea, but to prevent harm coming to our children. We had away games where we were met by armed guards along the roads. They had to give us a military escort. But via sport, we went to Moldovans and Moldovans came to us. War separated us but sport united us. But that doesn't mean it wasn't dangerous. All travel in and out of Bendery was dangerous.'

On 21 July 1992, the President of Russia, Boris Yeltsin, and the President of Moldova, Mircea Snegur, signed an agreement in Moscow, in the presence of the Transnistrian President, Igor Smirnov. The decree led to a declaration of a frail peace. The following month, normal life began to continue in Bendery, 'in order to forget this horrible time', says Khodykin.

Tighina were relegated from the Divizia Națională in 1999, and spent the next fifteen seasons bouncing between the top two divisions, save for a brief spell in the third tier.

In 2014, the side's financial shortfalls caught up with them, and they ceased to exist altogether, and spent three years playing as an amateur team in Moldova's lower leagues.

Under Transnistria's previous President, Yevgeny Shevchuk, sports funding in Bendery was wiped out. The Tighina coaches met with city officials, not to ask about salaries or restoring the stadium, but to request funds for a team bus.

The facilities that had helped the town recover from the traumas of the war – which left a disenfranchised youth population, disillusioned by unemployment, drugs and crime – were left to go to ruin under Shevchuk.

'Under him, there was absolutely nothing,' lambasts Khodykin. 'There was no financing. When we did go to financers to ask about funding, we didn't ask about wages or the stadium, we asked about money to get the bus to our next game. My wife was furious because I gave up my pension to pay for a new bus,' he says with a wry smile. 'Five years without football is like five years in prison. But now the club is returned to life.'

The current President, Vadim Krasnoselsky, made a manifesto promise ahead of his election in 2016 to restore the stadium at Bendery and to invest in FC Tighina to help the side recover its place in the Divizia Națională.

'The time after the war was a very criminal time,' explains Khodykin. 'There were a lot of youth with no work and little to do. It was important Tighina existed to ease Bendery's social problems.'

The President's promises have been followed up. In spring 2017, work began with architects and technology sourced from across Europe to create a state-of-the-art facility for young athletes, as well as for the senior football club. The structures were designed and built by specialists from Germany and Belarus, whilst the pitch was laid by technicians from FC Chernomorets in the Ukrainian city of Odessa. The city of Bendery has been rejuvenated as a result.

'Bendery has a great football tradition from Soviet times,' says Khodykin. 'They used to call this stadium the graveyard under Shevchuk. Look at it now.'

* * *

It's only around 15km from Bendery to Transnistria's capital Tiraspol. My fixer Andriy uses the drive to indoctrinate me about his theories on the meaning of life in this paranoid pseudo-republic.

'Ask not what Transnistria can do for you, ask what you can do for Transnistria,' he preaches. This is the first in a volume of Andriy's philosophical epigrams that are deserving of an explanation that never arrives.

'Do you know who said that?' he asks. 'President Kennedy.' I nod politely, and turn my face towards the window to hide my bewilderment.

Andriy used to be a broadcaster for the state radio company in Tiraspol. The station's mission, in his words, was to transmit programmes to Western Europe that spread the message of 'what Transnistria is trying to achieve'. A few years ago, Moscow pulled funding for the project, so now he spends his days 'welcoming' the few hardy travellers that make it as far as this joyless Stalinist backwater.

'The bastards in Chişinău made this war,' he says of the 1992 conflict. 'The hubris of Moldovan politicians was responsible. They would not negotiate. For Transnistrian leaders, it was like talking to a brick. Actually, it was worse. At least the brick won't shoot at you.'

This was not a conflict driven forward by ethnic hate. At the moment the USSR collapsed, Transnistrian separatism was unique in this respect.

The sliver of land at Moldova's eastern border represented a plurality of hopes and expectations of what a post-Soviet future could be. There was no nationalistic fury, no bloodlust or constructed national past leading people into a blind fight.

Transnistrian separatism, therefore, was a question of interests.

Russian and Ukrainian speakers comprised roughly two thirds of the land east of the Dniester. And they had seen enough in the peacocking of Moldovan nationalism in the late 1980s to legitimately fear that Chișinău would seek unification with its ethnic cousin, Romania.

There were also historical grounds on which to predicate separation. Moldova's ancestor, Bessarabia, had between 1918 and 1940 been a part of the Romanian kingdom. The Nazi-Soviet Pact of 1939, signed in secret between the emissaries of Hitler and Stalin, uncoupled Bessarabia from Romania and handed it to the USSR. The Moldavian Soviet Socialist Republic was thus created by welding newly acquired Bessarabia onto the Slavic lands of the Dniester region.

When Chișinău declared independence in 1990, it adopted the position of nullifying the 1939 pact, thus rescinding Moscow's sovereignty, yet it saw no contradiction in seceding within the borders the agreement had drawn up.

Those in the east considered those borders that wrapped Romanian Bessarabia and Slavic Transnistria together in one state to have been invalidated, and began planning for a future as a member republic of a devolved, federal Soviet Union.

In that sense, it was never truly independence that Transnistria was chasing, only independence from Moldova. Its aim then was the same as its aim now, to seek protection from and opportunities within the Russian world, of which it feels intrinsically a part, with sufficient autonomy to be able to freely react to the challenges that its own unique geopolitical circumstances pose.

* * *

From the fifth floor of the Butylka museum in the village of Tîrnauca, the surrounding countryside looks tatty and wild.

During the Second World War, there was a Soviet military base here. Now, Tîrnauca is a place of stillness and peace.

To the north-east, a view of Tiraspol interrupts the calm. From here the 12,000-seater Sheriff Stadium on the outskirts of Tiraspol looks grey and imposing, an angry concrete lump sketched in amongst the serenity and the quiet.

There are two other stadiums visible from the top of the Butylka. Dinamo Stadium, home of FC Tighina in Bendery, also shows itself, as does the ground of local club, FC Dinamo-Auto Tiraspol, just half a kilometre or so back up the road.

It is apt that so many grounds are visible from here. The Butylka's owner, the textiles magnate and pioneer of the republic's new capitalist frontier in the 1990s, Grigory Korzun, is a holy figure in the complicated gospel that is Transnistria's history.

They all talk about him, from the pen-pushing football bureaucrats in Chișinău to the indolent administrators rotting away in desk jobs in Tiraspol. To me, an outsider, his apostles share the word of his work with reverential duty.

Korzun was atypical amongst businessmen under the Soviet system, a maverick. He was one of the first entrepreneurs permitted to run a private enterprise during the last days of Communism, he acquired FC Tiligul Tiraspol from the city administration in 1991 during the late-Soviet privatisation blitz, and bankrolled the club from the wealth he had garnered in the production of textiles and sportswear.

In this act, he fell incurably, unaccountably in love with Tiligul. As an owner, he was every football manager's dream, even if at times he became a bit of an interfering nightmare. He orchestrated his team's performances from the touchline, and he once remonstrated forcefully enough with a referee that he was banished from the stadium.

During matches, he sat on the substitutes bench swigging cognac from a flask and chain-smoking cigarettes. Once, before a European game away at FC Sion in Switzerland, the home team brought a crate of wine to the Tiligul dressing room, which the players duly indulged in before kick-off. When Korzun found out, he read his team the riot act.

'Did you come here to play football, or to drink wine?' he frothed in a rage that was all too familiar to the players of Tiligul. Later, he nevertheless sat on the bench, sipping from not one, but two bottles of brandy.

As Korzun's son Stanislav explains, only his father's love of booze could rival his affection for football. Housed at the Butylka is Korzun's vast collection of liquor bottles – more than 10,000 – harvested from over a hundred countries. The players of Tiligul have brought back bottles for the collection from their footballing travels around the world and the archive ranges from the whimsically obscure to the fantastically and sexually obscene.

Such was the barmy dialectic between his twin passions that when money was tight, as it often was in post-Communist Tiraspol, Korzun would pay his players in cognac or sugar, sometimes even US dollars and German deutschmarks. Former Tiligul midfielder Igor Oprea, who played for the club during the transition from the Soviet system to the Moldovan, said in a 2017 interview with the website MoldFootball: 'Korzun told us, "Today salaries are deutschmarks, but paid at the dollar rate." He was cunning like that.'

Tiligul were one of the biggest losers when the USSR collapsed. In 1991, they finished the season in second place in the Soviet second tier, which would have been enough to secure a coveted first-ever promotion to the Top League. But it was a prize that could not be claimed.

Within weeks of the end of the season, the union had been

dissolved and the clubs were repatriated to the newly formed republican leagues. They say that in Tiraspol, the people grieved harder over Tiligul missing out on promotion than they did for the collapse of Communism.

'The Soviet Top League was one of the best in Europe in 1991,' said Oprea in that 2017 interview. 'There was a real football boom in Tiraspol then. It was a huge summer for us. Tiligul were loved by the people.'

I'm being guided around the Butylka's bizarre collection by Stanislav and my friend from the Tiraspol American Centre, Olga. Olga is a dry-witted girl with tempting striking eyes and a snappish sharp tongue who speaks in charming colloquial English with the ready command of a native speaker. On the drive to Tîrnauca, we had talked about the Butylka's ludicrous Guinness recognition as the tallest bottle-shaped building in the world. 'Ridiculous,' she admonishes in her Americanised Russian accent as we step down from the cab at the gates of the complex. 'It doesn't look a thing like a bottle.' I disguise my laughter by raising my notebook to my face.

This probably isn't something that Stanislav wants to hear. Though wealthy by Transnistria's standards, the Korzun estate has been suffering hard times of late. 'The hotel here was repossessed by the bank and sold off years ago,' states Stanislav candidly. His father may have built an empire, but Tiligul was the labour of love that virtually pulled it to the ground.

And yet, he has left an indelible legacy here. In the highly sensitive aftermath of the war, it was Korzun that successfully lobbied the nascent state authorities in Tiraspol to forgo the founding of a Transnistrian football league and to join instead with Moldova. It's a collaboration that remains today.

'His legacy was that he brought Moldova and Transnistria together in football,' Stanislav proudly remarks. 'He persuaded our leaders to cooperate with Moldova at a time when things were very politically delicate. Without him, football would not have survived in Transnistria.'

The irony is that, without Korzun's union, there would almost certainly have been no FC Sheriff Tiraspol; the financial and footballing giant that emerged in 1997 that ended up destroying Tiligul.

'He knew there was no point in trying to compete with Sheriff's riches,' says Stanislav. 'That's why he eventually sold the club.'

But there is also a story that says Tiligul were just one more club that could no longer be supported by a football economy that simply doesn't work. Tiligul's eventual collapse in 2009 was the thirty-sixth time since independence that a team resigned from the Moldovan league citing financial troubles.

Moldovan football is broke. Clubs cannot survive – less still compete – without substantial private backing from third parties. Yet during the 1990s, Korzun's investments were generous enough to ensure Tiligul remained in the country's top two; they finished second in six of the first seven Divizia Națională seasons.

The side enjoyed a thrilling rivalry with Moldova's leading club, FC Zimbru of Chişinău, who were themselves propped up by a Moldovan oil magnate, Nicolae Ciornîi, whose money had come from the Russian energy giant LUKOIL, a company that had struck a deal in the early 1990s with the Chişinău government that allowed them to enter the Moldovan market in exchange for massive investment in sports infrastructure.

Only the Transnistrian war prevented Tiligul from beating Zimbru to a league and cup double in the first Moldovan season in 1992. Days before the end of the season, the football authorities in Chişinău decreed that it was no longer safe for clubs to travel to and from Tiraspol, and Tiligul's final two fixtures were cancelled. This meant that there was a stalemate at the top of the table, and the

Moldovan Football Federation announced a play-off in the city of Bălți to decide the champions.

Embittered by the federation's handing of events, Korzun simply refused to let his team participate. 'I don't remember all the secrets,' said Oprea in 2017. 'But we felt insulted by the federation's decision.' A technical victory was awarded, and the maiden title went to Zimbru. Tiligul have never been able to wrest the title from Chișinău.

Oprea recalls, '1992 was a tragic year in Moldova. But despite the fighting, everywhere in the country that Tiligul went, we were received well. There was no bias against us. It was a golden time in Tiraspol for football.'

In early 1993, political leaders from Tiraspol and Chișinău began the dirty work of figuring out how the two republics could live together in a state of frozen conflict. The obstinacy demonstrated on the battlefield was brought to the negotiating table. Moldova proposed a loose federation with autonomous powers for Transnistria, declaring a vision for 'one people, two states'. The separatists, predictably, declared that they would settle for nothing less than full independence, rendering the talks doomed before they had begun.

Meanwhile, football in Transnistria had also gone international for the first time. In 1994, Tiligul entered the UEFA Cup Winners' Cup in the preliminary rounds, facing off against AC Omonia from Cyprus, though their giddiness got the better of them – for the away leg in Nicosia the team were forced to wear their opponent's colours, having failed to pack the correct kit for the trip. 'Still, it was a wonder playing in Europe,' said Oprea. 'It was a new experience for Moldovans. It was so exciting.'

The Divizia Națională became Moldova v. Transnistria – the derby across the Dniester. In 1993 and 1994, Zimbru and Tiligul were separated at the top by three points; in 1995, by just one. Zimbru fans would sing, 'We have one rival – Tiligul. We beat them, we win the league' (admittedly this is not as catchy and loses some of its impact in translation).

This was around the time that Zimbru were acquired by the oil magnate Ciornîi. Ironically, Ciornîi was funding his team using money from a Russian energy firm, LUKOIL, whilst Korzun's own fortune had been acquired by trading in Moldova. In football though, they supported opposite sides. The two giants from Chişinău and Tiraspol would even donate kits to other teams in the league, since they were the only two clubs in the country that had any money.

Tiligul's riches were a stark contrast to life for the ordinary people of Tiraspol. As the 1990s rolled on, inflation turned the republic's currency to shrapnel, bread prices soared, and wages nose-dived until they hit rock bottom. The exhilaration following independence had, by 1994, given way to the slow drudge of reality and the realisation that this was not so much independence as dependence on Mother Russia. Moscow provided free gas and fuel for citizens of Transnistria, as well as paying up pension pots in full.

Internal hardships fused with central propaganda to foment a siege mentality, which preached that the demonising influence of Moldova and the West, rather than the republic's own economic backwardness, had turned daily life into a relentless struggle. Slowly, Transnistria hardened into an 'idea', pursued for its ideological purity rather than its expediency as a route to prosperity, a mandate in which it was patently failing.

A cultish belief in the ordained destiny of Sovietism kept the people of Tiraspol going, rigorously fetishising a past that had manifestly disappeared, but of which there was enough of the rusty, broken remains left behind to feel real and palpable.

Korzun kept his players living like kings beneath the fluttering icon of the hammer and sickle. Consequently, the oneness of the struggle between the city and its football team was diminished. Manager Efim Shkolnikov, who led the team into their first European campaign in 1994, claimed to have earned more during his six-month spell managing Tiligul than he had in the previous ten years combined working for teams in Ukraine. On arriving in Tiraspol, he was dumbstruck by the standard of facilities with which the team operated.

Vladimir Kosse was another Moldovan international brought to Tiligul by Korzun. He arrived from Yaroslavl in Russia in 1992 at a time when public life in Transnistria was beset by lawlessness, mismanagement and poverty. Yet the owner's maniacal charisma – and deep pockets – drew him to Tiraspol.

'That was the time when Moldovan football came into contact with great European football [for the first time],' said Kosse in 2017. 'Tiligul, though it represented Transnistria, also represented Moldova. And that was very inspiring.'

Yet that very same month, whilst Kosse and his teammates were fantasising about the prospect of bridging the Dniester through football, President Yeltsin agreed a deal with Chişinău for the withdrawal of Russia's 15,000 troops stationed in Transnistria; a killer move in an attempt to assert Chişinău's sovereignty and loosen Tiraspol's footing.

It was a time of contractions. In Moldova's first-ever competitive game, a 3–2 win against Wales in October 1994, Tiligul Tiraspol players scored all three goals at the Republican Stadium in Chişinău. The same ground even hosted Tiligul's European debut match against Omonia, though few local fans turned out to watch. Football may have found common ground where the negotiators had found none, but it is hard to avoid the conclusion that the union with Moldova was a strategic arrangement for Tiligul.

Alexander Verevkin was at Tiligul for the good times, first as a player and latterly as one of Korzun's coaches. He's one of the few members of that side still slogging it out here on Transnistrian soil. He doesn't share the rose-tinted nostalgia of his old comrades.

'After the Soviet Union collapsed, the level of football here decreased,' Verevkin tells me. The interview with Verevkin was one of the strangest I have ever done. It took place in my fixer Andriy's car with me in the passenger seat and Verevkin immediately behind. Andriy was unwilling to step out into the rain storm that was pounding Tiraspol that morning, and so translated from the driver's seat. Every few minutes, Verevkin would break off from what he was saying to remark about the *'ochen Anglii pagoda'* ('very English weather'), as though the country exported it to the rest of the world. 'It was a much lower quality than before. The conflict added to that decline, because a lot of people left Tiraspol. Many young people and footballers left for Ukraine and Russia.'

By the second half of the 1990s, it had become clear that a state of relative security had settled on Transnistria. The ceasefire with Moldova had held, and though the people lived with the twin miseries of hyperinflation and an autocratic political regime, a clear sense of Transnistrian statehood had started to develop.

In late 1997, a wave of posters began appearing around Tiraspol bearing the slogans of the self-styled 'Defenders of Transnistria'. They called on President Igor Smirnov to 'defend the independence of the Transnistrian republic against becoming a province of Romania, against losing our language and becoming ashamed of our nationality ... and against repaying the West for the Republic of Moldova's many billions in loans.' Finally, they called on the President to 'remain faithful to the oath of allegiance to the people of Transnistria'.

That the republic survived at all is surprising. It relied financially and militarily on a protector state from which it was geographically isolated. It suffered under intense economic strain, internal political corruption and external pressure from neighbours to rejoin Moldova.

Yet regardless of perceptions in Moldova and the West – and of allegations that Transnistria's economic viability was wholly dependent on the fact that it sat outside of the system of international law and could therefore sell cheap weapons to grubby African dictators – Tiraspol choreographed the formation, not only of a functioning state, but of a society with an observable national consciousness.

By the end of the 1990s, that consciousness was no longer linked to Tiligul's pursuit of Zimbru. Korzun was finding it harder to keep up with the investments being made in Chişinău by Ciornîi and LUKOIL. In a final roll of the dice, he took out a massive bank loan in order to erect a new stadium in Tîrnauca.

But it was an investment in a future that never arrived. The arrival in the Divizia Naţională of a new rival, FC Sheriff Tiraspol, in 1998 backed by the infinitely wealthy Sheriff LLC corporation, spelled the end.

'Grigory Korzun understood that it no longer made sense to try and compete with FC Sheriff,' explains Verevkin. 'He saw how big their stadium was, he knew that it was better then to sell the club.' A local businessman, Peter Reich, took the team on, but was unable to stop them tumbling down the league and eventually out of the top flight.

It all ended with a whimper. The club's final throw of the dice came when it posted an advertisement on a Moldovan football blog site pleading for investors to save the club.

The 200-word ad boasted that the club's stadium had gas, electricity and a kitchen. Unsurprisingly, nobody came forward.

In 2009, the team was denied a licence to compete professionally, and transferred its material assets to FC Olimpi from the city of Bălţi.

* * *

It isn't hard to see why Korzun thought his baby deserved something more special than its tired and shabby old ground. The Republican Stadium in Tiraspol is a dust bowl, all blotchy stone and cheap concrete, and radiates all the old-world charm of a council-run leisure centre.

It's tucked away, out of sight, off the grid. 'Nothing to see here', it proclaims, or rather mumbles under its breath away in its corner. It recalls the days when football under Communism was a kickabout between teams representing the city's factories.

Nearby is some of this colourless city's only greenery. Victory Park is just large enough that from its centre one can almost block out the sight of the mechanical greyness that characterises Tiraspol's streets.

Of course, there is the obligatory Eastern European abandoned Ferris wheel watching vacantly over the patchy grass, the like of which seems to have been erected without rhyme or reason in every city park east of old Berlin. It gives the place a Pripyat-esque atmosphere of having been evacuated after a nuclear crisis.

On a synthetic pitch next to the main stadium, players kick seven shades out of each other in a chaotic five-a-side rough and tumble. This, says my fixer Andriy, is the closest Transnistria gets to a regular football league, though it looks like the players are bigger fans of kickboxing than they are of football.

I've been in Tiraspol for four days, long enough to have learned its rule of thumb; anything that is owned, run or maintained by the city authorities will, without fail, be broken. Not unusable, necessarily. Just bits missing, or parts bolted on wrong. The building where I collected my press licence looked like it had been looted from the inside out and stripped in readiness for demolition. I have also learned to time my daily shower with the lunchtime window when the hotel has hot water.

We're here at the Republican Stadium to meet with Pavel Prokudin, president of the Transnistrian Football Federation.

Prokudin is a safe pair of hands. In the world of Western capitalism, he could be a steady middle-management type, all suit and trousers, a disciple of the clunk-clunk of the chain of command. In this universe, he is an archetype of the post-Soviet bureaucrat, young enough to have avoided inheriting the nakedly self-serving habits of the Communist management world but old enough to have inherited a passive respect for its compliant dreariness.

Between 2015 and 2016, he was a dutiful Prime Minister to Transnistria's reform-minded President, Yevgeny Shevchuk. Once he was swept out of office, he scooped the consolation prize of head of football.

He greets me with a white-toothed smile and a smart pair of pressed lapels, one of which sports a glistening brooch bearing the Transnistrian green and red flag. The golden hammer and sickle catching the sun on the corner of the badge remind me of the significance of the past in this part of the world.

This famous motif of the USSR proudly adorns billboards and buildings all around Tiraspol. A huge statue of Lenin watches over the city from his plinth outside the parliamentary building. Battered old Ladas rumble along the potholed roads. Tiraspol is a colour board of grey, grey and more grey, punctuated only by the red and green Transnistrian flags that flutter from almost every building, invariably accompanied by the tricolour of Vladimir Putin's Russia.

'We may be on a capitalist path nowadays,' Prokudin begins. 'But we still feel very respectful for the Soviet times.' We take a moment to exchange observations about the implausibility of Tiraspol's bloodless austerity. 'That's why you see what you see in the streets. We respect our history. We respect our Russian heritage.'

I find it hard to believe that Prokudin thinks the situation in Tiraspol is normal. Outside, the streets are deserted, made empty by a mass human exodus. Those that remained loiter without intent, because Tiraspol cannot sustain them in a fulfilled existence. Life here is not life, rather it is the checking-off of days, a recitation performed in sham synchronicity with a Soviet past that has gone and isn't coming back.

'In Transnistria, it's difficult to develop football because we are not recognised and we don't have money,' argues Prokudin, framing football's place in this broken machine. 'The authorities have to look at the welfare of the people first. Then maybe third or fourth priority is football.'

There is no Transnistrian national team for people here to support during the never-ending winters, no football league to look forward to on a Saturday and pick apart at work on Monday mornings. Fans can watch FC Sheriff Tiraspol play in the Moldovan league, but the team have won almost every Divizia Națională title for the last twenty years, and those spectators that still bother to turn up seem bored rigid by the routine. Still, Prokudin is undeterred. He talks about making Transnistria a 'football republic'.

'Do you know what the budget of Manchester United is?' he asks. I say I think it's around half a billion pounds. He laughs. 'Our budget for the entire Transnistrian state in a year is around $330 million. Amongst that, we have to find the money for stadiums and infrastructure and football development.'

But Prokudin intends to get to work. There are hopeful plans detailing ambitious figures for the number of people the federation wants to get playing the game; part of a strategic task to spread a love of football to 20,000 people in Transnistria.

'There are about 500,000 people here, so our aim is to get 5 per cent of them actively involved. Professional football accounts for about 2 per cent of the players in Transnistria. The rest is amateur. All we're trying to do is to help people to fall in love with football.'

Yet the spectre of isolation stalks this proto-republic. Politically, its leaders have spent years on and off sanctions lists drawn up by the international community. It enjoys diplomatic relationships with no one. In football, there is no recognition from UEFA or from FIFA. When it comes to cosying up with Transnistria, no one outside of these borders wants to know.

Rather than make football the martyr for a futile campaign for recognition, the leaders of Transnistria have chosen another path. 'UEFA doesn't recognise us, so we will form a union with Moldova instead,' declares Prokudin. 'We talk in one football language. Football is not politics.' He tells me that it was the president of the Moldovan Football Federation, Pavel Cebanu, who said football unites the two banks of the Dniester. In turn, I remind him of the situations in Nagorno-Karabakh, Abkhazia and South Ossetia, where football is used to declare identity in the language of fierce nationalist contests. Why is Transnistria different?

'The 1992 conflict wasn't ordinary people against other ordinary people. This was a war made by politicians. The conflict wasn't supported by the people of Moldova. The legacy of that is that we're able to have good relationship in terms of our cultures. My mother is Moldovan. My father is Ukrainian. We don't have conflict at the ordinary level. Let me say again, politicians made this war.'

At this moment, the sunlight streaming through the window catches off the red and green Transnistrian flag pinned to Prokudin's suit jacket, crystallising his contradiction. He was, after all, a political representative of the partition that this war created, and he is a direct beneficiary of the divisions it helps to sustain. 'But let's get back to the football,' he urges, batting off my enquiry with a furtiveness to which I am becoming used.

Since 2014, there have been annual matches organised for war veteran charities between representative sides from Chişinău and Tiraspol, hosted here in the Transnistrian capital. An amateur team representing Transnistria will compete in a national competition in Moldova for the right to enter the UEFA Regions' Cup, for non-professional players. Ex-Tiligul player Alexander Verevkin will coach the team. Everyone I speak to here, Verevkin included, talks about Prokudin as being the man who has put President Vadim Krasnoselsky's plan to revive football in the republic into action. 'Krasnoselsky participates actively in football,' states Verevkin. 'He takes Transnistrian sport seriously. He wants to create infrastructure, and Prokudin is making it happen.'

Which is fine, as far as it goes. It's just that, this all feels too much like I'm waiting for the reveal. Transnistria's political leaders have played dirty to keep Moldova's guardsmen far from Tiraspol's door. The republic stands accused internationally of terrible crimes, of directing a global weapons trade that supplies terror cells and arms foul despots, all with the end game of clinging on to sovereignty by a couple of dirty fingernails. Why go to these lengths? Why construct a distrusted, feral state only to then buddy up with the enemy at large on the football pitch, a place where the passions of the nation are most easily aroused? Why eschew that great signifier of a proudly independent people – the national football team – in favour of being wilfully swallowed up by Moldovan football, which has its own culture, traditions and identity?

Transnistrian football's loyalty to Chişinău has been tested to its limit, and passed. In April 2003, when Moldova's own Republican Stadium had all but fallen down through neglect, the Moldovan national anthem played in Transnistria, and the Moldovan tricolour flew from the roof of Tiraspol's Sheriff Stadium, as the national team from over the river travelled across the border to play a European Championship qualifier. They lost narrowly to the Netherlands, but the house was packed, and there was no trouble in the stands or on the streets. When clubs from Tiraspol play in UEFA's European competitions, they can only do so as Moldovan teams. Transnistria's most successful club, FC Sheriff, have competed in Europe against heavyweight sides from England, Russia, Ukraine and the Netherlands, yet in the foreign coverage they receive, Transnistria never gets a mention. UEFA doesn't recognise the republic's existence.

'You ask about sadness that we aren't represented,' begins Prokudin. 'We don't feel it that way. When our sports people win internationally, we still feel proud. The same goes for when Sheriff Tiraspol play in the European competitions. We have this unresolved conflict, but no one has died for nearly thirty years. Whereas, look at Ukraine. A recognised state, but look at how unsafe it is in Donetsk and Luhansk. So which is better? To be recognised or to be safe?'

The leaders of Transnistrian football are drawn from a small pool, and think with one mind. Prokudin, for instance, went to school with Grigory Korzun, and speaks fondly of his friend's work with Tiligul Tiraspol and their 1991 promotion to the Soviet Top League.

'For some people, they were terribly sad that Tiligul would not get the chance to play against Spartak Moscow and Dynamo Kyiv. They were more upset about the collapse of the Soviet football league than about the collapse of the USSR itself.'

So, which was the more damaging for football? The collapse of the Soviet Union, or the political partition from Moldova?

'The collapse of the union,' he says without the slightest hesitation. 'Because the conflict was a result of the end of the USSR.

This was the thing that caused all of our problems, and especially in football.'

'We had three options after the USSR collapsed,' explains Prokudin's colleague, Sergei Ursul, who has slipped in to join our discussion. 'The first was to join the Russian league. The second was to form an independent league. And the third was to join with Moldova. And we chose the latter, because the ball unites the right and left bank.'

And yet the republic itself leans towards Russia, as it did in 1992 when this decision was first made. Was there never any pressure to unite in football as in political life?

'I think in the 1990s there were some discussions. But that's forgotten. The relationship works very well now. The first step in uniting the two banks was taken by Pavel Cebanu in Chişinău. He offered the hand. It works well because it means our clubs get to play in the Champions League and the Europa League.'

III

On Karl Leibknecht Street, the main road through Tiraspol, a palace rises up from amongst the empty fields and craggy dirt tracks.

A little along from the obligatory 'Welcome to Tiraspol' road sign, the resplendent home of FC Sheriff Tiraspol appears, glistening against the overcast sky.

FC Sheriff are the kings of Moldovan football. But they rule over a poverty-stricken land. Since their founding in 1997 and promotion to the Divizia Naţională the following year, they have won seventeen out of twenty-one league championships.

Their stadium, with its surrounding training and hotel complex, was completed in 2002 at a cost of around $200 million and is so large it could form its own sub-district of Tiraspol. For context, only one other team in Moldovan football owns its own stadium.

The club have shot to the zenith of Moldovan football like a bullet. The Divizia Națională is a colourless sham, though that is only partially the fault of Sheriff. A stale state of ambivalent half-interest amongst fans prevails here.

When I visited Sheriff Stadium in April 2019 to watch the hosts play FC Milsami from the city of Orhei, the place was barely a quarter full. Those that had turned up gave the impression of having done so simply to pass the time, and watched the game silently and glassy-eyed. There is nothing else to do in Tiraspol on a Sunday evening.

Arriving at the ground shortly after kick-off, I was greeted by a gaggle of military men (or maybe just police – it's impossible to tell the difference in this part of the world) who, realising that I spoke little Russian, waved me on my way to the gates. There, another gang of khaki-clad officials were waiting ready to perform a full body search before I was allowed in. There is no entry charge to watch the champions play.

The Milsami fans were outnumbered by a small platoon of Soviet-looking soldiers congregated in one corner, who appeared not to be doing any actual policing but rather enjoying the game and taking turns to take group photographs.

However, the forty or so visiting fans who made the journey to Transnistria made more noise than the rest of the stadium combined, especially so when the final whistle sounded to signal a surprise 1–0 win for Milsami. It wasn't enough to knock Sheriff off top spot in the league, nor is it likely to prevent them winning another championship this campaign.

Back in the late 1990s, it was anticipated that the arrival of Sheriff would open up a new era of competition. FC Zimbru from Chişinău dominated the first decade of the league with eight title wins in the first nine seasons after independence. The gap between them and the usual runners-up, FC Tiligul, had started to grow.

Sheriff challenged the status quo. In the spring of 2000, the upstart team led the table by two points with three games to play, before collapsing during an away game against Olimpia Bălţi and handing the title to Zimbru. The following season, it was the team from Chişinău's turn to suffer the agony of blowing the championship, losing against the new pretenders on the home straight to miss out by a single point.

Rather than signal a new age of lively competition, Sheriff began to dominate. In 2001/02, the gap between Sheriff and third-place Zimbru had grown to twenty-one points. Between 2005 and 2008, the team lost just two of the ninety-four league games they played. Moldovan football had, like a ninepin, fallen to the oligarch class.

At the same time, the club's transfer policy diversified. Players were signed from a dozen different countries, introducing the Divizia Naţională to exotic faces from all over the world. Supporters started to fill the team's 12,000-seater arena, a grand palace that mocked Moldovan football through its scale and comfort. In Europe too, the team made rapid progress, in 2009, 2010 and 2013 the side came within a single game of qualifying for the lucrative group stages of the UEFA Champions League, the dream ticket for any emerging European football club.

The scope of the team's monopoly transcends usual football arrangements. Sheriff – which is the second-largest company of Transnistria, and is behind FC Sheriff Tiraspol – used to own fellow Divizia Naţională side FC Tiraspol, until UEFA stepped in to put a stop to dual ownership of clubs in the same competition.

'There could be no "farm teams", UEFA said,' I'm told by Petr Lulenov, a board member of the Football Federation of Transnistria and ex-general secretary of the other professional club in the city, FC Dinamo-Auto Tiraspol. We meet with him in his office at the high school where he works as the principal and which, by coincidence, is the same school that Andriy attended as a teenager.

'So Interdnestrcom, the branch of Sheriff LLC that owned FC Tiraspol, were told they could no longer own the club.' The given reason for FC Tiraspol's erasure was a lack of financing. This appears to be at variance with what the team's former general manager Sergei Ursul had told me when I met him in the office of Pavel Prokudin in the Transnistrian Football Federation.

Lulenov claims this is smoke and mirrors: 'The club was made to correspond with correct moral concepts. The psychology of people is different in Transnistria. Sometimes, the owner wishes that only one team is the champion, all the time. So they try to influence. But if you weaken the opposition in the league, how can you expect to do well in the European competitions?'

Lulenov is a tall, gentle man with kind eyes and a bald head, and for the first hour of our meeting he talks in meandering and exhaustive detail about his career in mini football, a game that was taken seriously here in Soviet times.

He and fixer Andriy talk at length amongst themselves between translations, and frustratingly little of it seems to make its way back to me. In fact, Andriy seems to be smitten with Lulenov, hanging on his words like an expectant grandchild.

'The problem of Sheriff is that the foreigners who come into the team are not patriots,' says Lulenov, during a momentary pause from bonding with his new protégé. 'There is a certain arrogance of the foreign players. They think they are more professional. But the players of say, Milsami, as you saw, are more motivated. They try harder against the foreigners. The problem of Sheriff is that it is a business plan. But football is more than money. Money is good, but football philosophy must be more than just this. For the guys who finance Sheriff, they see it as just the next business project.'

The club was founded by two former KGB officers who got rich off the privatisation gold rush that accompanied the end of the Soviet Union. In 1993, Viktor Gushan and Ilya Kazmaly set up a holding company, Sheriff LLC, a glorified smuggling operation established as a charity seemingly to assist the families of police veterans. Kazmaly ceased to be listed as a director of the company in 2012, but Gushan, who was once a senior security officer in the criminal investigations department, remains the man ultimately calling the shots at both the corporation and the football club.

Back in the early 1990s, Sheriff LLC was rumoured to have links with the black market for cigarettes, alcohol and sundry goods coming into the country across its porous borders from Ukraine. Contraband channels that had hitherto been peddled by small-time importers were industrialised to create a highly mechanised and devastatingly efficient commercial network,. This was the Wild West of oligarchic empire building.

Today, the corporation dominates every corner of public life, from banking and telecoms to the media and the republic's Parliament. Sheriff supermarkets, bearing the company's unmistakable five-point star, seem to sit on every street corner. They even bought the city's cherished cognac-producing KVINT distillery.

In 1996, three years after the company's founding, the Tiraspol government granted favourable conditions to Gushan that virtually excused him from paying any excise on what Sheriff brought over the border to sell. With competition vanquished and monopoly assured, he did what any self-respecting post-Soviet oligarch does with his riches. FC Sheriff Tiraspol was born.

'The club is run at a loss,' believes Lulenov. 'They created this structure in order to make money. The plan was to build infrastructure.'

The theory was sound enough. The all-weather pitches of the Sheriff Sports Complex were supposed to be money spinners in a country like Moldova where the winters bite long and deep. There were plans for the superpower teams from Russia and Ukraine – Spartak Moscow, Dynamo Kyiv and the rest – to use Sheriff's world-class facilities, and for legendary rivalries to develop across the borders between Tiraspol and the great footballing cities of the former Soviet world. 'Some teams did come,' states Lulenov. 'In the early days.'

The club pursued a policy of signing promising young players from Africa and South America, with the hope of moving them on to wealthier rivals in Russia, Ukraine and beyond. Other clubs in Eastern Europe have become successful stepping stones between far-off leagues and the promised land of European football. Ukraine's Shakhtar Donetsk have made millions from selling South American talent to teams in England, Spain and Italy. Making his name at CSKA Moscow, Nigerian international Chidi Odiah is a Sheriff graduate, as are former Wolves and FC Rostov defender Isaac Okoronkwo, Stanislav Ivanov who played for FC Moscow and Lokomotiv Moscow and Austrian side Sturm Graz's David Mujiri. Sheriff's current squad boasts nineteen overseas players, compared to just five from Moldova (the world governing body, FIFA, doesn't recognise Transnistrian citizenship). Amongst that number are players from as far afield as Brazil, Liberia, Cameroon, Colombia and Switzerland. Yet despite their initial success, the club now finds it almost impossible to attract buyers for their foreign imports.

The grand intentions of the management to create rivalries with clubs across the Russian-speaking world, and to produce a factory of international talent providing Eastern European football with future world stars, have long since faltered, leaving behind a bloated monument to a washed-out ambition.

The club has been left scrambling to squeeze every cent out of its assets. In April 2019, the team's star winger, Belgium youth international Ziguy Badibanga, walked out after a standoff with club management. 'Badibanga was a really good player for Sheriff,' describes Lulenov. 'But he refused to sign a contract extension, which meant that Sheriff wouldn't be entitled to a transfer fee for him when he was sold. So, they banished him to the reserve team, to try and put pressure on him to sign.'

But Badibanga called the club's bluff, ran down his contract and left as a free agent. When he signed for a new team in Kazakhstan, Sheriff received nothing. 'Now, there is no successful business model in buying players from abroad and selling at a profit,' says Lulenov. 'They're lucky if they can sell for the same money they paid.'

Today, the club are further than ever from their goal of reaching the Champions League. In the summer of 2019, despite winning both the domestic league and cup, they were knocked out in European qualifying by Georgian minnows Saburtalo Tbilisi, dismantled 3–0 at their expensive home ground in front of a few thousand largely silent supporters.

A paranoid secrecy surrounds Sheriff. When my colleague James Montague reported on the team for the *New York Times* in 2012, he was told in no uncertain terms that nobody from the club would be made available for interview. '[Sheriff's] officials treat basic details of the club's operations – even the recent successes that have brought it to the verge of joining Europe's soccer elite – like classified material,' he wrote for the publication.

My own correspondence with the club had been promising, until I moved from the subject of matchday accreditation towards meeting somebody from the senior management, after which the replies to my emails abruptly stopped.

The team's press attaché sidestepped any attempt to make contact with me by phone or via my network of contacts in Chişinău and Tiraspol, and he is still the only press officer I have encountered anywhere in the world whose job is to keep reporters from finding out about the club.

Unfortunately for the Sheriff gatekeepers, there is always someone with access ready to pull back the curtain and tell the un-curated version of the story. For me, that person was Octavian Țîcu, a historian and former sports minister in the Moldovan government.

'Because of the historical trade relationship between Chişinău and Odessa [a port city on Ukraine's Black Sea coast], Sheriff have been able to accumulate huge resources of contraband,' Țîcu tells me over lunch, reminding me about the importance of Tiraspol's geographic location, bang in the middle of the route from the Moldovan capital to the Black Sea. Țîcu is one of the more remarkable characters I crossed paths with. A five-time Moldovan national boxing champion in his younger days, Țîcu is now a highly regarded academic, holding posts at Moldova's Institute of History and the Moldova State University. He is one of those frustratingly brilliant people that excels at everything they turn their hand to, and his insights into the workings of the Transnistrian state are delivered with a surly authority.

'Weapons, cigarettes, meat. They take it from Odessa, and they export it to Moldova, and to Russia. Sheriff have made an economic empire this way. They have made a monopoly of provisions,' explains Țîcu. Odessa – a stopping-off point for produce travelling across Eurasia – is around 81km from the Transnistrian border, an ocean gateway to a world of often illicit riches.

Rosian Vasiloi is ex-deputy head of the Moldovan Border Police

Department. In a 2019 interview with the European Observatory on Illicit Trade (Eurobsit), he said, 'Smuggling through Transnistria remains an enormous problem, allowing the separatist leaders to enrich themselves off the proceeds. That regime remains in total control of all illegal activities in the region.' Eurobsit reports that customs officials at the Transnistrian border can earn up to $100,000 per month by accepting payments to allow certain businesses to bring in their goods. Sheriff's was a new kind of wild capitalism, built on post-Soviet lack of proper government control.

There are, however, changes underway in this corner of Eastern Europe. Entrenched processes and systems that have held fast for decades are beginning to loosen.

The 2014 civil war in Ukraine and the subsequent partition of the country near its eastern border with Russia prompted a re-evaluation of border policy in the region, and of the ease with which criminal enterprises operate here. This has inspired a new motivation to tame the wild frontiers that facilitate separatist causes.

'In Transnistria, they have no rules,' states Țîcu. 'But they need the complicity of Ukrainian factors. Some local factors, but also central powers. Kyiv had interest in maintaining this.'

Those interests go to the summit of power in Ukraine. The country's former President, Petro Poroshenko, owns a controlling stake in the Ukrainian company Roshen, which, according to customs records obtained by the NGO Rise Moldova, exported $3 million of food products to Transnistria via Sheriff LLC between 2014 and 2017 (Poroshenko relinquished his control over Roshen during his time as President of Ukraine). The company publicly denies doing business with companies in Transnistria. Yulia Marushevskaya, head of the Odessa regional customs division, said in 2016, '[The situation] is suitable for contrabandists, and for high-ranking officials in Chişinău and Kyiv. This is a matter of political will, both for the Ukrainian authorities and for the Moldovan authorities.'

'Since 2016, the situation has become more complicated,' explains Ţîcu. 'Because of their own civil war, the position of Ukraine is different. Moldova too has taken a different approach to Transnistria. The golden age of Sheriff is over as a result.'

Anatolii Dirun is professor of political science at Tiraspol Interregional University. He has observed a tightening of Kyiv's resolve to secure its borders. 'Crossing the border between Transnistria and Ukraine has become more controlled,' he tells me.

'For example, after 2014, Ukraine stopped Russian men aged eighteen to fifty-five from entering Ukraine. So any Transnistrians with Russian citizenship were affected by this. Another change in our relationship with Kyiv has been economic. Trade negotiations have been negatively affected by the war in Ukraine because, between 2014 and 2017, nobody there was buying our products. That market was shut down. The Ukrainian market is still not as attractive as it was five years ago.'

This has had a knock-on effect for Sheriff's owner Gushan, and for the corporation and the football club, all of which rely on the easy movement of goods between Tiraspol and Ukraine.

In 2017, the first checkpoint to be jointly administered by both Kyiv and Chişinău was installed along the sprawling 450km border between Ukraine and Transnistria near to the villages of Pervomaisc and Kuchurgan, and it finally gave Moldova a say over what comes in and out of its breakaway neighbour. Monitors estimate that 70 per cent of illegal trade between Tiraspol and Odessa was crossing the border at this point and Sheriff LLC controls this market.

'Don't confuse the football team with the corporation,' says Lulenov. 'They are not the same. But everything is connected. Football and economic trade move in parallel, and in the same direction. A bad result for one can mean bad results for the other. But if you do one thing well, you should do everything well.'

The ethics underpinning the creation of Eastern Europe's oligarch class – broadly attributable to the removal of price controls on state-owned assets which allowed a tiny few to grow incalculably rich, whilst the populace starved in their freezing homes – have long weighed heavy on the hearts of football fans on both sides of the former Iron Curtain.

Life was cheap during the first decade following the fall of Communism. Whether any of the major names who have funded football in Moldova and Transnistria since independence would pass the strictest ethical tests over the way they acquired and disposed of their millions, is a problem without a solution – nobody is asking these questions in this part of the world.

Russia's oligarchs, the co-signees of the so-called Davos Pact, who had bankrolled President Boris Yeltsin's re-election campaign in 1996, were booted from the political scene at the turn of the century by Vladimir Putin, who promised they could keep their riches – and their freedom – provided that they ceased being involved in Kremlin business. No such deals were made in Tiraspol, where Gushan stands alone in terms of the influence his company holds over public life.

Sheriff's political arm, the Renewal Party – Обновление – has enjoyed a secure majority in Transnistria's Parliament since 2005.

The party rose to prominence under ex-Sheriff director, Yevgeny Shevchuk, who later fell out with both the party and the corporation shortly before he was elected President of the republic in 2011.

Shevchuk – who is described as being different from the classic twitching, paranoid bureaucrats of the old Communist order – continued to feud with Sheriff once in power. However, not even the President's office outranks Gushan. In 2016, isolated in Parliament,

Shevchuk was ousted, fled the republic (either by taxi cab or in a speedboat via the Dniester, depending on which reports one believes) and was slapped with an international arrest warrant, allegedly at Gushan's behest, though Shevchuk claimed later that Sheriff had ordered his assassination.

He remains on the run, and is widely believed to be living comfortably with his family in Chişinău.

Shevchuk's replacement, Vadim Krasnoselsky, is a former head of security at Sheriff, and enjoys Gushan's personal backing. After a brief hiatus, the iron grip of the oligarchy is once again tightening on Transnistria. It is small wonder that critics caustically dub the place 'the Republic of Sheriff'.

'In the European competitions, nobody will ask how you came to be in first place,' says Lulenov.

'They know only that you are the champions and you are in Europe. Sherriff's main focus is its participation in Europe. In order to do that, it needs to continue to win in Moldova every season.'

But how does Transnistria benefit from having its most successful club compete in Europe under the flag of its political enemy Moldova?

'To some degree, it's a serious question,' begins Lulenov. 'But it is also a naïve question. We here in our republic, we don't ask this question at all. On the one hand, we're trying to achieve our sovereignty as a republic. But it's naïve because, well, let me ask you a question. What else should we do for twenty-seven years that we are not recognised? We want to participate in international competitions. And this is the only window through which we as Transnistrians can participate.

'The world is very unstable. We've all seen what's happened in Ukraine. We've seen what's happening in Britain, with Brexit. I cannot give you a date when we will have our independence recognised. Our immediate priority is to find common language with our immediate neighbours – Ukraine and Moldova.'

On the drive back from the school, Andriy confirms my suspicion that he has fallen hard for Lulenov. 'I trust men like him,' he admits admiringly. 'I would like to see men like him in control here. We've had enough of oligarchs in Transnistria. We're ready for a revolution – a revolution of ideas.' As he speaks these words, one of the wheels on his beloved Range Rover smashes down into one of the craterous potholes that scar Tiraspol's crumbling roads, and his face tightens into an excruciating grimace. 'Wealth only works when it works for the people.'

IV

The weather in Chișinău is unbearable. Although it's incredibly bright and sunny, the air is freezing, which creates the confusing and deeply unsettling sensation of being both too hot and too cold at the same time.

Legend traces Moldova's origins to the fourteenth century. The Romanian prince Dragoș allegedly pursued an aurochs – the now-extinct European bison – across the Carpathian Mountains. He chased the animal to the river at Baia in modern Romania, whereupon the prince's hunting dog Molda collapsed exhausted into the river and drowned. The grieving Dragoș named the river in the dog's memory, and the Principality of Moldavia eventually inherited the moniker.

The principality was pulled back and forth between the Ottoman and Russian empires for most of the next 400 years, until the modern republic's ancestor, the Governate of Bessarabia, was annexed to Romania from Russia in 1918, opening the door to the traumas and dramas that have coloured the republic and render it a fascinating, dangerous and deeply confusing nation.

Chişinău is known for its Soviet-era apartment blocks that stretch forever in every direction. In his book *The Fall of Yugoslavia*, Misha Glenny attributes the proliferation of these kinds of structures to an 'unshakable commandment in the bible of Eastern Europe's town planners', and certainly Chişinău is as scarred as any of the capital cities of the former Eastern Bloc with these grimy, Brutalist installations. There has been a desperate struggle to inject the city with colour in the years since independence, although it is clear that the battle has not yet been won. The bones of the city have been in place since the 1830s, but the dreary shade of Soviet grey has proven difficult to shift.

After arriving in Chişinău I quickly made the York, an inexplicably English-styled pub within a hop of the gorgeous Nativity Cathedral, my regular watering hole here. The barman on my first night explained how the owner had considered this to be an 'exotic theme' for a bar, a fantasy he may or may not have wished to revise after Welsh football fans smashed the place to pieces in 2017 when they came here for a World Cup qualifying match. The place is a twee mash-up of ham-fisted clichés, all Union Jacks and blotchy portraits of the Queen, in short, it is exactly how you would imagine a bar owner in Moldova would think English pubs look.

I make the point of asking what younger people here – the man serving me beer is no older than thirty – think about the Transnistria conflict. 'People don't care,' he replies plaintively. 'It's another country to us. We don't really understand what it's about.'

I'm in town this morning to meet a celebrity of Soviet Moldova.

Pavel Cebanu won hearts by becoming the country's best-ever footballer. He was born in Reni in what is now Ukraine in 1955. He played for Moldova's premier club, FC Nistru Chișinău, a provincial team within the USSR that punched well above its weight and won two promotions to the Soviet Top League in 1973 and 1982.

Nistru were the embodiment of Moldovan nationalism. The club badge bears an image of the country's national symbol, the legendary aurochs that was hounded by Prince Dragoș, known in the Romanian language as the *'zimbru'*.

In 1991, when Moldova gained its independence and the Divizia Națională was created, the club changed its name from Nistru – after the Romanian name for the country's river Dniester – to FC Zimbru, thus completing the metamorphosis into a bastion of the new Moldovan nation.

Cebanu broke into the team as a precocious seventeen-year-old, and he marshalled the side from the heart of midfield. He captained the team, and decades later etched himself into history as Moldova's greatest-ever player as voted by a national poll as part of UEFA's fiftieth anniversary celebrations in 2004.

He eschewed life as a foreigner in one of the other USSR republics and styled himself as a one-club man, sticking out his whole career at Nistru and becoming a revered figure in Moldova. A brilliant, dutiful technician blessed with the vision and touch of a gifted footballer, he obtained the nickname Zé Maria for his similarities to the great Brazilian playmaker.

Cebanu invited me to his office at the Moldovan Football Federation, only days before he resigned as the organisation's president. He is like a human experiment in testosterone therapy. His handshake almost crushes my knuckles, and throughout our meeting he sits with his legs parted at a full right angle, slightly slouched in his seat and peering over the top of imaginary spectacles. A televised re-run of last night's Premier League game between Wolves and Manchester United provides a quiet, if distracting backdrop to our meeting. I can only imagine it's been switched on for my benefit. Cebanu's office is probably the nicest room I have seen in Chișinău; bright, spacious and clean, a far cry from the state of my room at the crumbling Hotel Chișinău.

In 1997, this leering apparatchik was elected president of the MFF at a moment when young Moldova was economically on its knees. Independence in 1991 followed by the shift from a command economy to a free market had caused rapid and unsustainable inflation. This in turn brought a sharp rise in the rates of alcoholism, unemployment and poverty as the country's trade networks between the other Soviet republics – including its burgeoning wine market – collapsed.

On 2 March 1992, the United Nations formally recognised the new Moldovan republic. On the same day, Chișinău went to war with separatists near its eastern frontier for control of Transnistria; at stake were the Dniester region's arable land and the factories that accounted for roughly 40 per cent of Moldova's industrial and agricultural output, despite the fact that the area made up only around 20 per cent of the republic's territory.

The loss of Transnistria disconnected the country from its most viable path towards economic recovery. This was the abyss that preceded the formation of the new football federation.

'We had absolutely no infrastructure for football in Moldova after the USSR broke up,' explains Cebanu in a tone that sounds rehearsed. 'We were not like Russia, Ukraine, Kazakhstan and the other republics. We didn't have pitches, facilities; nothing. So that was the first challenge.'

When Moldova beat Wales 3–2 in their first competitive international in October 1994, they did so on a pitch that was virtually unplayable. The decisive element of surprise was the team's only weapon. Chişinău represented a new kind of foreign challenge for Western European footballers, the city was far-flung and mysterious, yet spartan and impoverished in a way that international footballers had not experienced before.

'Now, finally, the MFF has everything it needs to function as a normal football federation,' Cebanu boasts. 'We have headquarters, we have a national training academy where all fourteen of our age group national teams play and train, we have our indoor futsal hall, and we have beach soccer facilities.'

All this is very well and good, but what about the fact that as of April 2019 Moldova languishes ninth from bottom in the UEFA country rankings, with just a clutch of Europe's smallest countries beneath them? How about the sobering reality that since beating Wales, the team has won just eighteen competitive games in twenty-five years? Cebanu has overseen two and half decades of total stagnation, and I'm keen to know why.

'We didn't get a shred of government help to build all this,' he complains, gesturing to the wood-panelled walls and floors of the presidential office and all but ignoring the question. 'We did it all with money from FIFA and UEFA.'

It's a universal truth that is lost on the football bureaucrats of Eastern Europe that the one place where you are least likely to get an honest picture of what is going on with football in any given country is inside the plush and consistently overstaffed offices of its football federation.

Cebanu's landlocked country may have a state-of-the-art stadium for playing beach football, but the men's senior team is ranked 175 by FIFA. During the 2018 UEFA Nations League, the team were beaten 4–0 by tiny Luxembourg. They have never threatened to qualify for a major international championship, and that will not change any time soon. But the president is in no mood to deviate from the party line, and I quickly accept that our interview is spiralling into something resembling a public relations pitch for the MFF. Feeling slightly dejected, I wrap things up with Cebanu and shuffle next door to the York to process my frustration with a pint of Chișinău's insidiously strong local brew.

I get the answer to the question that Cebanu did not acknowledge early the next morning on my way out to breakfast. A copy of the Chișinău weekly newspaper, *Ziarul de Gardă*, has been discarded on the next table to where I have sat to eat my toast on the sidewalk of Ștefan cel Mare. It bears Cebanu's unmistakable smarmy glare across its front page, alongside mugshots of the federation vice-president and general secretary. The headline translates as 'Chiefs for life at the MFF – the business of football'.

My experiences in Eastern Europe tells me football administrators do not make the front pages on account of their good work.

Later today, I am due to meet with the other great monolithic figure of Moldovan football, who happens to be Cebanu's nemesis. Whatever the president is accused of in the pages of *Ziarul de Gardă*, I do not expect any pulled punches.

* * *

Ion Testemițanu speaks like a scholar, walks like a model and looks like a brick wall. Known affectionately as Ivan, he is the only Moldovan footballer to have played professionally in England – he spent three years at Bristol City between 1998 and 2001.

He was a few weeks into his career at Ashton Gate when a broken leg sustained during a game against West Brom scuppered his progress. He was never the same player again.

'They wanted me at Southampton before the injury,' he explains. 'It would have happened too. But after the injury, I never heard any more about it.'

When we meet at Café Karl Schmidt, just around the corner from Cebanu's office at the MFF, I'm quite happy for the ice breakers to last a little longer than usual owing to Testemiţanu's cultish status in England (as a West Brom supporter I offer my belated regrets for the tackle by van Blerk that scuppered his chance of a shot at the Premier League), but before we can settle in he's whipped out his copy of today's *Ziarul de Gardă* and is beginning his own personal inquest into president Cebanu's affairs.

'Football is dying in Moldova,' he snaps angrily. 'Cebanu had twenty-two years. In twenty-two years, you can grow a lot. But he only destroyed. Dying, dying, dying, every day. The championship is absolute bullshit. It's full of fixed matches. I know this because I investigated it. I was part of the federation and I was working also for the police. Cebanu never knew this. I was like an undercover policeman. They gave me protection at my house, because you never know who knows what you're doing.'

Testemiţanu used to be one of Cebanu's chieftains. He was persuaded by the president to join the MFF in 2009, and was handed a portfolio overseeing ethical practice. The plan, he believes, was ultimately to implicate Testemiţanu in the MFF's malpractices, thus discrediting him as a voice of opposition.

'My wife said, "Why? Why are you doing this?" Because I want to clean my national football. I had dreams of playing for Barcelona and playing in England. But players from Moldova, they don't have a chance. Because instead, young players are being bought off by match fixers. If you are a young player here in Moldova, you've got no chance.'

European football is changing apace. Unheralded nations like Albania, Iceland, Wales and Northern Ireland have all appeared at major international finals in recent years. Moldova, meanwhile, are going backwards, plummeting down FIFA's rankings. The team has finished bottom or second-bottom in all but one of the twelve qualifying tournaments they have entered.

Some Moldovans are angry. Most are just apathetic. Whatever enthusiasm existed when the team beat Wales in 1994 became boredom and indifference years ago.

'The money that comes from UEFA and FIFA is meant to be for developing football in Moldova,' says Testemiţanu, at which point he launches into a tirade:

'For schools, for coaches, for domestic clubs, for players. What Cebanu has done, he has built only for himself.

'In Moldova, the federation invests in only themselves. They built the Ciorescu Arena for futsal. They built Vadul lui Vodă, the national team training camp. They built the federation offices. But all of this stuff benefits only them. The training base, they only let it be used by people if they pay, a lot.

'UEFA and FIFA grants paid for all this. But the federation took a lot of that money. They say to FIFA they need €6 million for the futsal arena. But to build it, it costs only €2 million.

'Of course, there are no documents to prove this now. In 2009, when the Dniester burst its banks and flooded, the federation drove out there in the middle of the night and threw all the papers relating to the construction of Vadul lui Vodă in the river. The evidence is gone.'

Testemiţanu translates the highlights of the *Ziarul de Gardă* article for me with relish. The opening paragraph runs:

> Against the backdrop of sporting failures, those who have been at the forefront of our national sport, each with links to other prosperous businesses, have managed to build for themselves a fortune of millions through our football federation.

The case against Cebanu was strong. Officially, he received a salary of $1,000 per month and lived in a modest three-room apartment in central Chişinău, until his resignation. It was the same one that was given to him decades ago when he still played for Nistru. But *Ziarul de Gardă* claimed to have acquired a cache of documents relating to expensive property owned by him and members of his family. Much of this property is allegedly registered in the name of his partner, a former schoolteacher named Olga Latii.

According to *Ziarul de Gardă*, in 2003, one year after the construction of the €6 million Vadul lui Vodă national training academy, Latii purchased an expensive holding in a Bucharest apartment block, which changed hands repeatedly over the following two years between members of both Cebanu and Latii's immediate families. The current value of the property is listed by the Romanian land registry as being around $250,000, but the market value of the apartments is significantly higher.

Latii is also allegedly listed alongside a clutch of employees at the MFF as a partner in an assortment of private businesses. Those partners include the wife of former Moldova international and head of the MFF disciplinary committee, Marin Spinu. Spinu initially denied that either he or his wife had any business connection with Latii, before coming clean once he was confronted with publicly obtainable records that confirmed his involvement.

For Cebanu, the MFF has turned into a bit of a family affair. His son, Ilie, used to be a goalkeeper for the national team. Upon his retirement from playing at thirty-one, he was almost immediately made team manager of the national side, responsible for non-football matters. He is also listed as a director at a local company, GPI Invest, alongside colleagues at the MFF. A subsidiary, City Developments, is responsible for the purchase and development of valuable land around Chişinău. The ultimate source of financing for the GPI projects is unknown, but it's highly unlikely that the answer is Ilie's modest footballer's salary or the money he now earns in his MFF role.

Ilie also purchased an expensive 13.3-hectare plot of land in the desirable Apelor Valley in Codru in 2007 and built a house on it. The house is formally listed as being worth $67,000, but on current market values it is likely to be worth as much as three times that amount. In 2005, Latii purchased another house, also in Codru, which the land registry shows to have a current price of $280,000. Yet during the 1990s, she lived in a modest 50-square-metre apartment, which she donated to her daughter in 2004.

The question posed by *Ziarul de Gardă* is, how have Cebanu, Latii, Spinu and the others been able to finance substantial business investments and property purchases on the modest monthly stipends paid by the MFF?

'We suspect that this money for the company has been taken from the MFF,' claims one of the investigation's authors, Victor Mosneag, when I meet him at *Ziarul de Gardă*'s offices the evening after meeting Testemiţanu. 'Ilie's [Cebanu's] partners are people from the federation who have worked with [Pavel] Cebanu for many years. We also have reason to believe that Cebanu owns a lot of property abroad – nominally. It is all registered in Latii's name.

'He's smart. He drives an old Golf and lives in a small house. He doesn't flaunt that he has money.'

This isn't the first time the lid has been lifted on MFF practices. In 2009, a similar scandal rocked Moldovan football, with senior figures, including Cebanu, being accused of embezzlement in the press.

'Cebanu lost a lot of weight during those weeks,' describes Mosneag. 'He was very scared. After 2009, he changed his lifestyle. The two of them [Cebanu and Latii] sold off one of their bigger properties. He realised it was important for his political survival to not show off his wealth.'

The MFF as an institution is a reminder that, despite Moldova's courtship with the European Union, it remains a society torn between the ghosts of its Soviet past and attempts to realise its European ambitions.

In Cebanu and Testemiţanu, this conflict is given a human face. The president's mentality is a product of the old Communist system that created and curated a management class steeped in corrupt practices. The will of the nomenclature, the collective belief that the system should bend to the expediency of the management classes, whilst publicly bowing to the unshakable authority of the party, superseded the rule of law. In the language of the inquest into the one-party state, the only truth was the lie.

Testemiţanu, on the other hand, came of age at the end of the Communist period. He spent his best years in England and South Korea, liberal-democratic societies where chivalry and polite deference to the rule of law are virtually fetishised.

'Cebanu has been paying off the police to keep them away from his corruption,' alleges Testemiţanu, crystallising the entrenched corruption. 'The police are just as bad. Money went from the federation to the police each year to keep them away.' It was always a fantasy that Testemiţanu would be able to bring his ethics to bear on the rotten apparatus of the old order.

'Cebanu came to me in 2009 and said, "Ivan, I want you to be a vice-president in the federation." I said OK, but if I am in the federation, we will do things honestly. We will operate the way they do in England and in other countries where they do football properly. We will work towards sports principles.

'So what happened? The first year, I arrested people within the federation for trying to fix a Moldova under-fourteen's fixture in a UEFA development tournament. The coach called me and said someone offered him €8,000 to fix the last game. So we set it up with the police and a secret video, so that he went to meet with the person who had offered the money, we arrested them.

'And do you know the person who was most disturbed by this? It was Cebanu. Because he arranged that. Without his say-so, you cannot do anything. The federation is full of his people.'

* * *

The barter economy never disappeared in Moldova. In March 2019, residents in the Sectorul Botanica district of central Chișinău saw a chance to make some easy money.

World champions France were in town, headlining at the Zimbru Stadium in a Euro 2020 qualifier. The residents of the fourteen-storey apartment block next door that looms over the stadium offered ticketless fans a bird's-eye view of the match, for a price. Reports varied, but some say that a place on one of the upper floors cost as much as $100 for a spot. The police promptly moved in, and the enterprise was quickly shut down.

Over-subscription at football matches is rarely such a problem. On a cold April night just a few days after the France game, the stadium's usual occupiers FC Zimbru Chișinău play host to Speranța Nisporeni in the Divizia Națională.

Looking around the ground before kick-off it is not a difficult challenge for a bored, freezing spectator such as myself to count the number of fans in attendance. Barely a couple of hundred have turned out.

The Zimbru Stadium is a charmless arena constructed in 2006 to replace the crumbling Republican Stadium. The apartment blocks just beyond cast their grey shadows down on the pristinely tailored pitch, creating a sense of two disparate worlds clashing.

In one corner of the stands a small number of ultras, clad in the famous green and yellow of Zimbru, bang drums and bellow throaty songs, in an attempt to create some atmosphere in an otherwise silent concrete amphitheatre. However, the noise has all but evaporated into the night before it gets anywhere near the rows of empty seats on the side of the ground where I am sitting.

I watch the game with the club's administrative manager, Emil Pisarenco, a thin, likeable young guy in his late twenties who doubles up as in-house club historian.

'My team is West Ham,' he explains as he regards me with bloodshot eyes. 'I like that film *Football Factory* with Danny Dyer where he plays a football hooligan. What a great actor. So now I support West Ham.' Over the course of the ninety minutes, Pisarenco paints a sorry picture of the state of Moldovan domestic football and his club's declining relevance to it.

'All clubs in the top league are obliged to run a youth academy,' he explains. 'But instead teams just approach a football school in their city, get them to sign a document for the MFF that says they will work together, and then they never hear from them again. They don't even provide the school with a few footballs.' Tonight's visitors Speranţa Nisporeni are amongst the worst offenders in the league claims Pisarenco.

'Zimbru and Sheriff Tiraspol are the only clubs that take youth development seriously. But that's only because they're the only clubs that own any facilities. Every other team just rents training pitches and stadiums from municipal authorities.'

I ask Pisarenco why there is a team bus belonging to Divizia Națională side FC Milsami in the stadium car park when the team aren't due to play here today. 'They've nowhere else to keep it,' he laughs. 'They have no stadium, no training centre. The bus is the only thing they own.'

Zimbru lost 2–0 to Speranța Nisporeni thanks to a penalty for the visitors in each half, and there is precious little on display to persuade the majority who say the team will be relegated this season that they are wrong. No money, no support and after the first three games of the league no points and not one goal scored.

Once, Zimbru dominated Moldovan football, winning eight of the first nine domestic titles following independence. Their last they were league champions was in 2000. They haven't lifted the title since.

Recently, the club have been selling off their land in downtown Chișinău. The estate used to sit across seven hectares, but this is much reduced now since the owner, the local oil magnate Nicolae Ciornîi who is vice-president of the multinational corporation LUKOIL, sold the land that housed the club museum and accommodation facilities to the international school next door. It is no secret here that Ciornîi wants shot of the club in order to cash in on the rest of the estate.

Such is his waning interest, the team could only prove to the MFF that they had sufficient funding to last the 2019 season on the day before their league campaign was due to start.

Two main phenomena have contributed to the club's decline. The first is a general process of regionalisation that occurred across the states on the margins of the former Soviet Union – the redistribution of resources, power and influence from the republican capital cities to the regions – in the decade after the socialist one-party state collapsed. These are the same forces that caused the balance of power to shift in Ukraine from thirteen-time Soviet league champions Dynamo Kyiv to Shakhtar Donetsk, in Romania from 1986 European Cup winners Steaua Bucharest to CFR Cluj, and in Bulgaria from CSKA Sofia to Ludogorets Razgrad. Market economies contributed to the creation of a dictatorship of an oligarch class, the members of which chose to throw their money at provincial football clubs as a way of undermining and unseating the traditional power centres.

The second is that the reliance of clubs on a single backer to finance their activities has become harder to bear. At the time he took control of Zimbru, Ciornîi was a regional vice-president of the Russian oil giant LUKOIL. The company had been one of the single greatest beneficiaries of the dismantling of the Soviet state; inheriting the producing sites at three of Siberia's most profitable oil fields and becoming the largest non-state controlled energy supplier in the world. Ciornîi, who was born in the Ukrainian city of Odessa and educated in Moscow, had a brief to manage LUKOIL's expansion in the Balkans, a portfolio that extended as far east as his native Moldova. In exchange for a licence to trade and grow their business in the country, Ciornîi helped broker a deal between the government in Chișinău and LUKOIL that would see the company invest $25 million per year in sporting development in Moldova.

What he failed to disclose to his bosses was that he had a controlling interest in Moldova's biggest private sporting institution – Zimbru. The club had been registered in the names of members of Ciornîi's family, and legally there was no record of his connection to the club. Between 1994 and 2009, unbeknownst to the company, Ciornîi channelled money from LUKOIL's donations into things like stadium renovation and to cover the club's running costs.

When LUKOIL's executives found out, they cancelled the deal, sacked Ciornîi and left Zimbru to the sole financial responsibility of a man who had never had any interest in football to begin with, and had only taken the team on because he coveted the land that came with it.

Ciornîi has been desperate to offload the club for a number of years. Some here believe Zimbru is destined to fall into the hands of Vladimir Plahotniuc, Moldova's richest and most influential man. A ruthless tycoon with vast political influence, most people refuse to talk on the record about Plahotniuc. If he takes on the club, it is believed that it will be the end of the team's seventy-year existence, though the sensitivity that surrounds the Zimbru land means the government is likely to do everything it can to keep the club away from Plahotniuc. The situation became more serious in March 2020 when Zimbru finally collapsed, leaving the fate of the club and the land attached to it up in the air.

Despite what's happened, there remains an unbreakable historical link between the club and the state.

When the USSR collapsed, the government initially retained ownership of the team. It was a hugely difficult climate for any state-owned institution, as the whole of Moldova was rocked by the economic shockwaves of being uncoupled from Moscow.

Zimbru were so poor that between 1991 and 1994 they took to paying their players in wine acquired from Chişinău's famous Mileştii Mici winery. Most players gave the wine to their families, who for a time were able to keep afloat by selling the wine on at local markets and, for those with contacts, internationally. Ironically, it was the collapse of the wine trade between Chişinău and Moscow that had contributed to the economic collapse in the first place.

'Nobody seemed to understand why it was happening,' recalls Ivan Testemiţanu of the poverty that came to Chişinău. 'And nobody seemed to know what the consequences would be. Nobody understood. After independence, life got much worse. There was no work, no salaries. We just tried to survive. There were a lot of criminals here after independence that were all looking to find ways to hide their money and keep it from the state. These are the people who benefited from privatisation.'

The only team to interrupt Zimbru's dominance of the Divizia Naţională in the 1990s, FC Constructorul Chişinău, were founded and financed by one such figure, the notorious mafia kingpin Valeriu Rotari, commonly known by his underworld nickname 'Zelioni'. A respected and feared criminal influencer, he was known to operate as a mediator in disputes between gangland factions; he also has over a decade of prison time against his name.

With his millions, he backed Constructorul to the hilt, guiding the team from the third division to the first in just two years and winning the title in their first top-flight season in 1996/97. The following year, they became Moldova's second-ever representatives in the Champions League, losing a first-round thriller 4–3 against Slavia Mozyr from Belarus.

Zelioni was assassinated in February 2000 when his car was hit by a volley of Kalashnikov bullets as he drove home from a casino not far from the Republican Stadium. A selection of names from Moldova's criminal underworld were accused of his murder, with some reports alleging that a high-ranking Chişinău dignitary had ordered the killing over a debt owed to Zelioni by his son. Still, no one was ever charged over his murder.

Following the assassination of its owner, Constructorul was acquired by the Sheriff corporation in Transnistria – the owners of

FC Sheriff Tiraspol – who moved the club east across the de facto border and rebranded them as a feeder club, FC Tiraspol.

'They say that it was this guy [Zelioni] that made Pavel Cebanu run for president of the football federation,' claims Testemiţanu. 'They say he controlled the president.'

The lucrative land attached to Zimbru was the attraction for Ciornîi when he acquired the team and its assets in 1994, nominally for free.

This being post-Soviet Moldova, however, there was a catch. In order to seal the deal, Ciornîi agreed in private to pay the country's then President Mircea Snegur an ongoing personal stipend of $5,000 per month. Though Snegur is long gone from office, Testemiţanu alleges the remunerations have continued well into this century, and the former president still holds a seat on the Zimbru board.

Nevertheless, the club recovered under the stewardship of Ciornîi. As well as a procession of Divizia Naţională titles, they reached the UEFA Cup second round in 1995. And finally, the players began to receive financial remunerations once again.

Sergei Cleşcenco was the hotshot young centre-forward in this resurgent Zimbru side. He arrived in the team in 1990 aged just eighteen, and played through the awkward transitionary period towards Moldovan independence.

'It was a very good level of football in Moldova immediately after the union collapsed,' recalls Sergei Cleşcenco when we meet at the MFF offices in Chişinău. 'We had Zimbru, there was Tiligul playing in Tiraspol, there was a good team in Bendery and in Comrat. [From] 1991 to 1994, Zimbru had good results, but the situation at the club was really not good at all. There were big financial problems. There were many occasions when we didn't receive a salary.

'Then in 1994, Ciornîi took the club on, and the situation stabilised. Suddenly we were getting good salaries, and they arrived on time. We had money to buy apartments in Chişinău. I am hugely thankful to Mr Ciornîi, because he changed our lives.'

Ciornîi changed the lives of those players fortunate enough to have been saved from poverty by his patronage. But the platitudes of Sergei Cleşcenco, Testemiţanu and others don't mask the fact that football under Communism was almost entirely unaccountable at this time. Today, it seems not to have recovered from the post-Soviet shock therapy that crippled it nearly thirty years ago.

I had come to Moldova with preconceptions about how the business of football worked.

Several years ago whilst working as a freelancer for *Vice*, I interviewed the former Arsenal and Tottenham midfielder Rohan Ricketts about the mistreatment he suffered whilst contracted to the now-defunct Divizia Naţională team FC Dacia Chişinău.

Dacia are one of two clubs responsible for denying Sheriff the league title in the last two decades (Milsami Orhei in 2015 are the other), and won their only championship in 2011 following an uncharacteristically tight three-way fight for the title against Milsami and Sheriff (the three finished level on points and Dacia were made champions based on their head-to-head record).

Dacia had been founded in 1999 by Marin Livadaru, a businessman and failed parliamentary candidate whose political movement, the Progressive Society Party, is somewhere on the fringes of Moldovan politics.

Generously supported by Livadaru's millions – the same money that simultaneously funded the operations of FC Iskra-Stal Rîbniţa, the team in the village that houses northern Transnistria's Soviet ammunitions dump – Dacia made steady progress, coming close to winning the league a couple of times before finally tripping up their rivals from the Dniester in 2011.

Ricketts, an Arsenal academy graduate who was briefly a regular at Tottenham in the 2003/04 season, had by 2010 made a small-time reputation for himself as a journeyman, playing for teams in Canada and England before accepting a contract to play for Dacia at the beginning of what would become their title-winning year.

When I spoke to him in 2017, he was at the heavy end of six years of litigation with Dacia over unpaid wages, a process that by then had sucked in FIFA, the Professional Footballers' Association and the Court of Arbitration for Sport.

To say this was a simple dispute over pay would be to undercut Ricketts' trauma. The problem started because it was claimed that one of the agents involved in brokering the deal had led Dacia to believe Ricketts was a striker. When he told them that he was actually an attacking midfielder, the club tried to wriggle their way out of their commitment, and drew up a document entitling him to one month's salary provided he packed his bags that same day and left.

'That was a good document for me to have,' an upset Ricketts told me. 'It proved that it was them, the club, who wanted to get rid of me. Then, after about twenty minutes, they walked back in the room and said, "Rohan, we've made a mistake, we just need to go and correct it," and they took the document from me. But it wasn't a mistake – they just didn't want me to have the document, because they knew it would have let them off.'

He spent three and a half months in Chișinău, training on his own and getting nowhere near the Dacia first team. He received no payment during that period. At the end of three months without a wage, he began the process of severing ties.

The case went before the Court of Arbitration for Sport and Ricketts, backed by the Professional Footballers' Association in London, was awarded $100,000 in damages, to be paid by the club within twenty-one days. But Dacia weren't finished.

'The club never paid,' stated Ricketts. 'They appealed the decision on the grounds that I had been fraudulent.'

Tax regulations in parts of Eastern Europe mean that it is common practice for clubs to sign up players on two contracts simultaneously. In Ricketts's case, this meant one document under which he was to be paid $7,000 across three years, and another that entitled him to the bulk of his salary. Dacia's allegation was that Ricketts had faked the second of the two contracts.

'That means I would have had to have agreed to be paid $7,000, split over three years. You can't live anywhere on that. It's the most ridiculous story ever.'

Dacia also alleged that Ricketts drew up this contract himself – in English and Romanian – used the club's official stamp and faked the signatures of officials.

'They said I did all that, just to have a club in Moldova.' The club brought in a handwriting expert to examine the contracts, and the expert's verdict was that the second contract could have been signed by someone else, other than the club. Consequently, the court found in favour of Dacia. The case was upheld and Ricketts was made to pay the appeal fee.

He wondered how the court could have reached such a decision, 'because the case doesn't even make sense. I agreed to go somewhere for $7,000, broken down over thirty-six months? How has someone come to that understanding? It should have been impossible to lose that case.'

As I write this, Moldova have just gone 4–0 down at home to Turkey in a Euro 2020 qualifying match. The footage from Chişinău makes me a tiny bit nostalgic for the Brutalist grey concrete apartments hanging over the Zimbru Stadium, and it is sad to see the national team go down so easily.

The performance has been hopeless. The four-man defence play like they are strangers, the strikers wander about aimlessly – which turned out to be irrelevant because the ball never gets anywhere near them – and the midfield is full of holes that Turkey's creative players easily exploit. Last week, Moldova lost 3–0 to international minnows Iceland, a nation a fraction of Moldova's size, but with football authorities that have invested thoroughly and efficiently to produce a ruddy and healthy football ecology.

Moldova's now former coach, the implausibly named Semen Altman, dodders about on the touchline, out of ideas. Greying and well into his seventies, he's part of the Soviet old guard whose cynicism has led the country into this wilderness.

Who is going to lead them out?

PART FIVE

AFTER HADES: UKRAINE AND THE DONBASS

The blackbird of your eyelashes is taking off
And taking my confidence away to an unknown place
The halfstep is being left unwalked
The half a breath is getting stuck in my throat
HRYHORIY CHUBAI, UKRAINIAN POET

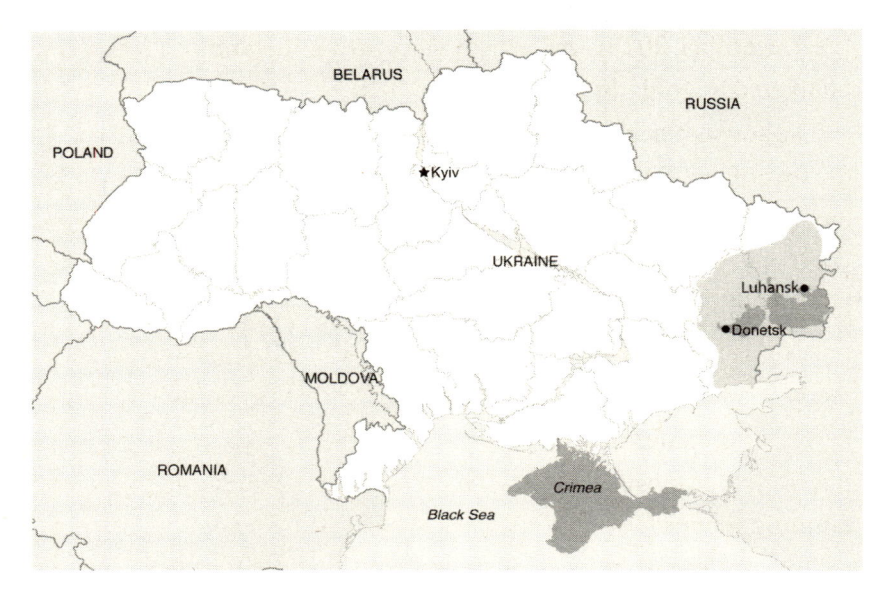

© Donbass: Бровар / CC

I

It's December 2018, and Vlasovsky Lane in downtown Kharkiv is blanketed in cold, dirty snow.

The loose black slurry along the pavement has been churned by the feet of evening commuters into a wretched slippery mire, and the moisture has long since seeped through the stitching of my boots. Each step I take sends an icy spray shooting upwards, coating my legs in a thin layer of cold.

It's not long after 5 p.m. in Ukraine's second-largest city, but already it's nearly pitch dark, the dim orange glow of the streetlights barely illuminates the flecks of snow that have been steadily cascading from the sky since midday. Kharkiv is at the beginning of a long, draining winter.

The city seems built to be permanently cold. Once the capital of Soviet Ukraine, it is an austere mash-up of Constructivist ugliness and Stalinist pomp.

The Kharkiv National University, a blustering concrete mass that sits off the city's gigantic Freedom Square, was partially rebuilt after being damaged during the Second World War to incorporate the new style of Stalin's architectural peacocking with an affronting brutality.

Back on Vlasovsky Lane stands the giant yellow exoskeleton of the Metalist Stadium that is home to the city's football club FC Metalist Kharkiv. The angular frames of its roof stanchions point their skeletal joints upwards into the wintry sky like the frail legs of insects. Set here in the biting cold of Kharkiv, the stadium looks like some bewildered giant cockroach scavenging for morsels at the end of a nuclear winter.

Whatever beauty there is to be found amongst the bleak cold of snow-swept Eastern Europe has deserted Kharkiv tonight, rendering it depressingly Soviet as the temperature falls as the last of the daylight disappears. As I set foot in the road to cross, a silver Mercedes zips around the corner and zooms across my path, showering me in brown icy water from the gutter.

Once inside the stadium, the walls of the reception area are mostly glossy and bare, save for a few action shots of the players of FC Metalist. The team's complexion is a familiar one in Ukrainian football, a mélange of Eastern European faces with slightly more exotic figures of around half a dozen Latin American signings. This is the face of Ukrainian football since the fall of Communism. The country has become an unlikely halfway house for players from Africa and the Americas attempting to enter the lucrative world of elite football in the West.

The front desk is manned by a sour man with flabby jowls that obscure where his neck ends and his head begins. '*Zdravstvuyte* – I'm here to see Anton Ivanov,' I explain with all the cheer I can muster from my frozen bones.

'I don't know where he is,' grunts the man, just about paying me the respect of lazily raising his eyes to meet mine. I enquire whether there might not be someone else in the stadium that does know where he is, and the man shrugs an apathetic shrug.

I explain that the meeting with Ivanov is the reason why I have travelled to Kharkiv. Before he can heave his shoulders into a second disinterested shrug, an elderly man in a Metalist hoody emerges from the back room, and following an exchange in Russian between the pair a phone call is made; minutes later a short, portly gentleman in a blue tracksuit enters through the main stadium doors and introduces himself as Anton Ivanov. We leave the man on reception to return to his daydream.

'I like England,' offers Ivanov almost in apology as we ride the lift to the stadium's executive lounge. He is the general manager of Metalist, and possesses all of the burly swagger that I have come to expect from Eastern European football bureaucrats.

'I spent an exchange programme in Shrewsbury when I was a schoolboy.' I suspect the Middle Englanders of parochial Shropshire were a comparative treat for Ivanov if the 'receptionist' on the stadium front desk is a typical representative of the Kharkiv citizenry.

Metalist's stadium should have been preparing to host Shakhtar Donetsk from neighbouring Donbass in the Champions League tomorrow night. The Ukrainian champions play their home games in Kharkiv on account of the Donbass War that forced them to leave their hometown and which continues to rage in Ukraine's far east.

Instead, a flare-up of tensions between Kyiv and Moscow in the disputed Crimean region earlier this month has meant that the game has been moved 500km west to the capital, with Kharkiv placed in a state of emergency and deemed an unsafe location by UEFA.

Tonight, in Kharkiv, a city on the front line of where Ukraine's authority ends and revolutionary Donbass begins, there is none of the busy activity that should accompany the countdown to a game in the Champions League. The stadium is dark and quiet, and the executive lounge is bare of festivities save for a sad, lonely Christmas tree, which is listing miserably in one corner. A single distracted barman slovenly props up the counter, rallying briefly to bring Ivanov and me a cup each of sweet berry tea, which sends an instant warmth fizzing through my frozen muscles.

Metalist Kharkiv plays an unwilling role in this war. The club is a revival of the Ukrainian Premier League team of the same name that went to the wall and was liquidated in 2016, wiped off the map by the hubris of one of its former owners, the international fugitive Sergei Kurchenko.

'We can say that our club collapsed because of the Ukrainian revolution,' states Ivanov. 'But I cannot say the revolution was bad, because it changed Ukraine. My aim now is to renew Metalist within the new Ukraine.'

The team was founded in 1925 as the worker side of one of the city's locomotive factories, and was traditionally a middling club in the Ukrainian Soviet Socialist Republic, winning promotion to the Soviet Top League in 1960 and spending more time in it than out of it over the next thirty years.

'Metalist is a great example for the other clubs in Ukraine to change their financial philosophy,' states Ivanov. 'We need to make our football community healthier, so that we spend only what we earn, not what we are given by oligarchs.'

Today, the club is propped up by a consortium of eighteen private and public backers, none of which owns a share of the business greater than 15 per cent. This defends the club against the vagaries of single-party ownership, the kind that ultimately brought the club to its knees when the previous owner, the presidential protégé turned international fugitive Kurchenko – variously described as 'the wallet' of impeached former Ukrainian President Viktor Yanukovych – pulled his vast fortune out of his Ukrainian business interests during the revolution.

Kurchenko has since been implicated in the financial scandals that contributed to the toppling of Yanukovych from office, and in October 2017 the remaining assets attached to the holding company that owned Metalist, including the stadium, were confiscated by the state.

Following the court's decision to return the club to public ownership, the Ukrainian Prosecutor General Yuriy Lutsenko triumphantly summed up the mood in Kharkiv: 'We can proudly inform residents of Kharkiv that FC Metalist will belong to them not fugitive kleptocrats.' Kurchenko himself remains on the international most-wanted list, his whereabouts unknown.

Ivanov remains part of an ongoing civil case regarding outstanding debts owed to him by the old company. He's not alone – creditors are queuing up over money owed following Kurchenko's midnight flit. But the general manager hasn't been dissuaded.

'With the club having so many sources for funding, there is no risk of another collapse if one person pulls out,' he declares defiantly. 'We're not like Shakhtar, who are owned and paid for by the richest man in Ukraine.'

The business models used by clubs in Ukrainian football invite financial catastrophe. The man that Ivanov is referring to is Rinat Akhmetov, a close ally of Chelsea owner Roman Abramovich, who through his financial power transformed Shakhtar's fortunes between 1996 and 2014.

Like Abramovich, Akhmetov got rich off the fire sale of Soviet state assets when the USSR disintegrated and its former leaders sold off massive state utilities for a fraction of their value to favoured insiders, and his club Shakhtar has since become one of the success stories of post-independence Ukraine, shattering the dominance of the once-untouchable Dynamo Kyiv and becoming something close to a European force. But this model leaves teams at the mercy of a volatile and unpredictable political ecology, where a single change in political winds can have cataclysmic consequences for clubs that have become reliant on the private fortunes of apparatchiks and crooks.

Like Metalist, Shakhtar represent one side of a definitive cultural divide in Ukraine. The club is a descendant of the Soviet coal industry, hence their orange and black shirts that mimic the sight of underground workers emerging from the mines into the light.

The Donets Basin (Donbass) from which they hail is a Russian-speaking corner of Ukraine. The region's historical, linguistic and cultural practices differ from those of the metropolitan aesthetes of Kyiv and the west of the country.

The civil war that followed the 2014 overthrow of Yanukovych owes its genesis to this geographical and cultural division. It is a crisis with roots that reach back centuries.

Ukraine literally means 'borderland', a place where East meets

West. It is this middle-ness that is at the beating heart of the 2014 revolution and subsequent partition of the country. Because for most of the first thirteen years after independence, and indeed for many years before this moment, by and large there was no agreed idea about what it meant to be 'Ukrainian'. The reality is that the confusion over the essence of Ukraine's national identity is what has prevented a consensus from being reached over whether the country should align itself with Europe to the west or Russian to the east.

Modern Ukraine's capital was once the centre of the first great eastern Slavic civilisation, Kievan Rus', believed to have been founded by Scandinavian crusaders in the ninth century to bring order upon the tribespeople of the region and to exploit the commercial possibilities of the Dnieper River, which connected northern Europe with the Black Sea. Kievan Rus' fell to the Mongol Horde in the thirteenth century and its people migrated north towards Muscovy (Moscow), and it's here where the battle between historians begins.

Russians say that the city's population and culture moved northwards, and thus it is Russia that is heir to Kievan Rus' and the capital of the eastern Slavic world. Ukrainians say that the physical city of Kyiv can trace its heritage directly to the age of Kievan Rus', and therefore it owes no cultural bond to Moscow. Russians and Ukrainians do not agree historically on which of their nations is the allegorical 'older brother' of the two.

Physically Ukraine is divided in two at the Dnieper, the river that runs through the heart of Kyiv and historically separated Russian Ukraine in the sixteenth and seventeenth centuries from the western half that was ruled by Poland. Proponents of 'Ukrainian-ness' existed in this period as reactionary antagonists to Russian and Polish rule, rebelling at the local level against imperial control and striving to keep their language and cultural practices alive in spite of attempts from the centre to assimilate them as Russians and Poles.

To the south of these lived the marauding Muslim Tartars of Crimea and the Black Sea steppe. Between them, these were all of the lands that eventually came to be the modern Ukrainian state.

By 1800, Poland had been wiped off the map, divided up between the empires of Russia and Austria-Hungary, the latter of which took ownership of the province of Galicia in what is now western Ukraine, whilst the eastern and central parts were ruled by Saint Petersburg.

Late in the previous century, Russia's empress Catherine II had finally conquered the northern shores of the Black Sea and tamed the fertile 'wild field' that sat between her empire and the Tartars, on which land her emissaries would soon build key industrial and port settlements. Meanwhile in the west, Galicia remained a dominion of the Habsburg Empire, until the collapse of the great powers and restoration of Poland in 1918 made it a possession of Warsaw, and it stayed so until 1945 when at the end of the Great Patriotic War it was handed to the Soviet Union and incorporated into the Ukrainian Soviet Socialist Republic.

Thus, the question arises, what is Ukraine? The heir to a great civilisation, later conquered by Russians, Austrians and Poles and constantly fighting to survive as a national idea amongst the oppression? Or an ethnic cousin to the Russian world, sharing a common history and religion and speaking a quaint, but primitive linguistic dialect (which is how many Russians view the status of the Ukrainian language)?

Certainly, Ukrainian politicians cannot agree on an answer to this question. Before the revolution of 2014 there were two distinct notions of Ukraine: one, a 'monist' unitarism that borrowed ideas about 'integral nationalism', the idea of the Ukrainian nation as the backbone of the political unit, whereby the nation and the state become indivisible. At its extreme edges monist unitarism has a hard-right flavour, and its exercise in history by the various rebellious Ukrainian nationalists who fought against imperial oppressors certainly did betray fascist tendencies – indeed, the Organisation of Ukrainian

Nationalists headed by Stepan Bandera in the 1930s and 1940s were active collaborators with the Nazis.

This history, together with a perceived theology of Ukrainianism that mobilises the functions of the state in a nationalist cause, is why the insurrectionaries in the Donbass since 2014 have enjoyed such success in persuading local people into believing that the Kyiv government holds an openly fascist agenda.

The second model, adopted by the Russophone people of the south and east of the country, says that Ukraine is by its very nature federal, owing to its patchwork construction as a hodgepodge of different peoples, languages and cultures. This, they argue, better reflects the historical realities of the territory of modern Ukraine and its Russian, Polish, Austrian and Tartar genesis, not to mention the fragments of the country that were variously under Romanian, Hungarian and Czech rule during the twentieth century. These groups would seek a federal, compartmentalised Ukraine, composed of local autonomies based on ethnic realities.

The federal model affords a stage to those who would argue both Russians and Ukrainians share a common ancestor in Kievan Rus', and it is precisely these sympathies that were preyed upon by Russia's agents of destabilisation in Ukraine's south-east and Crimea following the 'Euromaidan' revolution of 2013. That revolution began in November when President Viktor Yanukovych made a sudden reversal on an association agreement with the EU under pressure of sanctions from Moscow.

Furious that their government had spurned a golden opportunity to break free of Russian influence and to pursue Ukraine's ambitions in Europe, protesters flocked in their tens of thousands to Kyiv's central Independence Square – Майдан Незалежності – to demand the 'traitor' Yanukovych's removal.

Their grievances were against a government steeped in alleged corruption and the cravenness of the regime in giving in to demands from Putin and for ripping up the contract with Europe.

Within a fortnight, the demonstrations had reached 300,000 strong, and a semi-permanent platform was erected in the square as demonstrators travelled hundreds of miles from the regions to stake their allegiance to Europe.

After a tense winter, violent clashes between protesters and the authorities re-erupted in February, during which the government authorised the police to use live rounds against the Euromaidan crowds, resulting in the deaths of dozens of protesters when uniformed snipers opened fire on the crowd.

This proved to be the final catalyst for the collapse of the government. As 20,000 furious rioters descended on the parliamentary building to demand a return to the constitution of the Orange Revolution of 2004, President Yanukovych fled the capital for Moscow, and a hastily installed provisional government voted unanimously to impeach him on the grounds of mass murder of protesters and corruption in office.

Kharkiv has shown itself to be largely immune to the convulsions of the eastern Ukraine's separatist rebellion. However, this doesn't mean the place isn't deeply affected by the revolution. Just ask fans of FC Metalist.

One of the rebellion's most curious precipitates occurred in April 2014 with the bizarre sight of fans of Metalist and FC Dnipro, the team's arch-rivals from the nearby industrial city of Dnepropetrovsk, marching through the streets of Kharkiv in tandem in vocal support of a united Ukraine, perhaps the only occasion in living memory when the two sets of supporters have come together without untrammelled violence breaking out. Instead, the violence was started by pro-Russian saboteurs who attacked the demonstrators in the centre of Kharkiv as they belted out anti-Putin chants.

In January 2014, the ultras of Dynamo Kyiv had triumphantly proclaimed from the Euromaidan, 'We are coming out – for our city, for our country, for our honour.'

Within days, all fifteen of Ukraine's top-flight teams (a sixteenth team, Arsenal Kyiv, had been declared bankrupt and expelled from the league a few weeks earlier) had pledged support for the Dynamo ultras and the cause of a united Ukraine, which gave birth to a unique period of self-organisation within ultras culture.

All cross-party hostilities were suspended in favour of a peaceful, civil collective based on the principle of Ukrainian nationhood, and representatives of all Premier League clubs were dispatched to the Euromaidan.

For a brief moment, football became one of the most demonstrative spaces for the cause of Ukrainian unitarism, with swathes of traditional rivals suspending hostilities and marching together before and after football matches in support of a united, European Ukraine.

All of this changed on 2 May 2014 on a day of tragedy in the Black Sea port city of Odessa. More than forty people, mostly anti-Euromaidan Russophile activists, were burned to death when violence broke out during a unity march between activists of the local team FC Chernomorets and Metalist. Some 700 Kharkivite ultras had made the journey to Odessa for the Premier League game against Chernomorets, partly to support the team, partly to join in the March for the unity of Ukraine. En route to the ground, supporters marched side-by-side chanting anti-Putin slogans and taunting the saboteurs.

Before kick-off, street fighting broke out between the protesters and a pro-Russian camp at Kulikov Square that had been erected in front of the Odessa local administration building. Most of those that were killed were members of the separatist group. They perished after becoming trapped on the upper floors of a former Soviet trade union building that had been set alight by Molotov cocktails that had been hurled through the windows.

As the building burned, Metalist played out a 1–1 draw at Chernomorets Stadium, dropping two points that gifted the league's final Champions League place to, of all teams, Dnipro. Once the scale of what had happened in the fire of Kulikov Square became known, no one was talking about football.

'Everything that happened was like in a horror movie,' one Chernomorets ultra, who had marched with Metalist fans, told Reuters. 'We never expected an ambush on such a scale and for the police to do so little.'

One Kharkiv ultra later recalled how he'd seen a young Chernomorets supporter shot in the head. A rival fan took the dead boy's phone from his pocket and called his mother to tell her that her son had been killed.

The tragic events in Odessa were a turning point for football's role in the revolution. Before 2 May, supporters had set aside rivalries to march together against a national threat.

After Odessa, the idea that football could be a safe space for expression of the unitary movement was shown to be a fiction. The following week, the Football Federation of Ukraine forced all league matches to be played behind closed doors to prevent the eruption of a second Odessa.

Whilst the war in Donbass raged, the corresponding fixture between Metalist and Chernomorets the following season was cancelled altogether by decree of the Ministry of Internal Affairs, so deep was the wound across Ukrainian society that was inflicted by the 2 May massacres.

II

Life was hard in post-Communist Ukraine. Life in football was hard, too.

Metalist passed through a succession of hands in its first years as a private business and not all of these owners had the club's best interests at heart.

The team yo-yoed between the top two divisions until finally in 2005 a clean, stable investor was found, the charismatic and popular local businessman, Oleksandr Yaroslavsky. Under Yaroslavsky, Metalist became one of the best-run clubs in Ukraine, and established itself as the strongest team outside of the top-two duopoly of Dynamo Kyiv and Shakhtar Donetsk; it also briefly broke into that elite club when it finished as runner-up in the league in 2013.

'Yaroslavsky didn't bring superstars,' explains Ivanov. 'He invested in infrastructure. Within a couple of years, it brought results, and we became the third power in Ukraine.'

Yaroslavsky was instrumental in securing Kharkiv's place as a host city for the 2012 European Championships, which brought with it massive investments in the city's infrastructure, including the crumbling Kharkiv airport.

The crowning jewel in the town's renovation was Metalist Stadium, a joint investment between Yaroslavsky and the regional Oblast administration – the magnate put in 30 per cent of the project's funding – the stadium's future subsequently became a matter of public interest when Kurchenko's assets were frozen after the revolution and he fled abroad.

In 2014, Yaroslavsky left Ukraine and became a member of London's Eastern European oligarch class, alongside his close friend and confidant Roman Abramovich. He married his long-term partner Marina in a lavish ceremony at the Ritz Hotel in April 2018.

Yaroslavsky never declared his reason for abruptly selling Metalist to the upstart Kurchenko. The most popular theory is that he was embroiled in disputed allegations of alleged match-fixing with the mayor of Kharkiv, Hennadiy Kernes – a known pro-Russian sympathiser who was shot in the back by a sniper (and lived to tell the tale) whilst out cycling during the confusing days that followed the seizure by separatists of the oblast administration in April 2014 – over the ownership of Metalist Stadium.

Another theory goes that President Yanukovych intervened personally to place the club in the hands of his protégé Kurchenko.

The most plausible reason behind the sale is that Yaroslavsky had invested in the club and in the city for Euro 2012 purely in the hope of currying favour with powerful figures in government, and that his relationship with the team had been above all a business one. Still, those close to Yaroslavsky speak glowingly of his sincere affection for both Metalist and for football, and by handing the reins to Kurchenko he was placing the club in an indisputably healthier financial position than he himself could ever get it in.

'The truth is somewhere in between,' states Ivanov as we tick off the possibilities. Either way, Metalist was swimming into dangerous waters. It left them sitting ducks when the presidential regime was toppled two years later.

When Kurchenko took control of the club in 2012, the recruitment policy changed. Metalist began to follow the example of the clubs that they were trying to catch up with, and in came a roster of talent from Argentina, Brazil and Africa.

The team achieved its goal of breaking the duopoly, and in 2013 ousted Dynamo Kyiv to finish in the top two and qualify for the Champions League. Kurchenko even bought the remaining shares in the stadium that were still owned by the Kharkiv Oblast. Everything seemed set up for a bright future rivalling Ukraine's top powers.

'At first everything was good,' says Ivanov. 'Kurchenko doubled the playing budget, brought in bigger-name players. At the end of that first year, we came second in the league.'

In the event, the club was disqualified from playing in the following season's Champions League over an outstanding match-fixing allegation dating back to 2008.

'We lost a lot of our best players over the decision,' says Ivanov. 'Ambitious players want to play in the Champions League. The Court of Arbitration for Sport decision was the beginning of the end for Metalist.'

When the revolution began, Kurchenko pulled his money out of Ukraine. His holding company, VETEK, was seized by early 2014 following the toppling of Yanukovych, by which time Metalist's players claimed not to have received any wages for three months. 'That was the final phase of the death of the club,' argues Ivanov. 'We still finished third, incredibly, despite everyone's wages being cut and a lot of players walking out.'

The following season, with most of the players sold off and the club's management structure crumbling, Metalist plummeted down the league; once again allegations of match fixing began to haunt the side as officials scrambled to halt the slide by foul means or fair.

Following a failed, last-ditch plea for Yaroslavsky to return to save the club, Metalist were finally thrown out of the league and declared bankrupt in 2016.

The sale of the club to Kurchenko had been a shock, not least of all because virtually no one in the country at that time knew who he was.

He had graduated in law from the University of Kharkiv in 2011, and at just twenty-seven years old was catapulted suddenly into the public eye. He was soon being described in the national press as 'that young genius' and the 'right arm and wallet' of President Viktor Yanukovych.

When everything came crashing down, Kurchenko was accused of having built his petroleum empire by exploiting smuggled gas and faked import licences, which for some observers finally resolved the enigma of how he had risen to become one of the most influential faces in the country before he was thirty.

Today, he appears on the international wanted list for financial theft from the Ukrainian government totalling 2 billion hryvnias (approximately $80 million dollars), as well as on a list of US and EU sanctioned individuals owing to his alleged role in contributing to the destabilisation of Ukraine in its conflict with Russia. He is also the subject of a US and EU asset freeze.

'Kurchenko was like the wallet for Yanukovych,' claims Ivanov. 'His businesses made a lot of money for the President. Now, no one even knows where he is.'

This meant the beginning of the end for Metalist. When their patron evaporated into thin air, the side fell fast and hard into the financial abyss. Only now, with the new investment model designed and implemented by the general manager, are the club looking like returning to the Ukrainian Premier League.

'Hopefully in the future, clubs will live off only what they earn,' remarks Ivanov optimistically. 'Football shouldn't rely on living month to month on handouts from rich men. But it's a prestige thing. A rich man who wants to be on top in Ukraine has to own a football club.'

* * *

In the industrial Russophile east, Ukraine's pro-Moscow President Viktor Yanukovych enjoyed a strong supporter base. The population in this part of the country watched the events of February 2014 unfolding in Kyiv with extreme unease.

Soon, furious counter-protests erupted against the 'fascists and terrorists' of the Euromaidan, fuelled by an incendiary cocktail of ethno-linguistic patronage – 75 per cent of Donetsk Oblast was Russian speaking – years of economic drudgery, to which union with Moscow was widely deemed to be the only solution, and sensationalist fear-mongering that pitted the European 'autocracy' in Brussels as an aggressively expansionist super-state intent on subverting the forces of culture and decency (one popular, but patently ludicrous rumour warned that a pro-Europe Kyiv would seek to replace the 9 May Victory Day parade with a gay pride festival).

Throughout the course of April, pro-Russian gunmen and separatists steadily took over the institutions of government, building by building, in the major cities of the Donbass – Donetsk and Luhansk – and declared independent republics.

By the end of the month, Kyiv conceded it no longer held control in Donbass, and two new proto-republics were born along Eastern Europe's tumultuous post-Soviet faultline.

When Kyiv's authority began to break down in eastern Ukraine in the spring of 2014 following the Euromaidan protests, Kharkiv was a hub of unrest.

On 7 April, the central government building was briefly occupied by pro-Russian separatists, and the flag of the so-called 'People's Republic of Kharkiv' was raised above the building of the city administration, though local observers contended that the rebels were hired hands brought in from outside the city rather than born and bred Kharkivites. Within two days, Ukrainian police, whose collaboration with the separatists in Donetsk and Luhansk had been a deciding factor in the outcome, had retaken the building in a bloodless operation during which barely a shot was fired, and the city's brief flirtation with cessation was ended.

Kharkiv, a city of merchants and traders, is of a different breed to neighbouring industrial Donetsk. One local journalist has compared the two cities to the differences between a worker and a bureaucrat; one is measured, collected and reasoned, the other is forceful, impulsive and swears loudly.

Metalist Kharkiv waited a long time for football success under Yaroslavsky and Kurchenko. The team was never consistently one of Ukraine's top three sides in the Soviet league, though frustratingly their bitter rivals Dnipro Dnepropetrovsk had more success, winning the Soviet Top League in 1983 and 1988. The rivalry was an industrial as well as a sporting one – both clubs were founded in the early twentieth century by metallurgic workers at state-owned factories not much more than 160km apart.

Kharkiv is big football country. Since 2016, the city has hosted Shakhtar at Metalist Stadium after they departed their temporary home in the fiercely nationalist city of Lviv, where they had not been made welcome on account of Donetsk's Russian sympathies.

Yet Metalist's second division fixtures typically draw bigger crowds than Shakhtar can manage in exile. Only for Champions League games do the league victors get their numbers up into five figures.

Even though Shakhtar pays a fair rent, the deal doesn't work for everyone. The city has been a willing host, but it hasn't played into Metalist's hands to have regular top-flight and Champions League games here soaking up the attention and the money of local supporters. Shakhtar pay to maintain the pitch, but this is not really a bonus when there are fewer fans than there ought to be paying to watch Metalist matches in the stands.

'Our aim is to help them feel at home whilst not forgetting that they are guests,' explains Ivanov. Nonetheless, the number of supporters who come out to support Metalist is almost double the amount that turn out to watch Shakhtar. Ivanov continues:

'Nobody feels like Shakhtar is a refugee team. This war came into all our lives very suddenly, but we are still one nation. There are about 200,000 refugees in Kharkiv from Donbass. They are Kharkiv citizens now. We're happy to have Shakhtar because they bring the Champions League here and because they bring the Ukrainian Premier League here.'

Kharkiv was the capital of Ukraine until 1934, the city's fine architecture and reputable university bestowing upon it the assumed responsibility of being an academic hub. The city is also largely sympathetic to Ukrainian nationalists. The street unrest that preceded the seizure of the government building in April was not joined en masse by local Kharkivites and instead relied on pro-Russian agitators who had been shipped into the city in minivans.

It has since been established that the Kharkiv People's Republic was orchestrated by native Russians and members of Oplot, a local pro-Russian fight club that sought to play to the sympathies of those Russians that lived and worked in the city who were fearful of the shift towards Western Europe.

The closure of the border between Kharkiv and Russia soon afterwards effectively put down the last rumblings of separatist mutterings in the city, and rubber-stamped the local opinion that Kharkiv did not have the DNA for a separatist rising.

I had originally planned to come to Kharkiv to watch Shakhtar play against Olympique Lyon in the Champions League. After a ropey start to their campaign, Shakhtar had hauled themselves into contention to qualify for the knockout rounds with a dramatic late win against the German side Hoffenheim on the penultimate match-day, and a couple of days in the country's second city seemed like a decent opportunity to assess the impact that the war was having in the Kyiv-controlled east.

But circumstance interceded. A couple of weeks before the game, a group of Ukrainian sailors were arrested by Russian police in the Sea of Azov off the Crimean Peninsula, creating a massive diplomatic flare-up between Kyiv and Moscow. Somewhat hysterically, the Ukrainian President Petro Poroshenko responded to the standoff by declaring a state of emergency in all regions bordering Russia and Russian-controlled territories of Ukraine, including the Kharkiv Oblast.

The surest sign that this would disrupt football came a week later, when UEFA announced the Europa League game between Arsenal and FC Vorskla, from the city of Poltava, would be moved to Kyiv for safety reasons, despite the fact that Poltava was nowhere near the regions affected by martial law (there were rumours that the governing body cowed to pressure from Arsenal over where the game should be played, and certainly both Vorskla and the city itself were caustic in their reaction to losing out on the chance to welcome a Premier League team for no justifiable sporting reason).

The inevitable decree that the game between Shakhtar and Lyon in Kharkiv would be moved to the capital came just a few days before the game was due to happen (ludicrously, since it had been clear to everyone that UEFA could not allow Kharkiv to host a Champions League match once they had said no to Poltava) after the Lyon club president complained his team had been unable to find a company willing to charter a private flight to the affected regions.

I'd decided to follow through on my plan to go to Kharkiv and to then make the 500km journey to Kyiv on the day of the game. Predictably, UEFA's last-minute dallying had placed a massive demand on the tickets on the rail and air routes, which left me with the only option of travelling for ten hours through the night by bus in the blizzards that had carpeted most of the route with six inches of snow.

'You can see in the streets, things are normal,' states Ivanov. 'Martial law, they call it. It was a big mistake from the President. It's affected no one except a few soldiers, but why could we not play football here?'

The idea that Kharkiv had been unsafe to host an international football match was clearly ludicrous. The party line from Kyiv was that there had been an increase in soldiers being deployed on the streets – though this was hardly apparent – and that the presidency had assumed increased powers to limit internet communications should the authorities see fit.

Neither of these measures should have been a barrier to football. The formal reason for the declaration of martial law was that the skirmish in the Sea of Azov had created a legitimate risk of a ground invasion from Russia, but few in the country's press lent this idea any credibility. The more popular theory that some people believed was that Poroshenko was hoping to drag the emergency out long enough to postpone the upcoming presidential elections that most felt he was destined to lose (Poroshenko was voted out of office in April 2019 in favour of the current President, comedian turned politician Volodymyr Zelensky).

Indeed, I encountered fewer armed military personnel during the twenty-four hours that I spent in Kharkiv than I would have expected on an average day in central London. I did come across one pair of young-looking soldiers in khaki gear, which was at around 3 a.m. as I fought my way through a blizzard in the deserted streets towards the central bus station. After walking past them I turned the corner to find a ten-metre long cock and balls had been freshly drawn in the snow.

The long trip to Kyiv wasn't really worth it in the end. No one at the stadium wanted to talk to me about Shakhtar, not even other journalists in the press box. The club itself refused to provide anyone to be interviewed, a position they maintained for more than a year afterwards despite my repeated requests. The match at the Olympic Stadium was a let-down too. Shakhtar drew 1–1 with Lyon in the snow, a result that saw them knocked out of the Champions League, though I watched the second half on a TV in the press room for fear I might freeze to death in the exposed media gantry.

There was talk in the football press in Ukraine during my stay of Shakhtar relocating permanently to Kyiv. Certainly, in the current political climate there is no hope of them returning to Donetsk any time soon.

III

A little after 10 p.m. and there's no one to be seen on the streets of Donetsk. There's still an hour to go before the citywide military curfew descends, by which time you'd better be off the streets or prepared to face the ire of gun-toting lawmen.

Still, no one's taking any chances. The city is already slipping into a state of quiet, eerie stasis. It won't stir again till 5 a.m. tomorrow when the curfew is lifted.

Why this is necessary, nobody seems able or willing to say. The people of Donetsk are in a state of inertia, their spirits have been weakened by years of conflict and isolation that has now turned to a degenerative stalemate.

Dead-eyed soldiers guard the city's borders with zealous dedication. Even the sites of the town's once bustling nightlife have been claimed by gunmen, repurposed for shadowy activities euphemistically termed 'military intelligence'.

Welcome to Donetsk, formerly free and fizzing with life, now a pawn in a prolonged and convoluted proxy war.

After my lengthy detention at the Donetsk border as I'd tried to enter from Rostov-on-Don in Russia, I was eventually rescued by my fixer Mikhail, who drove two hours to the camp to bail me out. After a hasty dinner during which we made our plans for the next few days, I set off into town to see what has survived of life here since the war.

After an hour of traipsing the streets I find the only pub in the city still open, and sit down thirstily at the bar to order a glass of whatever beer they're still able to import into the separatist Donetsk People's Republic (DPR). The beer is fine but the service is dour, a glassy-eyed, skinhead muscle-man slams my drink down on the counter without meeting my gaze, and flatly ignores my attempt to strike up a conversation about the Ajax v. PAOK Salonika Champions League match flickering on the TV.

The people of Donetsk have lost the thing they loved most. Shakhtar Donetsk, champions of Ukraine and European heavyweight, are long gone from the city. They last played here, at their glorious 50,000-capacity Donbass Arena, in May 2014, in a 3–1 win against Illichivets Mariupol to claim a fifth straight league title. Barely 18,000 turned up to see the game, which was down to human survival as the city braced for war rather than supporter apathy.

Two days later, the flag of the self-proclaimed DPR was raised – illegally – over the city's police headquarters. Ukraine retaliated against the separatists with a bombardment of shelling.

The club have continued to dominate the league, despite being refugees in their new temporary home 300km away in Kharkiv, and have been racking up domestic titles like they've been going out of fashion.

But it is Shakhtar's European record that its fans most cherish. In 2009, they became the first Ukrainian club since independence to win on the continent when they beat Werder Bremen to lift the UEFA Cup, and two years later they reached the Champions League quarter-final where they faced the mighty Barcelona. In their final season in Donetsk, they held Manchester United to a hard-fought draw at the Donbass Arena, and put four goals past Spanish high-flyers Real Sociedad.

Only one thing matters more to the club than winning, and that's winning against their bitterest rival, Dynamo Kyiv. As one old Shakhtar song goes, 'just as coal becomes dust, we will grind down Kyiv's will'.

Dynamo Kyiv were the team associated with the Soviet interior ministry, and under their legendary coach Valeriy Lobanovskyi won more USSR league titles than any other club. Even post-independence Dynamo were a team of international significance. In 1999, coached by Lobanovskyi and led by a young Andriy Shevchenko, they reached the semi-finals of the Champions League. Had they hung on to the 3–1 lead they raced into in the first leg in Kyiv it would have been them and not Bayern Munich that advanced to play Manchester United in the tournament's most famous final.

Meanwhile, Shakhtar had their origins in the coal industry, and came from a city built by miners, for miners. And aside from a couple of runners-up finishes and a handful of Soviet Cup wins, they never troubled the USSR's elite outfits, and it was not until the economic liberalisation of the post-Communist 1990s that they started to seriously rival Kyiv as a football power.

Shakhtar v. Dynamo is a microcosm of the conflict that created the 2014 Donbass War; the Russified industrial hard men of the east versus the capital's bloodless Ukrainian nationalists. In Soviet times Shakhtar were the uncouth, noisy upstarts, whilst Dynamo were grandees of the whole USSR, and had won thirteen national titles through the ordained benefactors of the Communist Party of Ukraine. One club was built with soot and calluses, powered by honest, unpretentious Soviet industry; the other by city bureaucrats and metropolitan intellectuals.

As was chronicled by Jonathan Wilson in his book *Behind the Curtain*, former Shakhtar vice-president Mark Levytsky encapsulated the difference between his club and Dynamo by scoffing 'let them read Balzac, we will concentrate on football' after being told that his Kyiv counterpart had framed their rivalry with some high-culture literary reference.

Since Ukrainian independence in 1991, the teams have fought it out at the top of the league; in recent years one has been weighed down by its own expectations, whilst the other has been elevated by an oligarch grandee with bottomless pockets and an unshakable desire to see his hometown burn down the old order. Dynamo have failed to live up to the record set by their legendary grand master, the tactical savant

Lobanovskyi who is still idolised in Kyiv, because they have not been able to detach from his myth. Shakhtar, meanwhile, have gratefully splurged the millions gifted to them by their president, the Donbass industrialist and Ukraine's richest man, Rinat Akhmetov, and have become a member of European football's cosmopolitan elite.

The crisis in eastern Ukraine and Shakhtar's abandonment of the city of Donetsk are part of a political earthquake, at the centre of which sits Eastern Europe's most visceral football rivalry.

'The people aren't angry about Shakhtar leaving. They're just in pain.' Oleg Antipov, former press secretary at the club and now a member of the DPR Football Union, is doing a stoic job of masking a broken heart. He's bearing up – just.

In the USSR, the relationship between Shakhtar and its fans was so tight that after a bad result the club would send players into the mineshafts for 'feedback' sessions with angry workers.

The mining communities of Donbass built the old club. Its players were the sons of pit workers, and its supporters watched their games from atop slag heaps with coal-blackened faces from the day's work. When the team abandoned their home ground in 2014 they left behind regret, recriminations and a $500 million hole in the ground.

I meet Antipov on my first sun-kissed morning in Donetsk at the start of a long, hazy summer. They're used to temperature extremes here. It's one of the few things they've been able to rely on since peace turned to war in 2014. But this has been a particularly oppressive few weeks as the heatwaves that have been sweeping east across the continent have turned the flatlands of Eastern Europe into sweating, restless dust bowls.

Having failed to find a room at the fancy Shakhtar Plaza, which was built for the Euro 2012 championships and is still in surprising demand given the city's circumstances, I booked into the Hotel Ekonomic, which lives up to the meagre promise of its name. After my hellish experience at the border, I would have greeted the most spartan lodgings with ready glee, and I politely decline the offer of an upgrade at the expense of the DPR's Ministry of Sport. The modest facilities offered by the Ekonomic are more than sufficient.

Despite the forty-degree heat, I have not seen Antipov dressed in anything but a colourless cotton shirt and sad, toneless slacks. His salt and pepper hair matches the lines of his aged face; seasoned and functional.

He is popular. Every hour like clockwork his phone chimes with a call from some long-held acquaintances in the meandering world of modern life in the new Donetsk. He also has a way of casually making Donetsk's tragedy sound like it is poetry.

'You hear the sound of the glass breaking,' he says of the air raids that started in mid-2014. 'Your house is shaking. You're standing in your hall thinking, "Please let it pass. Please not me this time." Then you hear the sound of the bomb exploding next to you.'

Despite his beige appearance, Antipov is relentlessly charismatic. His deep love and knowledge of his Donetsk, and of Shakhtar, is his key animator. If something happened in this city, Antipov can tell you about it. He is at once patriot, patriarch and footballing cognoscenti.

One of those phone calls comes from Ihor Petrov, a former Shakhtar captain and now president of the DPR's Football Union. He wore the skipper's armband when independent Ukraine played its first competitive match, a 2–0 European Championship qualifying defeat against Lithuania in Kyiv way back in 1994, and we are planning to meet him today at the city's old Olympic Stadium downtown.

That Lithuania game was played in an eerie atmosphere. A look at the video confirms only a smattering of fans turned out, spread across the huge sprawling terraces of Kyiv's Olympic Stadium, with both supporters and players obviously still coming to terms with the reality that they were no longer citizens of the Soviet Union.

Petrov hails from Horlovka, a settlement near the border where the DPR meets Ukraine proper that has been especially damaged by the conflict. He was signed to Shakhtar by the age of sixteen, and but for a short spell playing in Israel during the 1990s has known nothing but Donetsk and Shakhtar all his life.

Horlovka, Antipov tells me, is one of the most devastated parts of Donetsk Oblast, but the town has responded by having by far the strongest attendances in the DPR's amateur football league. 'The people crave normality,' he states wryly. 'This is how they find it.'

When we meet Petrov on the stadium forecourt, he is surprisingly diminutive. He is a full foot shorter than me and not nearly as broad. His voice is wispy and shrill, and I find it hard to imagine this is the man that led Shakhtar to their first trophy post-independence – a Ukrainian Cup win in 1995 – or for that matter the figure who went on those powerful midfield bursts that I had seen on the tapes of the Lithuania match.

I want to know what motivated him to stick it out in a warzone and team up with the rebel government, rather than duck out and watch the war on TV from Ukraine or Russia.

'I rejected offers from Kyiv and Moscow as a player, so why would I leave now?' asks Petrov, slightly offended by the question. This is the Donbass pride that Antipov had prepared me for. 'I made a decision to stay, no matter what. This is my home. I could have gone to Kyiv and extended my coaching licence. Now my licence has expired, I cannot go to Kyiv to renew it. My travel documents are no longer valid.'

The Ukraine team from 1994 was a troubled entity. After the fall of the USSR, many players couldn't decide whether they were Ukrainian or Russian, and there were players like the future Manchester United forward Andrei Kanchelskis, who represented Russia and the Commonwealth of Independent States.

Kanchelskis explained his decision in a 2018 interview with *FourFourTwo*: 'I chose to play for Russia rather than Ukraine. People in

Ukraine said bad things, shouting that I was born in Ukraine but played for Russia. But I wasn't the only one – Ukraine couldn't play at the 1994 World Cup, and six players born there chose to play for Russia instead.' The team was much weakened as a result.

This complicated sense of divided loyalty has afflicted Ukrainian political and social life in the twenty-five years since.

Here in the east of Ukraine, they speak Russian. Donbass looks to Moscow, not Kyiv, as its spiritual capital, and the people feel themselves to be intrinsically part of the Russian world. When Ukraine had its revolution and toppled the Donetsk hero and pro-Russian President Viktor Yanukovych from power, it was the final straw, the cue for the east to break away at any cost.

Five years into the conflict, the relationship between Donbass and the rest of the country would now appear to be completely non-existent. The Ukrainian government curates a website that lists individuals that are allegedly terrorists by dint of the merest association with the DPR. It includes the names of hundreds or politicians, sportspeople and public figures with known connections to the rebel state in Donetsk. Ihor Petrov's name is on it.

'As usual, sport has become mixed up with politics,' he states. 'I have been deemed to be assisting the "terrorists" of the DPR just by working here. If I try to enter Ukraine, I don't know what will happen. I suspect I will be arrested. The government of Ukraine are looking for people to blame. They have disqualified football coaches. They have disqualified players, regardless of past achievements in Ukraine. It's what happens when you mix up politics with sport.'

Petrov was once awarded the highest civilian honour in Ukraine for his services to football, having overseen the design and implementation of schools and academies for disadvantaged young footballers across the country. Now he dares not even approach the border.

'Even when I captained the national team, that feeling of being

Ukrainian was not born inside myself,' he explains. 'I still feel the USSR in my heart. I long more for the Russian Federation, because it represents that past. I never felt much for Ukraine.'

The dissonance between Kyiv and the Donbass dates to the first settlements here. In the last quarter of the eighteenth century, after Catherine II had made peace with Russia's historic adversaries, the Muslim Tartars of Crimea, she thus felt suitably secure in her frontiers to abolish the Ukrainian Cossack Hetmanate, the political unit surrounding Kyiv that despite being under Russian sovereignty had been allowed autonomy to live according to Ukrainian customs.

At the same time, the fertile 'wild field' that lay between Russia and the Black Sea steppe was made free from Tartar threat, and an intensive programme of agrarian and industrial development was embarked on in the territory Catherine dubbed '*Novorossia*' – 'New Russia'. The new programme saw the construction of two major new cities, Ekaterinoslav (now Dnepropetrovsk) and Odessa, but it was in the coal-rich flats of the Donets Basin that what was to become the empire's industrial engine room was established.

The Welsh metallurgic industrialist John Hughes was invited by the Russian government to found a steel plant in Novorossia in 1869. The settlement took the name 'Yuzovka' (a Russian rendering of 'Hughes-town'), and as migrant labourers flocked to the Donbass from across the empire, the region grew beneath its multifarious slag heaps to become Novorossia's bustling centre.

Their arrival riled the local Ukrainian-speaking farm communities. 'Local girls used to abscond from their communities and run off to the new settlements,' recalls Antipov. 'In any culture, that's going to cause problems. You're not going to feel much love. During the Russian Empire, incoming labour migrants would buy the land off the locals and set up new communities focused around the factories and mining shafts,' Antipov says of Shakhtar's origins. 'These were the migrant labour communities that eventually started the football club.'

The rise of the Donbass and the intermingling of Russian settlers with Ukrainian-speaking locals created friction, not helped by the continued Russification that was swiftly taking place amongst the native peoples of the dismantled Cossack Hetmanate, nicknamed '*Khokhali*' after the shaven-headed ponytails of the Ukrainian Cossacks.

Antipov, Petrov and I have walked to the Lenin Komsomol Park in the shadow of the Donbass Arena, which is surrounded by stones gathered from all over the unique geological landscape of the old city. The stadium sits 100 metres off, set against a rolling landscape that is dotted with slag heaps. You can clearly see the damage sustained when the arena was hit by shells that were fired by the Ukrainian army in 2014.

Even in the earliest origins of Shakhtar, the seeds of conflict were being sown. A national consciousness was forged that set the migrant workers of Donbass apart from other Ukrainians. Yuzovka (the town didn't acquire the name Donetsk until 1961) stood outside the formation of the Ukrainian nation, carried along by the growing confidence and social influence of the Donbass 'Little Russians' ('*Malorossians*').

'The first football game here happened in 1906, between engineers and technicians of the mineshafts,' describes Viktor Zvyahintsev, former Shakhtar skipper in the 1970s and a defender for the USSR national team. A decade later, 'a lot of German and Hungarian soldiers that were captured during the First World War settled here. They interacted with locals and taught them how to play football.'

During this time, football and mining became the rites of passage. Payday in Donbass meant a three-day riot. Amongst the slag heaps and pop-up villages, money was splurged on jewellery, gifts and booze in seventy-two hours of hard partying.

This became ritualistic; work hard, play hard, bread and spectacle, a celebration of the land and the fruits of labour. And of course, there was Shakhtar, the club created by the local Communist Party's All Union Council on Physical Culture and Sports.

Founded in 1936, the side was first called Stakhanovets after Alexei Stakhanov, the Donbass coalminer who became a Soviet propaganda poster boy due to his superhuman feats of labour. The Stakhanovite movement helped fuel the Stalinist five-year industrial plans of the 1930s, where workers drove their bodies into fits of exhaustion in the race to obliterate production quotas, in an attempt to modernise the backward USSR at breakneck speed.

Stakhanov was a symbol of Soviet iconography; the subjugation of the individual to the building of the new socialist world. The football club, renamed as FC Shakhtar, became a church for this new era.

'Football in Donetsk was truly international,' explains Zvyahintsev. 'The technicalities and strategies of different schools from all over were brought here by migrating workers. Every region of Europe has its own ideas on how to do things. All those ideas were brought to Donbass.'

For the first 100 years, Donbass took in wanderers and strays and churned out coal and footballers. In winning the Soviet Cup in 1961, Donetsk became known throughout the USSR as a football power.

The players from this era are now legends. The galloping full-back Vyacheslav Aliabiev, next to the rock-solid central defender Vladimir Salkov, were children of Donbass who learned to play the game amongst the region's slag heaps, and carried in them the spirit of the land. They were marshalled by the great coach Oleg Oshenkov from Saint Petersburg — Donbass steel combined with Russian guile was the formula for a uniquely effective football machine. They retained the cup in 1962.

'It helped that they were supported by the Soviet football structures that created links between the different generations,' states Antipov. 'Youngsters in the USSR were passed up through the age groups, doing things the same at each level. It was tightly controlled.'

Local hostilities between those living and working in the mining villages and the native citizens from the region were suspended during the years of the USSR.

But the Soviet Union's fragmentation in 1991 reminded people what and who they were deep down in their bones, and what and who their ancestors had been before Moscow had told them that they were Soviet. A countdown had started, even if nobody knew what it was counting towards.

* * *

When Inter Milan were having a particularly rough time in the early 2010s, AC Milan supporters goaded their great rivals with a huge banner at the San Siro stadium which read: 'When you are in hell, only the devil can help you out,' a reference to their former manager and public relations liability Roberto Mancini.

The implication was that re-appointing the hot-headed Italian, who had brought success to Inter but who also seemed to drag controversy with him, was their only way out of a deep hole.

I often think about Mancini and the Milan fans when I'm in Eastern Europe. The years after the fall of Communism were shadowy and dangerous. State property in the ex-Soviet republics was privatised at speed and with scant regard, and lucrative assets were flogged to speculative bidders with much to splurge and little to lose.

The architects of the old system's sickly corruption suddenly and unaccountably acquired huge personal wealth and as a result ruthless syndicates and mafia empires were created. Terrifying urban wars were fought over territory and the control of black markets.

Football clubs, meanwhile, were skint. Even mighty Dynamo Kyiv briefly found itself facing financial oblivion once its patron, the Communist Party, went up in smoke.

In Donetsk, Shakhtar had a choice to make; dance with the devil or go to the wall. There were plenty of investors from which to choose. A plea from the paper's editor printed in an edition of Donetsk local daily *Gorod* offers a chilling snapshot of life in post-Communist Donbass: 'Donetsk residents have a big request for you [the mafia]: Shoot and kill each other, but do not disturb civilians. Do not shoot from machine guns and grenade launchers in crowded places.'

One such individual to which this plea was aimed was a provincial entrepreneur of Volga Tartar descent named Akhat Bragin. 'Alik the Greek', as he was known in the underworld, acquired ownership of Shakhtar from the Donetsk city administration at the start of the 1990s at a time when the financial shock of privatisation threatened the club with bankruptcy. By 1995, Alik the Greek stood at the head of the largest financial and industrial group in Ukraine.

'The 1990s in the ex-Soviet republics were a scary time to live because of all the mafia and gang activity,' states Vyacheslav Sharafudinov. Before the war, Sharafudinov was one of the most respected voices in Ukrainian football, a TV pundit of thirty years and an incorrigible advocate of the footballing supremacy of the east. 'In Donetsk, criminals were dividing up the city into different empires. There were many murders committed.'

Eager for a flavour of the past, I've arranged for this afternoon's meeting with Sharafudinov to take place in Shcherbakov Central Park in order to visit the old Shakhtar Stadium. Back in November 2000 when I was twelve, I watched Arsenal lose 3–0 at this place on my parents' TV, during Shakhtar's Champions League debut season. It was a wild, misty night, and the broadcast captured with shimmering clarity the excitement of the crowd as they battered an Arsenal team featuring World Cup-winners Thierry Henry and Patrick Vieira.

Crumbling and decrepit, the ground was abandoned by Shakhtar long before the war in Donbass. Its white walls are cracked and covered with graffiti. Amongst the artless scrawling, I try to spot some act of protest, some expression of civil disobedience that mourns the wreck that this old temple to football has become. But there is none. The graffiti is just graffiti, created by vandals rather than social agitators. The Shakhtar Stadium is now just an easel for the brushstrokes of boredom and futility that has become life in Donetsk. At least today the sun is shining.

Sharafudinov cuts a rounded, stooped figure when I meet him on the bridge over Shcherbakov's green and peaceful lake, in the shadow of one of the stadium's floodlights. He has lived and worked all his life in Donetsk, curating and reporting on the rise to power of his beloved Shakhtar.

His large, balding head has caught the sun, and it is covered in a thin layer of sweat that gives it a dull, pinkish shine. However, this doesn't distract from his two gigantic dark-grey eyebrows that look like spiders trapped inside a thick wire mesh.

Since the club abandoned the city, he has served as chief executive in the DPR's Football Union, and as such is listed as a terrorist sympathiser by the government of Ukraine.

'Just at the moment when our club president [Bragin] was reviving the team, he was assassinated by his political enemies,' declares Sharafudinov. 'And it happened right here, at this stadium.'

At some point during Alik the Greek's rise to power, he encountered and crossed the Eastern European Bill Sikes in the Donetsk mafia land named Anatoliy Ryabin, a local thug with a hand in the business of contract killings.

After two initial attempts on Bragin's life failed, it was decided the only place where he would be sufficiently exposed would be at his beloved Shakhtar Stadium, where he never missed a game.

The operation was meticulous. Several weeks ahead of time, Ryabin's cronies spent three nights digging a hollow cavity in the concrete beneath the steps to the stadium's executive lounge, a few feet from where Sharafudinov and I are standing now. They filled it with 5kg of plastic explosives, then cemented over the hole and covered it with a wooden step. It was decided that the assassination would take place on the night of 28 September 1995, during a Cup Winners' Cup tie against Club Brugge of Belgium.

Almost unthinkably for a home game, Bragin failed to show, and the plan was postponed until three weeks later, the day of a Ukrainian Premier League match against FC Tavriya from Simferopol.

The hotly anticipated match was televised live on national TV – Shakhtar had been runners-up the previous season, and Tavriya had been the first champions of an independent Ukraine just a couple of years earlier.

The game had been going for five minutes when the bomb was detonated by remote control. Bragin, along with five of his aides, were killed instantly. The devastation was so gruesome that the president could only be identified by his trademark Rolex wristwatch that was still fastened around the wrist of his severed arm. Miraculously, none of the players or match-going supporters were hurt (although a waitress in the hospitality section was injured), and the game was quickly abandoned.

The assassination of Ukraine's most powerful oligarch was the formative event in the building of the financial-industrial complex of the Donbass, and of Ukraine. Rinat Akhmetov – who had been stuck in traffic at the moment the bomb went off – stepped into Bragin's shoes, both as president of Shakhtar and as inheritor of his boss's financial and industrial empire.

Alik the Greek discovered his protégé Akhmetov as a talented card player in their native village of Oktyabrsky when he was just out of school in around 1983, and drew him into his inner circle to take the place of a recently murdered associate.

Formally working as a butcher, Akhmetov learned the ways of the new private cooperatives pioneered by Bragin in the heady age of perestroika. The youngest member of this inner circle, Akhmetov lacked the physical and reputational standing of his new peers, but he quickly learned a wily knack for survival. Bragin gave him his first 'commercial' experience, which in 1980s Donbass was a euphemism for the Pandora's Box of opportunities that perestroika had cracked open.

An investigation in Ukraine in 2012 by the uncompromisingly entitled *Journal of Arbitrariness and Public Resistance to Illegal Acts* into the activities of the Bragin syndicate extracted testimony from locals of Oktyabrsky that claimed this mafioso circle earned its early money and power through the daylight extortion of ordinary working people. When asked about the young Akhmetov's personal involvement in the circle's business activities, the respondents to the journal's investigation had little to say.

This city was always the keystone to peace. During the 1990s, Ukraine's President Leonid Kuchma cut a deal with the governors of Donetsk, promising huge political and economic autonomy as well as the freedom to forge close ties with Russia in exchange for votes, so that he might create a stable government and stave off a bloody coup d'état threatened by the country's organised crime emperors.

In 2002, Kuchma chose the governor of Donetsk, a popular figure named Viktor Yanukovych to be his new Prime Minister.

Yanukovych, a Russian-speaker and Donbass native, had won the permanent loyalty of industrial eastern Ukraine by securing a huge government bailout in the mid-1990s after an economic slump forced dozens of mines and steel works to close.

He was also a massive and outspoken Shakhtar Donetsk fan – the club had won its first-ever title under the Italian coach Nevio Scala a few months before Yanukovych's appointment – as well as being a close political ally of the club's benefactor Akhmetov. The new Prime Minister was a regular at the Shcherbakov Park stadium for Shakhtar games, but he was also conscious of the political expediency of allying with the favoured football club in a workers' region like Donbass.

Yanukovych's political support in the south and east of the country helped him to secure a surprise win in the 2004 presidential election.

But the fabric of Ukraine was changing. A new generation of voters had emerged; young people who had come of age in a post-Soviet world and who had come to identify more with Europe than with Russia.

Corrupt Communist Party practices that had continued into the age of independence and blighted the government were rejected outright by the public. People no longer sanctioned their leaders to cut deals with criminals in order to keep the peace. A renewed Ukrainian nationalism was replacing the age-old kinship with Mother Russia.

Yanukovych's election win was sensationally thrown out by Ukraine's supreme court, which deemed that it had been rigged and blighted by fraud. As thousands set up camp in their tents on Independence Square in a furious protest at the direction the country was heading in, a second vote was held, and this time the disgraced Yanukovych was beaten to the presidency by the Ukrainian nationalist leader Viktor Yushchenko.

Everywhere in Ukraine, they call the events of 2004 the Orange Revolution. Except for in the east of the country, where they still bristle at the betrayal of their man Yanukovych and prefer the term 'Orange Putsch'.

If first the USSR, and latterly the clever premiership of President Kuchma, had kept the *Muskali* (the derogatory Ukrainian term for Russians) and *Khokhali* suspended in a state of enforced harmony – one country harbouring two distinct and opposing nations – then the Orange Revolution and election of Yushchenko was the grenade that blew it apart.

In politics, appearances are everything. 'Viktor Yushchenko rehabilitated fascism and nationalism during his time in power,' claims Sharafudinov. 'That ideology was not there before him. The people of east and west had been united before 2004. The political direction of Yushchenko, plus the fact that Shakhtar were becoming much stronger, created two concurrent negativities. The Kyiv government turned nationalists against Russian speakers, but also Shakhtar's success made them dislike us even more.'

Yushchenko's leadership began with a government decree that all national TV broadcasts, including football commentaries, were to be conducted in Ukrainian. 'In eastern Ukraine, the fans and the players all spoke Russian,' explains Sharafudinov.

'Yet I had to sit behind the microphone and commentate in Ukrainian. Even the foreign players coming here spoke Russian. The language law was forced on us. That's when we started to see the separation between the *Muskali* and the *Khokhali*. When we visited Western clubs, our South American and African players would get off the bus and ultras would shout, "*Muskali, Muskali*". The message was that anyone who wasn't from Ukraine was bad.'

Whether the changes that were beginning to take place in Ukrainian football exacerbated or were exacerbated by this political shift, is a matter about which everyone in Donetsk seems to agree. Nobody seriously doubts that the new success of Shakhtar played a role in deepening distrust felt by Kyiv towards the Russified east.

Akhmetov's millions had been making a slow, patchy job of rebuilding the team after the fall of Communism nearly left it bankrupt.

'It was hard to attract foreigners to a city that wasn't well known,' remarks Ihor Petrov, who captained Akhmetov's first squad in the 1980s. 'But the president and his partners were young and energetic. They were maybe twenty-seven, twenty-eight years old. Their business continued to grow after they came to Shakhtar, and they grew richer. This gave them more money to develop the club.'

Shakhtar finished second to Dynamo five seasons in a row between 1997 and 2001, during which time they made a first appearance in the Champions League.

Then, in 2001, the first foreign coach was appointed, the former Inter Milan player Nevio Scala, and the first true shift followed.

The manager may have been Italian, but the team was Donbass. Shakhtar's long-awaited first Ukrainian Premier League title was won by homegrown players. Baby-faced striker Andrei Vorobey – who scored with a sublime angled finish past David Seaman when Shakhtar raced into a 2–0 lead against Arsenal at Highbury in September 2000 (they eventually lost 3–2) – led the team from the front as a lithe and nippy striker raised in the shadow of the Donetsk slag heaps; he went on to score well over a hundred goals during his ten years at the club. A clip of his goal against Seaman flashed up on screen at the Donbass Arena museum when I visited with Antipov. 'Vorobey was a brilliant goal scorer for us,' he waxed, almost bleary-eyed with nostalgia. 'He was everything that is Shakhtar.'

Anatoliy Tymoshchuk, a fierce defensive midfielder who played 144 times for Ukraine, became one of Shakhtar's most successful exports during these golden years. He left the club in 2007, not for Dynamo Kyiv, but for Zenit Saint Petersburg and later Bayern Munich, though he had largely given Shakhtar the best years of his stellar career.

Oleksiy Byelik, a local boy who looked like a man twice his age, scored goals for fun, as Shakhtar raced into the last weeks of the 2001/02 season unbeaten in the league.

Tymoshchuk, Byelik and Vorobey, alongside a small clutch of imports from Nigeria, Senegal and other Eastern European nations, heralded the changing of the guard in Ukrainian football. It was the kind of story that belonged to another era, a team made up of a cohort of superstar players from within a stone's throw of the club's home ground. It all came to a head on the penultimate day of the season at the start of the summer of 2002.

Shakhtar trailed Dynamo in the league by two points when the champions from the capital travelled to Shcherbakov Central Park.

Scala's team knew that defeat would mean their great rivals would clinch the title on their pitch.

Whatever ghosts haunted Ukraine's second-best team were exorcised that day: own-goals from Kyiv's Sergei Fedorov and Goran Gavrančić gifted the hosts a 2–0 win that changed the course of Ukrainian football history. The following week, Shakhtar won 1–0 away at FC Zakarpattia in the Carpathians, the heart of Ukrainian nationalism, to lift the title for the very first time.

'We had taken a new confidence from the appointment of Scala,' recalls Petrov. 'The team had been getting stronger with Akhmetov, but we still weren't catching Dynamo. So the idea came to change the coach. As the first foreign manager, he brought something the club hadn't had before. It got the team out of old ways. It showed us that we could beat Dynamo Kyiv.'

Scala's title victory didn't create the dynasty Akhmetov had wanted. Instead, the Italian departed that summer, and the club re-hired its former coach from the 1980s and 1990s, Valeriy Yaremchenko, for a third spell in charge. Shakhtar enjoyed a healthy lead going into the final month of the season in spring 2003, before a 2–1 defeat to Dynamo on the run-in reopened old wounds and sent the title back to the capital.

The appointment of Romanian coach Mircea Lucescu proved to be the key that unlocked it all. As well as being an experienced international manager, Lucescu brought a cult of personality to Shakhtar and became the kind of authoritarian figurehead that was canonised in the Soviet world. Suddenly, the club had its own alchemist to rival the legend of the great Lobanovskyi at Kyiv.

'In the 2000s, Dynamo got stuck on the programme of Lobanovskyi,' says Antipov. 'He had his own mythology. But he would always adapt his programme to which players were available to him. The directors at Dynamo in the last few years weren't able to adapt the programme like Lobanovskyi could.'

As Dynamo followed the new trend of bringing in foreign imports, so the new players found themselves either unable or unwilling to adapt to the intensity of the old ways. Concurrently, the post-Soviet freedom of movement gave local players the choice to explore other football opportunities abroad.

'If the programme is right but the players are wrong, you will get no results,' states Antipov. 'That's what Dynamo have found now. The extra intense physical training of the Dynamo players that Lobanovskyi taught is too much for today's players,' adds Petrov. 'It is quite possible to get to a good level with only half of that physical pressure. But it's true that Dynamo failed to adapt.'

Dynamo continued to appoint coaches strictly from within their ranks well into this century, and this became a string of managers forever second-guessing the genius of their late mentor Lobanovskyi. Shakhtar, meanwhile, incautiously began to throw away its own handbook.

'Lucescu was the one who started bringing in young Brazilians and developing them to sell,' says Petrov. 'That was very profitable for the team, and we were able to develop more from that money. It was the work of Lucescu that turned Shakhtar into Ukraine's best team. The USSR used to have an ideal football system. Children were brought up and injected into the system. Each level was tightly controlled in the classical Soviet way.'

When the Soviet Union broke up, the education system for football became neglected. The connections between generations, ruthlessly forged through branches of the various Communist parties, started to fragment.

'Whoever was talented, they left for other countries,' explains Petrov of a post-independence exodus. 'By the time of 2005, there was no new generation coming through in Russia or Ukraine, so we made the choice to look at Brazil. When we look back, there was no other option.'

The last of the central trio of Vorobey, Tymoshchuk and Byelik finally left in 2009. Now, a network of agents and scouts placed all over South America has turned the new Shakhtar into the Brazil of Eastern Europe.

One of the first to arrive in eastern Ukraine in 2005 was the midfielder Jádson from Atlético Paranaense, who was the player who poked home the winner during extra time in the 2009 UEFA Cup final against Werder Bremen in Istanbul.

Other players have proved to be astute transfer market investments. The winger Douglas Costa became the most expensive player ever bought or sold by a Ukrainian team when Bayern Munich paid €30 million for him in 2015. The Chelsea and Brazil winger Willian, who left Shakhtar in 2013, has won the Premier League twice and played at two World Cups, and his compatriot Fernandinho has won three titles with Manchester City since he left Donetsk, also in 2013.

Away from the pitch, the club was also revolutionised, starting with the multimillion-dollar renovation of its stunning Kirsha training base. International consultants were hired to overhaul marketing, finance and youth development departments. A training centre for 3,000 children was opened, and Shakhtar became the first Ukrainian team to launch its own TV channel.

At the same time, the club was absorbed into Akhmetov's holding company, the multinational Systems Capital Management, which created a higher level of transparency and mimicked the business models used by Western clubs. The pace of modernisation in the Ukrainian football league during this period would have amazed even the Soviet industrial legend Alexei Stakhanov.

After 2004 and the increasing reliance on Brazilian imports, many older fans deserted the club. 'It used to be that the result didn't matter,' argues Antipov. 'All the fans wanted was to see local players giving everything for the spirit of Donbass. It's all changed now. All that matters is the result.'

'The club forgot its own legends,' claims Sharafudinov. 'That started in 2004, long before the war in Donbass. That's what upsets us the most.'

* * *

The Donbass Arena was the first UEFA four-star stadium built in Eastern Europe. The Euro 2012 semi-final was played there, the world champions Spain beating Portugal on penalties in front of more than 48,000 spectators and maybe a billion more watching on TV.

'It was built off the back of industry that we the people created and sustained,' enthuses Antipov, gazing off from the dugout towards the goal where those semi-final penalties were taken.

Shakhtar moved in to the Donbass Arena in 2009, swapping the crumbling 1930s terraces over at Shcherbakov Park for this glistening new amphitheatre. However, there is no football played here now though; the only sign there ever was is a polite 'Keep off the grass' notice planted at the edge of the recently re-laid pitch.

The stadium is spectacular, right down to the gleaming high-tech dressing rooms and medical facilities. It was here that Shakhtar's famous blind masseuse Vladimir Tkachenko worked his magic until 2014.

Tkachenko is one of those cultural luminaries that dot the history of football in Eastern Europe. Club legend recounts how his giant hands saved the career of the team's captain of the 1970s Mykhaylo Sokolovsky after curing an injury that had stumped the city's best medical minds.

Unlike a lot of new-build stadiums, Shakhtar have done a proper job of making this place home. There is even an empty frame in the home dressing room where there used to hang a decades-old Orthodox icon that was said to have brought the club good luck. All that's missing these days is the team.

The arena has suffered terrible damage, once when a shell aimed at the museum of the history of Donetsk city next door missed and crashed into the stadium, which started a fire, and again when a Ukrainian rocket landed nearby and the shockwaves literally shook the stadium's roof off. The arena has had rudimentary repairs, but there's a long way before the place can be considered safe.

'It was pretty costly to repair the roof after the blast pulled it off,' explains the stadium guide Victoria, a pale redheaded girl with a soft voice and a wily authority. Once, there would have been an army of guides employed to show visitors round. 'But the job needs finishing and that takes money we don't have.'

Stepping down the players' tunnel, we tread the concrete corridors where mountains of food and medical supplies had been stored just months before, shipped here in lorries from Ukraine as part of Rinat Akhmetov's 'Let's Help the Children' aid drive.

'The produce we were receiving from Akhmetov's foundation was of a terrible quality,' complains Antipov. 'The meats we received in the packages, even my cat refused to eat.

'Some lorries arrived at the stadium and instantly left without unloading. They took the stuff to fighters on the Ukrainian side of the front line. The only decent quality, reliable relief we received came from the Russian Federation.'

In 2017, the DPR began taking over private property all over the city. This included over forty factories and coalmines that were formerly under the management of Akhmetov's company Systems Capital Management and had been trading with businesses in Ukraine. Trade from these facilities had been pouring millions of dollars into Kyiv's state coffers, until a transport blockade set up by nationalists on the Ukrainian side of the border shut it down. Now, the mines trade with businesses in the neighbouring Luhansk People's Republic, and the tax revenue goes to the DPR.

The government took over the Donbass Arena, too. 'The DPR hasn't nationalised the stadium or removed it from its rightful owner,' explains Victoria. 'We have just taken responsibility to prevent the full shutdown of these facilities. It's a practical measure.' According to Akhmetov's foundation, this forced the shutdown of the humanitarian effort that was operating out of the stadium. But you'll hear little gratitude for the president's charity here.

'The people have disowned Akhmetov for abandoning us,' states Antipov. 'His money and influence could have helped the city. But he ran. What he did for the city means nothing now.' In the park next to the stadium, a Shakhtar supporter has scratched graffiti damning Akhmetov into a bench. 'I don't know the translation,' says Antipov. 'But it's very offensive.'

Shakhtar were made to leave as a result of the security situation when the separatists took control of the city.

They cannot go back, as to do so would give implicit recognition to the rebels. Besides, it would be impossible on matchdays for visiting teams to cross the militarised line between the DPR and Ukrainian fighters.

The club still owns substantial property in the DPR, including the Donbass Arena and the world-class training complex at Kirsha. Akhmetov remains the legal owner of more than half of the working mines in Donbass, although most of these have now been seized.

There are links between Shakhtar and some football schools here that still feed talented young players into the club's new base in Kyiv, but all this means little to people these days.

'It's all up to Mr Akhmetov,' I'm told by the DPR's Sports Minister Nikolai Tarapat. 'We can't comment on his decisions. For whatever business reasons he chose to sacrifice Donetsk and move the club away. Who knows? Maybe in the future, Shakhtar could become the key to peace.'

In 2017, a Ukraine nationalist veterans organisation issued shirts bearing supportive slogans for war veterans to be worn ahead of kick-off for all teams in Ukraine's Premier League. Seventeen of the eighteen teams wore them. The one team that did not was Shakhtar.

The organisation, somewhat dramatically, blamed the Football Federation of Ukraine for intervening on Shakhtar's behalf, saying, 'The reaction by the FFU again caused only negative feeling and shows that the lice from Moscow nits within Ukraine, which continues to drink blood from simple Ukrainian patriots and debases heroes, who are risking their own lives to protect the territorial integrity of Ukraine.' There was another incident in 2014 when the team were asked to wear shirts proclaiming 'Glory to the Ukrainian Army' before a game against Karparty Lviv. Once again, Shakhtar refused.

Even the squad is divided. The defender Yaroslav Rakitskiy, a Donbass native, left the club in January 2018 for Zenit Saint Petersburg, however, his face, frothing and wide-eyed in celebration, still drapes the exterior of the stadium, glaring madly over Lenin Komsomol Park.

Since the war, he has faced repeated questioning in the press about his refusal to sing the national anthem when he played for Ukraine. Now, this is no longer a problem. Since being sold to Zenit, he has not been picked to play for the national team.

Rakitskiy, who has the Donetsk rose, the city's enduring symbol, tattooed on his arm, is derided in Ukraine as a traitor following his transfer. Zenit are sponsored by the Russian state-owned energy giant Gazprom, which has been cutting off gas supplies to Ukraine since the conflict began. The team is partly paid for by the Russian state, which Ukraine accuses of prolonging the war.

All of this has caused irreparable damage to Rakitskiy's reputation, with 57 per cent of supporters polled by the Kyiv news site *Tribune* in 2019 stating that they believed the defender should never play for the national team again.

Is this the reason why Rakitskiy's face still adorns the walls of the stadium? As a heroic symbol of the city's defiance to Kyiv's claim to sovereignty?

'Not really,' says Tarapat. 'We just can't afford the money it would cost to take it down.'

* * *

Ukraine is the obsession that unites the people of Donetsk. That's why all trace of it has been wiped from its streets, as though the government of Kyiv were as remote from here as the lost civilisation of Kievan Rus', rather than the legal seat of power.

There is an old hotel in town called the Liverpool. Outside, a glittering Union Jack mosaic covers the wall, the kind that an English traveller who is far from home is lulled into posing beside with their arms wildly aloft, grinning insanely.

In my case, after the near-catastrophe of the border check, this proves to be a provocation too far. As my fixer Mikhail and I cross the road to walk away, we're ordered back by two heavily armed soldiers in khaki fatigues, with furrowed brows and furious scowls.

The next few minutes fly by in a blur. I surrender my passport, entry visa and press licence, and Mikhail gives up his Ministry of Foreign Affairs identity card. His credentials aren't enough to buy us out of whatever fix we're in, and a call is made by the lead soldier – the more miserly looking of the two – to his commander.

I try and read Mikhail's expression for a sense of what kind of trouble we're in, but he is poker-faced, and the drops of sweat on his forehead are just as likely to be as a result of the stifling heat as out of concern for our current predicament.

Eventually, the soldiers are satisfied that I am not a security threat, and we are hurriedly sent on our way. 'The hotel is a military intelligence building now,' explains Mikhail. 'They were discussing whether or not you could have been sent here by people in Ukraine. Obviously they thought not. If they thought that you had, this would have been a very different story.'

Why is this place still so tense? I ask Mikhail. It's been years since there was any military action directed on the city itself. Most of the fighting now is consigned to the borders of Donetsk Oblast where Ukrainian and DPR forces are still facing off. The Minsk accords of 2015 agreed a ceasefire, which was supposed to ensure peace in the region.

'Because the Ukrainians fired shots at their own people,' responds Mikhail. 'They dropped bombs on their own city.' This is the extent of his explanation, and put this way, I feel as though maybe we've gotten off lightly from our indiscretions outside the Liverpool Hotel.

In 2009, the chief of the Donetsk city administration, Nikolai Levchenko, caused a shock during a televised political debate when he compared Ukrainian President Viktor Yushchenko to Adolf Hitler.

Levchenko was an upstart provocateur, a fanatic who preached about justice for the working man whilst feathering his own nest through private entrepreneurship – illegal in Ukraine for civil servants.

The east blamed Kyiv for shoddy and dangerous working conditions, a lack of investment in industry and infrastructure, poor wages. But nobody questioned the $500 million that was found for the construction of the Donbass Arena. Whilst Donetsk as a city struggled by on scraps, Rinat Akhmetov booked Beyoncé to play a private concert for the stadium's grand opening party in 2009. Shakhtar was a balm for tired minds and aching backs in the never-ending struggle against Europe and Kyiv.

'With respect for our past, we look to our future,' chimed Levchenko robotically to the cameras. It's no wonder he chose these words. They are etched into the walkway on the approach to the Donbass Arena.

A 2010 film by German director Jakob Preuss entitled *The Other*

Chelsea: A Story from Donetsk charted the comparative growth of Donbass and Shakhtar. In it, Preuss asks, 'Is oligarchy a necessary stage as the new capitalism takes root?'

Throughout the film, the upwardly mobile Levchenko lavishes praise upon Akhmetov and Yanukovych. He has little interest in football he says, but he watches every home game from the VIP box, crooning, 'Shakhtar is important for our region, and its victories are the victories of the party of regions.'

'This is a classic. It's bread and circuses,' says one worker interviewed by Preuss, citing a maxim that was popularised during the Soviet era. 'People go to football, look at the Brazilian strikers and do not ask where Akhmetov took the money to buy them. When Jádson scored against Werder in the extra period, I was jubilant too. At that moment, I would probably also vote for Yanukovych.'

The idea in Donetsk of Ukraine as a fascist state is fostered by the Russian media, but it is rooted in old theories about 'integral nationalism' and the twentieth-century rebel leader Stepan Bandera's collaboration with the Nazi occupiers during the Second World War. Viktor Yushchenko's presidency was framed in the context of this aggressive form of Ukrainianism, so too were events surrounding the Euromaidan; this image was not helped by the fact that some of the more visibly militant protesters in the winter of 2013 to 2014 were in fact affiliated with parties and movements on the extreme right. Even so, the interpretation of the situation from Donetsk is paranoid, a product of cynical de-stabilisation by Moscow.

It's a mania that runs to the very top of the DPR command. The republic's Sports Minister, the cheery, bumbling Nikolai Tarapat, has voiced some of the most invective-laden opinions of anyone I met in Donetsk. I had hoped that as a member of the government he might provide some balance, but none was forthcoming.

'We don't agree with the promotion over the last ten years of the fascist ideology in Kyiv,' Tarapat told me, before reeling off an obscure list of despots that have tried to conquer the land here, everyone from Genghis Khan to Napoleon.

'Western media show completely the wrong picture of Donbass,' he argues. 'Do you see soldiers with guns in our streets? Or have you seen a normal city with peaceful people who are just trying to live their lives?' I consider telling him that twice in recent days I have been detained by soldiers with guns, but diplomacy gets the better of me.

The separatists' whole motivation seems to be to recreate the USSR. It's actually not as bonkers as it sounds.

The official line is that the Kyiv government was asleep on the job, neglecting public infrastructure in the regions, whilst cashing in on the common man's toils in the form of austerity.

'Before, the authorities were mostly thinking only of elite sport,' states Tarapat. 'They weren't investing in sport for the people, like had been done in Soviet times. Infrastructure used to take care of itself. We had thousands of players representing dozens of factories and mineshafts, all maintaining their own training and playing facilities in their towns and villages.

'The Ukrainian government undid all the good work of the Soviet generation in sports administration. For instance, the Donbass Arena was being built, but at the same time not a single hole in the children's sports schools was filled. They were falling apart.

'We care about building sports education for the masses. This Olympic Stadium, athletes can come here and use it free of charge. Under Kyiv, they had to pay a fee to use these facilities. How does that serve the people? We believe in accessibility.'

At least regular football has survived in the DPR. A ten-team championship runs during the summer months, though the league is officially amateur now that the region's professional players have been forced to move away to save their livelihoods. The 2018 champions, the appropriately named FK Gvardeets (the Guardsmen), play their games here in Donetsk city.

Matches are played at the Olympic Stadium, where just a few years ago Shakhtar played against European giants Barcelona, AC Milan and Roma in the Champions League in front of 25,000 fans. Now, games draw tiny attendances, with most matches attracting only a few hundred spectators.

It was Shakhtar's second-choice stadium for most of their history, but they played their historic runners-up season in the Soviet Top League in 1979 at this ground. Its stands are decked out in Shakhtar's gaudy orange and black colours, and the outline of its terraces rise and fall in gorgeous undulating contours. The stadium manager, a rounded, grandfatherly fellow named Gennady Laguteev, recalls how pro-Ukrainian former employees stole all kinds of essentials from the stadium in order to sabotage it when the war began.

'The war destroyed the football industry,' states Viktor Zvyahintsev, the former Soviet defender who now heads up the city's football administration. 'Nowadays, the players with potential have all left. All we have left here are the enthusiasts. Compared with before 2014, it's like the Stone Age. It costs millions of roubles to host even a single game at the Donbass Arena. The DPR cannot afford that.'

I meet Zvyahintsev in his tiny office in the basement of a ramshackle old building in Donetsk that looks like it's being held up by mud and matchsticks.

The bare concrete floors are coated in flakes of paint shed from the tatty walls, and cobwebs gently wave and wiggle in the corners of doorways as the skeleton staff here goes about its business.

These are the corridors of power of Donetsk football, but they resemble a haunted house, dusty and dark and crammed full with junk.

Zvyahintsev had a wonderful football career. He was Shakhtar's captain during the glorious 1970s when the team twice finished second in the USSR Top League and had its first adventures in Europe. He was also a seasoned international, charging up and down the wings from full-back with his classically Soviet, galloping gait.

He is not so mobile these days. As we exchange pleasantries, he lifts his shirt to reveal enormous surgical dressings across his chest. He is fresh from the operating table and the surgeon's knife and his torso is seemingly being held together with stitches, though I politely avoid enquiring what the surgeons were doing inside of him.

Zvyahintsev gives me the usual patter about having stayed in Donetsk out of loyalty to his hometown rather than some great patriotic urge towards the separatists, but he says he feels more Russian than Ukrainian. The interview takes place through a haze of cigarette smoke; no one is concerned that Zvyahintsev is smoking himself towards an early grave, least of all himself.

'The rivalry with Kyiv developed in this century with the rise of ultra culture,' he details.

The ultras are a movement descended from English hooliganism, but with a European twist. Usually, this involves the inclusion of some political message underscored by the thrill of putting on a spectacle. Performance is the beating heart of the ultras culture.

I had got a diluted taste of Ukrainian ultras culture several months earlier when Shakhtar played Lyon in a half-full Olympic Stadium in Kyiv. That night, the cold and the empty seats played a part in dampening the enthusiasm of the crowd, but a pocket of Shakhtar fans behind one goal still set off tear gas cannisters and managed to make a racket.

'In the 1990s, we witnessed the promotion of ultras ideology,' describes Zvyahintsev. 'It had never existed before. Artificially, these groups were motivated to grow. They became affiliated with clubs. The authorities encouraged it. It was directed from the top.'

The moment that Zvyahintsev and Antipov call the nadir of the proliferation of hooliganism was the Odessa massacre of 2 May 2014, on the day of the Premier League match between Chernomorets v. Metalist Kharkiv. However, they characterise it quite differently to how it was depicted in the Ukrainian press, where pro-Russian saboteurs allegedly attacked Ukrainian loyalist football fans.

'The ultras created the Odessa incident,' says Zvyahintsev. 'I told the authorities fifteen years ago – do not let this movement develop. They will cause us problems later. And look what's happened.'

With Kyiv depicted as the patron and protector for the ultras, the DPR holds Ukraine accountable for those who were burned to death at Odessa.

It's the kind of digestible fiction that has kept the siege mentality alive after the bombs stopped falling. The DPR calls Ukrainians fascist, but the contradiction – deriding far-right nationalists for their fascistic intolerance, whilst simultaneously mocking its sympathy for liberal European ideas like gay marriage and LGBT rights – is not acknowledged by anyone I have met here.

At the city's war museum, the chief researcher Dmitriy Vyazov curates an exhibition of spent weaponry that has been recovered from around the city. It includes vast rockets that were packed with explosives and nails and huge dirty bombs fired by Ukrainian soldiers at civilian targets, before the first Minsk accords banned the use of heavy artillery. One of the rocket housings he shows me is allegedly the one that tore the roof off the Donbass Arena.

The collection also includes objects that are said to have been recovered from Ukrainian prisoners of war, amongst them American flags and military manuals printed on US Navy-issue paper. Nazi paraphernalia allegedly recovered from Ukrainian soldiers, including a ring featuring the emblem of the SS, lie beside them.

Does Vyazov truly believe that Kyiv's army is collaborating with Nazi sympathisers? 'Of course,' he replies. 'You can see for yourself.'

For most in Donbass, the Cold War politics of the 1970s and 1980s never went away. On a wall outside the old city administration building, the one where DPR rebels forced out the Ukrainian authorities at gunpoint in May 2014, 'Fuck America' is still scrawled in hurried red lettering. Although the building is now abandoned, the barbed wire that was put up by the separatists still festoons the windows.

'The war wasn't inevitable until you consider NATO and Washington orchestrating the whole thing,' argues the pundit Vyacheslav Sharafudinov. 'There was a total media brainwash in favour of America. After that, it was no longer possible that Ukraine could remain one country.'

On my last night in Donetsk, after I've bid farewell to Mikhail over three or four local beers, I take the tram back over to Shcherbakov Central Park so I can watch the sun go down behind the old Shakhtar Stadium. It's probably an overly sentimental gesture to myself, some gentle consolation for having missed out on the days when the old place rocked with thousands of expectant fans in a football league that spanned the north Baltic shore to the central Asian steppes near the Chinese border.

I think about how the Communist world is still in the chaotic process of unravelling, even now, nearly thirty years after the document was signed in 1991 at the Belorussian retreat of Belavezha that brought the Soviet Union to an end.

The stadium looks pallid and dark as the fading sun casts it into silhouette. And somewhere over my shoulder the sound of children playing football in the park gently eases the feeling of loss.

CONCLUSION

It's October 2019, and I'm courageously dodging cars as I attempt a life-or-death dash across a four-lane highway in the centre of Sofia, Bulgaria. Waiting for me nearby outside a café at the city's archaeological museum are my fixer, Dimitar, and a man named Stepan, a spokesman for the ultras hooligan firm for the local club Levski Sofia. At last check, I was fifteen minutes late.

It's been two months since I flew from Rostov-on-Don in Russia to London's Heathrow Airport and brought the odyssey of countries, borders, visas and micro-aggressions that gave me the material to write this book to an end. But somehow, I've found myself sucked in again, persuaded by the *Times* sports desk to come to Bulgaria to spend an afternoon with the Levski fans who racially abused England's footballers in the European Championship qualifier here the week before. What I thought would be the end of my affair in the troubled terrains of Eastern Europe, I realise now was only the first chapter.

The fate of this region remains irrevocably tethered to our own. On the level of the ordinary football supporter, the shameful scenes at the Vasil Levski Stadium forced a re-appraisal of the English game's own relationship with racism; a sizeable, vocal section of our media turned the microscope on our own problems and started a long overdue inquest into the rotten underbelly of English football.

On the political level, there are potentially significant consequences and implications for the events discussed in these pages for those of us living in the West, seemingly light years away from the former Soviet Bloc. The recognition by the major Western powers of Kosovo's unilateral declaration of independence in 2008 has ramifications for independence movements in Catalonia and Scotland, not to mention in eastern Ukraine, which seems destined to remain an active front line between two increasingly recalcitrant poles of Europe. Russia's policy of destabilisation in the Donbass and the annexation of Crimea tested the waters of what Western Europe and the United States will tolerate regarding Moscow's re-encroachment into the 'near abroad'. Ukraine and Georgia and Azerbaijan in the Caucasus continue to seek political and commercial opportunities in the West, which works to de-motivate Moscow from any move to decrease its own military presence in Abkhazia, South Ossetia and deeper into Europe in Transnistria. That two of Europe's major oil pipelines pass only a matter of kilometres from the still simmering war over the status of Nagorno-Karabakh only adds to the geopolitical significance of a region with innate instabilities that could at any moment send shockwaves rippling westwards across the continent.

As for football – which has served as a central narrative thread that ties the book together, although it may sometimes have featured on the periphery – the days when teams from behind the old Iron Curtain harboured dreams of winning Europe's biggest prizes are long gone and they are not likely to return any time soon.

Steaua Bucharest won the Champions League in its former guise as the European Cup in 1986. Red Star Belgrade repeated the trick in 1991. Steaua have since suffered a financial collapse and been declared bankrupt, and Red Star were thrashed by the new-money tsars of Paris Saint Germain and Liverpool last season on their first return to the tournament in nearly thirty years. Dynamo Kyiv briefly threatened to re-establish the reputation of the teams of the former Soviet world when Andriy Shevchenko led them to a Champions League semi-final in 1999, but even the USSR's most successful club are a fraction of the side that was once assembled by the great master Valeriy Lobanovskyi.

For most clubs in the region, success is financial survival from one season to the next. Teams in Armenia and Georgia appear and vanish with alarming regularity, whilst only the gas boom from the Caspian oil fields keeps the football ecosystem in Azerbaijan running trouble free, at least relative to its impoverished Caucasian neighbours. Moldova has been laid waste by criminals and thugs; its football league is a plaything of hyper-rich former apparatchiks with money to burn and little care for competitive balance, whilst even Kosovo's excitement at taking its first steps into international football is not felt in its domestic league, where apathy and mismanagement continue to rule. Those promising young players that still come through in Eastern Europe are snapped up, invariably before they are ready, by talent farms for the continent's super-clubs, where most disappear into an impersonal, bloated system, which is far away from their families and familiar cultures.

I wrote in the introduction to this book that Communism, for all its glaring, inhumane flaws, as a system of social organisation lent itself well to the development of football. Hopefully this has been demonstrated, as much by the way the game has tottered and wavered since 1991 but persisted, as by any success achieved before it.

As for the future of the game behind the former Iron Curtain, much will depend on how far the global TV industry continues to eat into the slim supporter base of clubs in these countries, as many are lured away from spending their weekend afternoons on the terraces in

Pristina, Tbilisi and Chișinău in favour of sitting in front of a screen watching Bayern Munich, Manchester United and Real Madrid. The attention of the supporters will only stretch so far, and football as a digital commodity is stacked heavily in favour of the Hollywood leagues of England, Spain, Italy and Germany. A spate of Roman Abramovich-style takeovers at one or two of the better-supported clubs could raise the bar for a lucky handful of sides – as has been seen with Rinat Akhmetov at Shakhtar Donetsk and, to a lesser extent, Viktor Gushan at Sheriff Tiraspol and Azersun Holding at Qarabağ – but this will not benefit the national leagues as a whole. It is far more likely that football clubs in this part of the world will continue to survive on a wing and a prayer, holding on to the vestiges of their glorious past, whilst they are increasingly becoming relevant only to historians of the game rather than students of its future.

Much blood has been shed for the sake of the fragile, contested peace that currently exists across Eastern Europe, from Gjilan to Sumgait, from Kharkiv to Kapan. That the freedom to play the world's game is today enjoyed unhindered by almost all of the peoples of Europe is, at least, some small compensation for the trials and turmoil that this complicated continent has been made to endure.

TIMELINE OF KEY EVENTS

KOSOVO

October 1974 – The Autonomous Socialist Republic of Kosovo, a province of Serbia, is afforded equal rights with the six republics of the Yugoslavian federation.

March 1981 – Protests at the University of Pristina over discrimination against Kosovo's Albanian population turn violent, leading to a declaration of a state of emergency.

June 1981 – Béla Pálfi is appointed head coach of FC Prishtina.

May 1983 – FC Prishtina win promotion to the Yugoslav First League for the first time. They beat Serb rivals Red Star 3–1 in Belgrade.

March 1989 – Milošević revokes Kosovo's autonomous status within Serbia, and discrimination against the province's Albanians is formalised in law. A parallel government is formed by Kosovo's Albanian dissidents.

June 1989 – Milošević denounces the Kosovan Albanians as a threat to society at a Serb nationalist rally to mark the 600th anniversary of the Battle of Kosovo.

September 1991 – FC Prishtina resign from the Yugoslav Second League. All other Albanian football clubs in Kosovo follow, and a new football league is formed. The new clubs are banned from accessing stadiums under the ownership of Serb municipalities.

October 1991 – The deposed Kosovan Provincial Assembly unilaterally declares Kosovo's independence.

October 1991 – Croatia and Slovenia declare their independence from Yugoslavia, and the federation begins to violently collapse. By the end of 1992, Bosnia-Herzegovina and Macedonia also declare independence, leaving a rump state comprising of Serbia, Montenegro and the autonomous provinces of Kosovo and Vojvodina.

November 1995 – The Dayton Peace Accords bring an end to the wars in Croatia and Bosnia, but fail to include a settlement for Kosovo's Albanians. The Kosovo Liberation Army forms in Prekaz province.

7 March 1998 – Kosovo Liberation Army leader Adem Jashari is killed in Skënderaj, triggering a civil war between the Serbian government and the Albanian resistance.

March 1999 – NATO ground troops enter Kosovo after a prolonged aerial campaign. The Yugoslav army is driven out of Kosovo and the province is made a protectorate of the United Nations.

18 February 2008 – Kosovo unilaterally declares independence from Serbia for a second time, to partial international recognition. The Football Federation of Kosovo applies for UEFA membership, and is rejected.

3 May 2016 – The Football Federation of Kosovo's UEFA membership application is put to an assembly of the UEFA Congress, and passes narrowly. Days later, the federation is accepted as a member of FIFA.

5 September 2016 – Kosovo plays its first World Cup match, a 1–1 draw against Finland in Turku.

ARMENIA, AZERBAIJAN AND NAGORNO-KARABAKH

February 1988 – The Nagorno-Karabakh Supreme Soviet votes to detach from the Azerbaijan Soviet Socialist Republic and join Armenia. The vote is rejected by Moscow.

27 February 1988 – The Sumgait pogrom is waged by local Azerbaijanis against the city's Armenians. The death count is officially recorded as thirty-two.

28 February 1988 – Yerazank FC, from the Nagorno-Karabakh capital Stepanakert, refuse to travel to Sumgait to honour a league fixture against FK Khazar, citing safety concerns. The club ceases football activities.

23 March 1988 – Moscow renews its declaration that Nagorno-Karabakh's borders will not be changed. Soviet troops are dispatched to Stepanakert to disperse protesters.

November 1988 – Qarabağ FK win the regional Azerbaijani championship, gaining promotion to the Soviet third tier.

7 December 1988 – 25,000 people are killed when an earthquake strikes the Armenian town of Spitak. Azerbaijan blocks railway access to Armenia, holding up aid to the disaster zone.

August 1991 – Armenia and Azerbaijan declare their independence from the collapsing USSR, turning the dispute over the status of Nagorno-Karabakh into an international conflict.

26 February 1992 – 600 Azeri villagers are killed by Armenian snipers in the village of Khojaly.

May 1992 – Armenian forces capture the Azerbaijani-held city of Shushi, effectively winning the war.

14 June 1992 – Azerbaijani general and former Qarabağ coach Allahverdi Bagirov is killed in action.

23 July 1993 – Ağdam is abandoned to the Armenian army, which razes it to the ground.

1 August 1993 – FK Qarabağ, now playing in Baku after the destruction of the Imarat Stadium, win the first edition of the Azerbaijan Premier League.

May 1994 – A Russian-brokered ceasefire brings an end to active hostilities between Armenia and Azerbaijan over Nagorno-Karabakh.

2001 – FK Qarabağ are bought by the Azerbaijani food-processing giant Azersun, saving them from bankruptcy.

June 2007 – Two European Championship matches between Armenia and Azerbaijan are cancelled after the Baku government refuses to allow the Armenia team to enter the country.

June 2012 – The president of the Football Federation of Armenia Ruben Hayrapetyan is cleared of ordering the murder of a business associate in Yerevan.

October 2013 – Despite a good run, Armenia fail to qualify for the 2014 World Cup under manager Vardan Minasyan.

April 2014 – Qarabağ win the first of six consecutive Azerbaijan league titles.

September 2017 – Qarabağ become the first team from Azerbaijan to qualify for the Champions League, drawing international attention to their exile status.

GEORGIA, ABKHAZIA AND SOUTH OSSETIA

1978 – Popular protests in the Georgian capital Tbilisi win special status for the Georgian language in the USSR constitution.

Counter-protests erupt in the Abkhazian capital Sukhumi, winning formal privileges for Abkhaz education and media.

13 May 1981 – Dinamo Tbilisi become the first Soviet club to win a European trophy, defeating East Germany's Carl Zeiss Jena in the Cup Winners' Cup final in Dusseldorf.

18 March 1989 – Abkhaz nationalists present the Lykhny Declaration to Moscow demanding separation from the Georgian Soviet Socialist Republic.

9 April 1989 – Pro-independence demonstrations in Tbilisi are put down by Soviet troops resulting in the deaths of twenty-one protesters.

February 1990 – Georgia's football clubs resign from the Soviet championship and begin holding their own league competition. In Abkhazia, Dinamo Sukhumi splits in half between its Georgian and Abkhaz players, whilst in Georgia clubs reject their old Soviet names and adopt Georgian alternatives.

October 1990 – Nationalist dissident Zviad Gamsakhurdia effectively takes control of the Georgian Soviet Socialist Republic and announces the country's intention to secede from the Soviet Union.

November 1990 – Georgian nationalists march on the South Ossetian capital Tskhinvali. Gamsakhurdia revokes the region's autonomous status, and the city responds by forming a South Ossetian national guard.

TIMELINE OF KEY EVENTS

December 1991 – Gamsakhurdia is ousted from office in a coup d'état and a special military council assumes the presidency. Georgia collapses into civil war.

14 August 1992 – Georgia's National Guard invades Abkhazia and captures Sukhumi.

18 August 1993 – Dinamo Tbilisi become the first independent Georgian team to play in Europe, beating Linfield 2–1 in Tbilisi.

13 September 1993 – Abkhaz fighters, backed by Russian and North Caucasian volunteers, drive the Georgian National Guard and government officials out of Sukhumi. The city's mayor and founder of Georgian league club Tskhumi Sukhumi, Guram Gabiskiria, is executed by Abkhaz militia.

September 1999 – Abkhazia formally declares independence from Georgia.

November 2003 – The Rose Revolution ousts President Eduard Shevardnadze in Tbilisi. New President Mikheil Saakashvili promises to restore Georgian control over Abkhazia and South Ossetia.

July 2007 – FC Tskhinvali is formed in Georgian-controlled South Ossetia as part of a drive to promote reintegration of the breakaway territory.

April 2008 – Georgian troops shell Tskhinvali, leading to a Russian invasion of Georgia proper and a brief war between Moscow and Tbilisi. Russia recognises the independence of Abkhazia and South Ossetia.

MOLDOVA AND TRANSNISTRIA

September 1989 – The Supreme Soviet of the Moldovan Soviet Socialist Republic declares Romanian the official language of the republic, replacing Russian.

22 December 1989 – Romanian dictator Nicolae Ceaușescu is overthrown in Bucharest.

6 May 1990 – The Moldovan border with Romania is opened for the first time since the Soviet annexation, raising the prospect of political unification.

September 1990 – The Autonomous Pridnestrovian Moldavian Republic (Transnistria), a federal unit representing Moldova's Russian-speaking east, declares its separation from the Moldovan Soviet Socialist Republic.

November 1990 – Fighting breaks out in the town of Dubăsari near the Dniester River between pro-Russian fighters and Moldovan police. Low-level hostilities continue throughout 1991.

25 December 1991 – The USSR is formally dissolved and the Soviet Socialist Republic of Moldova is made independent, causing a nationwide collapse of the economy.

February 1992 – Tiligul Tiraspol owner Grigory Korzun persuades the Transnistria Supreme Soviet to allow the region's clubs to compete in Moldova.

March 1992 – Fighting breaks out in the town of Bendery near the

Moldovan-Transnistria border, the same day the newly independent football league of Moldova is due to begin.

May 1992 – The new Moldovan Football Federation cancels the final games of the season owing to the deteriorating security situation around Transnistria. Tiligul refuse to participate in a title-deciding play-off, handing the first championship to Zimbru Chișinău.

September 1994 – The Moldova national team beats Wales 3–2 in its first competitive international. The same month, Zimbru become the first independent Moldovan team to play in Europe.

April 1997 – FC Sheriff Tiraspol is founded in the Transnistrian capital by the food company Sheriff.

April 2001 – FC Sheriff win the first of the eighteen Moldovan league titles it will win over the next twenty years.

April 2003 – The Moldova national team plays its first-ever game in Tiraspol, losing 2–1 to the Netherlands in a European Championship qualifier.

UKRAINE AND THE DONBASS

April 2002 – Shakhtar Donetsk beat Soviet-era giants Dynamo Kyiv to the Ukrainian league title for the first time, signalling a power shift in Ukrainian football.

November 2004 – The Ukrainian election is won by the regime-backed candidate Viktor Yanukovych, defeating reformist opposition leader Viktor Yushchenko in a vote largely deemed to have been rigged. Protesters descend on Kyiv's Independence Square and the Orange Revolution begins.

December 2004 – The Ukrainian courts rule Yanukovych's victory to be null and a re-run is called. Yushchenko wins a majority and is elected President.

May 2009 – Months before new presidential elections, Shakhtar become the first team from independent Ukraine to win a European trophy, beating Werder Bremen to lift the UEFA Cup. Shakhtar fan Yanukovych addresses supporters in Donetsk and heralds the dawn of a new, united Ukraine.

February 2010 – Yanukovych is elected President of Ukraine in a fair vote after Yushchenko's government fails to deliver reform.

June to July 2012 – Ukraine co-hosts the European Championships with Poland. Shakhtar's state-of-the-art Donbass Arena welcomes fans from across Europe to a revitalised Donetsk to watch Spain beat Portugal in the semi-finals.

October 2013 – Yanukovych backs out of signing an association agreement with the European Union under threat of Russian sanctions. Protesters gather in Kyiv in what becomes known via TV broadcasts around the world as the Euromaidan. The number of demonstrators grows to over half a million, and similar pro-Europe protests break out around Ukraine.

20 February 2014 – government troops open fire on the Euromaidan crowds, causing the deaths of over a hundred protesters.

22 February 2014 – Yanukovych flees Kyiv for Russia, effectively resigning his post as President.

27 February 2014 – Russian troops in unmarked uniforms enter Ukraine's Crimean Peninsula and begin a bloodless takeover of government buildings. President Vladimir Putin publicly denies knowledge of the operation.

18 March 2014 – Putin signs an accession treaty annexing Crimea to the Russian Federation, and admits that Russian troops were behind the takeover.

7 April 2014 – Insurrection begins in the Donbass in south-east Ukraine. Armed men in unmarked uniforms seize the Donetsk city administration building and declare a Donetsk People's Republic.

2 May 2014 – Shakhtar beat Illichivets Mariupol 3–1 at the Donbass Arena to win the Ukrainian title in their final game in Donetsk. A week later, they relocate to Mykolaev on the Black Sea as fighting in Donbass intensifies.

2 May 2014 – Fighting erupts between pro-Kyiv and pro-Russian activists in Odessa before a league match between Metalist Kharkiv and Chernomorets. Forty-eight people are killed after a trade union building catches fire. The Ukrainian Football Federation bans football supporters from attending matches nationwide.

July 2014 – Shakhtar relocate permanently to Lviv in western Ukraine after the Donetsk People's Republic repels repeated attacks from government troops with support from Russia. Talks begin between Kyiv, Donetsk and international observers, but the ceasefire is frequently broken as the death toll passes 4,000.

July 2017 – Shakhtar relocate again, this time to Metalist Stadium in Kharkiv on the border of Donbass.

ACKNOWLEDGEMENTS

This book wouldn't have been written without the people willing to give up their time and energy to help a foreign stranger: Bajram Shala, who welcomed me on my first day; Edmond Rugova, whose words were a foundation for all the others; Valon Hoxha, who drank with me during sad stories; Nurlan Ibrahimov and Aydin Bagirov, who helped me understand the chaos of Baku; Sona Mirzoyan and Anush at Pyunik, for giving Yerevan its human face; Sergey Janjoyan, for forgiving my shady connections; Givi Todua, for his spotless translations; Zurab Tsurtsumia, for being flawlessly cool; Mamuka Kvaratskhelia, for sharing everything; Ion Testemiţanu, for relentless honesty; Victor Daghi, for ferocious efficiency; Andriy Smolensky, for his smarts; Olga Abahina, for hers; Mikhail Glukhov, for rescuing me from the storm; and Oleg Antipov, for proving that closed borders don't necessitate closed hearts.

Thanks also to Tim Baycroft, for introducing me to history and helping me try to write it; Darryl Samaraweera at Artellus, for persuading someone to publish something so strangely particular; Olivia Beattie at Biteback, for allowing herself to be persuaded; and James Lilford, who made sense of my rambling drafts and made them ready to read.

Thanks as well to Will Tidey, who gave me my start in journalism and read the early scribblings of this book; Ben Findon, Sean Fey Paul Hilliar and Glenn Moore, who read it and reassured me it wasn't a waste of time; thanks Todd Baker and Dave Innes for dragging me into adulthood and being my twin pillars.

And thanks Mom and Dad, for your tolerance; and thanks Nicky, Duncan and Lily. And thank you ASJ, for everything else and everything still to come.

INDEX

Abashidze, Sergo 167
Abkhaz Autonomous Soviet Socialist
  Republic 157
Abkhazia 148–61, 168–9, 170–71, 174–80
Abramovich, Roman 265, 272
Adamyan, Ashot 99, 101, 121–2
Adleiba, Astamur 177–9, 180
Ağdam, Azerbaijan 70–71, 73–4, 78, 80, 89–92
Ajinjal, Ruslan and Beslan 153–4
Akhalkatsi, Nodar 140–41
Akhmetov, Rinat 265, 284, 294–5, 297, 299,
  301, 303–4, 307–8
Alania Vladikavkaz, FC 189–90
Alans, the 185
Albania 18, 54–6
Albanians, Kosovo Muslim 8, 11–17, 20,
  23–4, 28, 33, 35–36, 43–5, 47
Aleksanyan, Samuel 108
Aliabiev, Vyacheslav 290
Aliyev, Heydar 84
Aliyev, Ilham 83–4
Almeyda, Richard 79
Altman, Semen 257
Amirani Ochamchire, FC 156
Andorra 104–5
Andriy (Moldova) 205, 207, 216, 227, 236
Anorthosis Famagusta FC 165
Antipov, Oleg 284–6, 289, 298–302, 304, 311
Anush (Armenia) 117
Ararat Yerevan, FC 66, 96, 99, 102, 109, 113
Ardzinba, Vladislav 174
Arifaj, Granit 10, 38
Arkan (Serb warlord) 18, 20
Armenia 65, 67–8, 82–3, 100, 104, 106–7,
  110–15, 125–6, 317

Armenian forces 77
Armenian Genocide 96
Armenians 71–2, 73
Arsenal FC 279, 292, 298
Arsenal Kyiv, FC 270
Arshba, Otari 174
Arshba, Valery 165–7, 176
Artsakh, FC 120–21, 124–6
Arzumanyan, Robert 114
Asadov, Oqtay 123
Asif, Fred 76, 90
Austria-Hungary 267
Azerbaijan 66–8, 78, 80, 82–3, 85, 102,
  106–7, 123, 125, 317
Azeris (Azerbaijanis) 71–2, 73
Azersun Arena, *Baku* 81–2
Azersun Holding 83–4

Babayan, Samvel 102
Badibanga, Ziguy 230
Bagapsh, Sergei 173
Bagdasarov, Mikhail 108
Bagdasaryan, Eduard 97–8, 100–103
Bagirov, Allahverdi 88, 88–91
Bagirova, Valide 88–9
Bajram Aliu Stadium, Skënderaj 7, 9–10
Baku, Azerbaijan 69–70, 85–7, 107–8
Baku Olympic Stadium, Azerbaijan 85
Baku United FC 107
Balaj, Bekim 55
Balkans, the 55
Banants (FC Urartu), FC 104–5, 108
Bandera, Stepan 308
Banishevskiy, Anatoliy 72
Barcelona, FC 282

333

Basayev, Shamil 163–4
Bayern Munich, FC 301
Belgium 112
Belgrade, Yugoslavia 45
Bendery, Moldova 198–206
Beria, Lavrentiy 136, 139, 151, 152
Bessarabia 208, 237
Blokhin, Oleg 3, 4, 142
Bolnisi Sioni, FC 190
Bolsheviks, the 140, 151, 186
Bor, FK 50
Boris Paichadze Dinamo Stadium, Tbilisi 93, 144, 165
Bosnia-Herzegovina 21
Bragin, Akhat 292–5
Buga, Ion 195
Bulgaria 250, 315–17
Busan IPark, South Korea 111
Butylka museum, Tîrnauca 208–9, 211
Byelik, Oleksiy 298, 301

Cana, Agim 18, 48
Cana, Lorik 54
Casals Rubio, Eloy 104
Cebanu, Ilie 245
Cebanu, Pavel 221, 224, 238–42, 246, 253
Celina, Bersant 60
Chernomorets, FC 270–71, 312
Chetnik forces 46
Chikhradze, Besik 166, 167–8
Chikhradze, Giorgi 155
Chikhradze, Goderdzi 163–8, 177
Chikhura Sachkhere, FC 162–3, 181, 183, 184, 191
Chişinău, Moldova 195–7, 199, 201, 207–8, 212–15, 231, 233, 236–9, 245, 250–52
Chubai, Hryhoriy 259
Cimili, Ramadan 48
Ciornîi, Nicolae 212, 217, 249–51, 253–4
Clemente, Javier 111, 115
Cleşcenco, Sergei 253
Club Brugge KV 294
Constructorul Chişinău, FC 252
Corruption Perception Index 83
Costa, Douglas 301
Crimea 125, 267
Crisci, Andrew 1
Croatia 21, 36, 59
CSKA Moscow, PFC 141–2, 229
Cyprus 165, 213
Czech Republic 115

Dacia Chişinău, FC 254–6

Daghi, Victor 195
Daraselia, Vitaly 94, 138, 157–8
Daraselia, Vitaly Jr 145, 158
David Petriashvili Stadium, Tbilisi 162, 181
'Davos Pact' 147–8, 234
Delijaj family 7
Denmark 115
Dinamo Auto-Tiraspol, FC 209
Dinamo Gagra 155, 164, 167
Dinamo Gandzha (Kirovabad) 77–8
Dinamo Stadium, Bendery 199, 202, 209
Dinamo Sukhumi 149–55, 157–60, 175, 177–81
Dinamo Tbilisi 93, 138–46, 151, 155–156, 159–60, 163, 187
Dinamo Zagreb 36, 41
Dirun, Anatolii 233
Dniester River 198, 199, 201–2, 235, 243
Dnipro, FC 269, 270, 276–7
Domi, Faruk 48
Donbass Arena, Donetsk 282, 302–4
Donbass, Ukraine 265, 276, 284, 287–9, 309
Donbass War 263, 275–6
Donetsk People's Republic (DPR) 281–2, 303–4, 312–13
Donetsk, Ukraine 276, 281–98, 306–8
Drenica, KF 7, 9–10, 19–22
Drita, KF 30, 30–32, 34, 36–8
Druzhba, FC 153
Duka, Armand 56
Dynamo Kyiv, FC 142, 166, 265, 269, 273, 282–3, 291, 297–300, 317
Dzapshba, Leonid 173–6, 177, 180

England 155
Enguri River, Georgia 133, 148–9, 160
Ergun, Reshad 84
Euromaidan, Kyiv 269–70, 275

Fedororov, Sergei 299
Fernandinho 301
FIFA 11, 56–7, 60, 102, 121, 179, 190, 240–41, 243
First Armenian Front 103, 105, 109, 117
Flamurtari, KF 14
Fomenko, Mykhaylo 144
Foster, Jonathan 119–20
France 247

Gabrielyan, Slava 121, 122, 124–5
Gagra, Abkhazia 161–7, 169
Gagra, FC 163, 164, 165–7, 177, 185
Gali, Abkhazia 170–71

INDEX

Gamsakhurdia, Zviad 138, 146, 156
Gandzasar Kapan, FC 116–18
Garibashvili, Irakli 187
Gavrančić, Goran 299
Gazzaev, Valery 190
Geci, Daut 19–22
Georgia 67–8, 133–8, 140, 155, 162, 167, 176, 317
Gerasimets, Sergey 142
Gabiskaria, Guram 154–5
Gjakova massacre 3–5
Gjilan, Kosovo 33, 35
Gjilani, SC 30, 33–4, 38
Glenny, Misha 237
Gori, Georgia 66, 134, 185, 187–8
Gornje Obrinje massacre 6, 7
Gozal, Abdolbari 83
Gozal, Hasan 83–4
Gračanica, Kosovo 32
Great Migration (1689) 24
Grigoryan, Loris 99, 101, 121–2
Gubliya, Beslan 149–50, 152–3, 155
Gudauta, Abkhazia 149–50
Gumilla (football coach) 153
Guria Lanchkuti, FC 137, 141–6
Gushan, Viktor 228, 233, 234–5
Gutsaev, Vladimir 94, 138, 142–6, 188–90
Guzun, Alexandru 198–200, 204
Gvardeets, FK 310

Harea, Gheorghe 200, 203, 204
Hayk the Great 96
Hayrapetyan, Ruben 97, 103–4, 108–109, 114
Horlovka, Ukraine 285–6
Hotel Nistru siege, Moldova 199–201
Hoxha, Enver 38
Hoxha, Genc 3–4
Hoxha, Valon 15–16, 18–19
Hrazdan Stadium, Armenia 96
Hughes, John 288
Huseynov, Mehman 84
Huseynov, Mushfig 72–7, 91

Ibrahimov, Nurlan 70–71, 82, 84, 86, 88
Illichivets Mariupol, FC 282
Imarat Stadium, Ağdam 74–5, 77
İnşaatçı Sabirabad FK 77
Intelektualët (fan group) *31–2, 35*
Inter Baku 78
Inter Milan 291
Ioseliani, Jaba 147
Ireland, Republic of 115
Iskra-Stal Rîbnița, FC 254

Isufi, Fisnik 30–32, 34–9
Italy 115
Ivanishvili, Bidzina 188
Ivanov, Anton 262–5, 272–5, 277
Ivanov, Stanislav 229

Jádson 301, 308
Jashari, Adem 10, 21
Jashari family 22
Johnson, Donald 198
Jones, Tom 111–16
Jordania, Merab 142

Kaladze, Kakha 94, 187, 188
Kanchelskis, Andrei 286–7
Kapan, Armenia 116
Karabakh movement (1988) 72
Karadžić, Tomislav 57
Karapetyan, Samuel 118–20, 126
Kartli-Kakheti, Kingdom of 185
Kasanov, Shahid 75
Kazakhstan 112
Kazmaly, Ilya 228
Kernes, Hennadiy 272
Khajimba, Raul 174
Kharkiv, Ukraine 261–3, 269, 272, 276–80
Khashig, Inal 150, 151, 154, 176–7
Khazar Sumgait, FK 78
Khlus, Viktor 142–3, 144–5
Khodykin, Yuri 204–6
Khojaly massacre 89–90
Khutchua, Irakli 166
Kinkladze, Georgi 93–4
Kipiani, David 94, 138, 146
Kitovani, Tengiz 158, 163
Kokoity, Eduard 182, 189, 190
Koloskov, Vyacheslav 140
Korzun, Grigory 209–18, 223
Korzun, Stanislav 210
Kosovo 3–61, 317
Kosovo, Battle of (1389) 9, 14, 23
Kosovo Liberation Army (KLA) 7, 21
Kosovo War 19–20
Kosse, Vladimir 215
Kostava, Merab 140
Krasniqi, Ramiz 48, 52
Krasnoselsky, Vadim 206, 222, 235
Kuban Krasnodar 108
Kuchma, Leonid 295, 296
Kulumbegov, Alan (Kantidze) 147
Kurchenko, Sergei 263, 264, 272–5
Kutaisi, Georgia 162

335

Kvaratskhelia, Mamuka 139–41, 143–7, 154, 155, 159–60, 167
Kyiv, Ukraine 266–9, 275–6

Laguteev, Gennady 310
Lakoba, Nestor 152
Lalic, Kosta 28–9, 53
Lanchkuti, Georgia 142, 143, 144
Latii, Olga 244, 245
Lernayin Artsakh FC 107
Levchenko, Nikolai 307–8
Levytsky, Mark 283
Liakhvi-Tskhinvali, FC 187–8
Likovac, Kosovo 6
Liria, KF 3
Lithuania 285
Livadaru, Marin 254
Liverpool FC 31, 94, 108
Ljukovčan, Živan 52
Lobanovskyi, Valeriy 282, 284, 299, 300, 317
Lokomotiv Tbilisi, FC 166, 190
Lominadze, Shota 150–51
Lucescu, Mircea 299, 300
Luhansk, Ukraine 276
LUKOIL 212, 214, 217, 249–51
Lulenov, Petr 227, 229, 230, 233–6
Lutsenko, Yuriy 264

Macedonia 16, 48
Mahmadov, Habib 82
Manchester United FC 220
Mancini, Roberto 291
Mandelstam, Osip 63
Mandžukić, Mario 60
Margaryan, Gurgen 68
match-fixing 145, 243
MCOP Lokomotiv Tbilisi 75
Meireles, Raul 113
Mensheviks, the 186
Mertskhali Ozurgeti, FC 155
Meskhi, Mikheil 163
Metalist Kharkiv, FC 144–5, 262–5, 269–7, 312
Metalist Stadium, Kharkiv 261–3, 272
Metreveli, Slava 163
Mika, FC 108
Mikhail (Ukraine) 281, 306–7, 313
Milan, AC 291
Milanic, Milan 48
Milošević, Slobodan 11–12, 14, 27, 39
Milsami, FC 225, 227–8, 249, 254
Minasyan, Vardan 111–12, 114–15
Minsk accords 307, 312
Mitrovic, Stefan 54

Mkhitaryan, Hamlet 113
Mkhitaryan, Henrikh 108, 113, 121, 129
Mkrtchyan, Levon 100, 108, 121–2, 125–6
Moldova 195–257, 317
Montague, James 230
Mosneag, Victor 245–6
Mujiri, David 229
Munishi, Kushtrim 15, 16–18, 61
Muriqi, Fadil 42, 43–4, 47, 48, 51

Nadirov, Adil 87–8
Nadirov, Vüqar 79–81, 87
Nagorno-Karabakh Republic 65–6, 82–3, 102, 107–8, 123, 135
Nagorno-Karabakh War 71, 87–8, 99–100, 117, 119, 122
Narbekovas, Arminas 145
Nart Sukhumi 177
Natavan, Khurshidbanu 74–5
NATO 5, 186
Neftçi Baku 66, 72, 78, 79
Nizam, Asif 90
NK Osijek 50
North Ossetia 189–90
Nyva, FC 199, 204

Obilić, KF 25, 43
Obilić, Kosovo 23
Obilić, Milos 23, 32
Ochamchire, Abkhazia 157–8
Odessa massacre 270–71, 311–12
Odessa, Ukraine 231
Odiah, Chidi 229
Odlar Yurdu Organisation 107
OFK Titograd 50
Okoronkwo, Isaac 229
Okriashvili, Tornike 167
Olga (Moldova) 211
Olimpi, FC 179–80, 217
Olympic Stadium, Kyiv 280, 285, 309, 310, 311
Olympique Lyon 278, 279, 280, 311
Omonia, AC 213, 215
Oprea, Igor 210, 213
Orange Revolution 269, 296
Ordzhonikidze, Sergo 136
Orujov, Hidayat 124
Oshenkov, Oleg 290
Osipov, Omari (Tetradze) 147
Osmani, Selami 37–8, 39
Ottoman Empire 24, 96

Pachajyan, Levon 113

INDEX

Paichadze, Boris 93
Pálfi, Béla 45–9, 51
Partizan Belgrade 41, 46
Partizan forces 46
Pashayev (Bagirov's son-in-law) 90–91
Patriarchate of Peć Monastery, Kosovo 45
Peć, Kosovo 24
Pelister, FK 52
Perdedaj, Fanol 60
Petrov, Ihor 285–9, 297, 299, 300
Pisarenco, Emil 248–9
Plahotniuc, Vladimir 251
Poland 110, 112, 115, 266–7
Poltava, Ukraine 279
Poroshenko, Petro 278, 280
Porterfield, Ian 110–16, 118
Portugal 111, 112–14, 302
Preuss, Jakob 307–8
Prishtina, FC 6, 10, 14–18, 25–30, 38, 41–53, 61
Pristina, Kosovo 12, 15–16, 39–40, 51
Prokudin, Pavel 219–24, 227
Putin, Vladimir 234
Pyunik, FC 97, 102–4, 108–9, 116–18

Qarabağ FK 70–72, 74–9, 81–9, 92, 106–7, 126, 128–9

Rad, FK 51
Rakitskiy, Yaroslav 305–6
Rashica, Milot 60
Red Star Belgrade 35–6, 41–2, 46, 316–17
Reich, Peter 217
Republican Stadium, Tiraspol 218–19
Rîbnița 197
Ricketts, Rohan 254–6
Ritsa Gudauta 150
Romania 201, 208, 236–8, 250
Romelashvili, Zaz 187–8
Rotari, Valeriu (Zelioni) 252
Rugova, Edmond 26–30, 41–4, 49–50, 52–3
Rugova, Ibrahim 15, 21, 38
Russia 72, 156, 219, 267
Rustaveli Avenue, Tbilisi 137, 140, 146
Rustavi, FC 180, 190
Ryabin, Anatoliy 293–4

Saakashvili, Mikheil 188
Saburtalo Tbilisi 230
Sadygov, Rashad 79
Safarov, Ramil 68–9, 83
Sahakyan, Arman 108
Sahit (Kosovan cameraman) 6–7

Salihu, Eroll 12–13, 15, 18, 56–7, 58–61
Salkov, Vladimir 290
Sanakoyev, Ashkar 181–4
Sanakoyev, Dimitry 181–3, 184, 185
Santa Coloma, FC 104
Scala, Nevio 295, 298
Seaman, David 298
Serb forces 7, 22
Serbia 8, 9, 13, 23–4, 36, 42, 44, 54–6, 111, 114–15
Serbian population 23–4, 33
Seroj (Armenia) 104, 105–9, 116
Shakhtar Donetsk, FC 108, 229, 263, 265, 277–86, 290, 292–4, 297–302, 305, 308, 310
Shakhtar Stadium, Donetsk 292–3, 313
Shakohoxha, Cimi 55
Shala, Bajram 17
Shaqiri, Xherdan 33, 38, 60
Sharafudinov, Vyacheslav 292–4, 296–7, 302, 313
Shearer, Alan 155
Sheriff LLC 226–7, 228, 234
Sheriff Stadium, Tiraspol 209, 224–5, 229
Sheriff Tiraspol, FC 209, 217, 220, 223–35, 248–9, 253, 254
Shevchenko, Andriy 282–3, 317
Shevchuk, Yevgeny 205–6, 219, 234–5
Shevardnadze, Eduard 137, 147–8, 159
Shevardnadze, Evgrapi 137, 141, 143, 145
Shirak, FC 108
Shkodër, Albania 58
Shkolnikov, Efim 215
Shusha massacre 90–91, 99, 122
Sikharuli, FC 167–8
Simonyan, Nikita 150
Skënderaj, Kosovo 5–6, 22
Skënderbau, George Kastrioti 23
Slavia Mozyr 252
Sloboda Tuzla, FK 50
Slovakia 115
Smirnov, Igor 205, 216
Snegur, Mircea 205, 253
Sofia, Bulgaria 315–17
Sokolovsky, Mykhaylo 302
South Ossetia 182–7, 188–9
Southampton FC 31, 242
Soviet Union 72, 178, 219, 223–4
Spain 302
Speranța Nisporeni 247, 248–9
Spinu, Marin 244
Stakhanov, Alexei 290, 301
Stalin, Josef 72, 136, 152, 261

337

Stavropol Krai 153–4
Steaua Bucharest 250, 316
Stepanakert, Nagorno-Karabakh Republic 74, 90, 102, 118, 120
Sukhumi, Abkhazia 148, 150, 155–60, 168–9, 171–3
Sumgait, Azerbaijan 86–7, 123–4
Sumgait pogrom, Azerbaijan 73
Sutjeska, FK 29, 53
Switzerland 210

Tadevosyan, Albert 109
Taktakishvili, David 179–80
Tamarasheni, Georgia 187
Tarapat, Nikolai 304, 306, 308–9
Tavriya, FC 294
Tbilisi, Georgia 93–4, 136–7, 148, 162
Testemiţanu, Ion 241–7, 252–4
Teteks, FK 50, 51
Ţicu, Octavian 231, 233
Tighina, FC 198–206, 209
Tiligul Tiraspol, FC 203, 209–17, 223, 226
Tiraspol, Transnistria 197, 199, 207, 209–20, 224–5, 231, 233, 236
Tîrnauca, Transnistria 208–9
Tito, Josip Broz 25, 42, 46
Tkachenko, Vladimir 302
Torpedo Kutaisi, FC 162–3, 165, 181, 183, 184, 190–91
Tortoshi, Jusuf 25–8, 43, 48
Tottenham Hotspur FC 107
Transcaucasian Democratic Federative Republic 68
Transnistria 195–239
Transnistria War 199–203, 239
Trepča '89, KF 6, 14, 17, 20, 33–4, 38, 48
Trotsky, Leon 172
Tsitsernakaberd, Yerevan 95, 96
Tskhinvali (FC Spartak), FC 166, 181, 183–5, 187
Tskhinvali, South Ossetia 183
Tskhumi Sukhumi, FC 154–5, 156, 179
Turkey 41, 71, 72
Tymoshchuk, Anatoliy 298, 301

UEFA 10–11, 55–56, 120, 125–6, 221, 227, 240–41, 243, 279
Ukraine 61, 108, 223, 233, 250, 261–313
United Nations (UN) 9, 57
Ursul, Sergei 224, 227
USSR 137, 139, 141–2

Vanyan, Karen 125

Vasiloi, Rosian 231–2
Vëllaznimi, FK 3, 48
Verevkin, Alexander 216, 217, 222
Victoria (Ukraine) 303–4
Vokrri, Fadil 29, 41–2, 48, 57
Vorobey, Andrei 298, 301
Vorskla, FC 279
Vyazov, Dmitriy 312

Waal, Thomas de 66
Wales 196, 215, 240
Werder Bremen, SV 282, 301, 308
West Ham 248
Willian 301
Wilson, Jonathan 283

Xhaka, Granit 60

Yanukovych, Viktor 264, 265, 268–9, 273–5, 295–6, 308
Yaremchenko, Valeriy 299
Yaroslavsky, Oleksandr 272–3
Yeltsin, Boris 148, 205, 215
Yerazank FC 97–103, 123, 124
Yerevan, Armenia 94–8, 105
Yugoslavia 13, 34–6, 44, 50, 51
Yushchenko, Viktor 296–7, 307, 308

Zakarpattia, FC 299
Žalgiris Vilnius 145
Zaqaryan (Armenia) 106–7, 109
Zelensky, Volodymyr 280
Zenit Saint Petersburg, FC 96, 305
Ziarul de Gardă 241, 242, 244–5
Zimbru (FC Nistru Chişinău), FC 203, 212–14, 226, 238, 247–53
Zimbru Stadium, Chişinău 247–8
Zugdidi, Georgia 133–4
Zurab (Abkhazia) 170–71
Zvyahintsev, Viktor 289, 290, 310–12